コ *ko*	フ コ			
サ *sa*	一 サ			
シ *shi*	゙ ミ シ	し *shi*	し	
ス *su*	フ ス	す *su*	一 す	
セ *se*	⌐ セ	せ *se*	一 ナ せ	
ソ *so*	ヽ ソ	そ *so*	´ ヱ そ	
タ *ta*	ノ ク タ	た *ta*	一 ナ た た	
チ *chi*	´ ニ チ	ち *chi*	一 ち	
ツ *tsu*	ヽ ヽ ツ	つ *tsu*	つ	
テ *te*	ー ニ テ	て *te*	⌐ て	
ト *to*	｜ ト	と *to*	ヽ と	

(Continued on back endpapers)

About the authors

Florence Sakade was a renowned editor and author of numerous books about Japan's language and culture, including *Origami: Japanese Paper Folding* and *Japanese Children's Favorite Stories*.

Janet Ikeda is Associate Professor of Japanese at Washington and Lee University in Virginia. She served as president of the American Association of Teachers of Japanese, and is currently on the Board of the AATJ. Ikeda is also a member of the U.S.-Japan Council and served on the Japanese American Leadership Delegation (JALD).

A Guide to Reading and Writing

JAPANESE

FOURTH EDITION

A COMPREHENSIVE GUIDE TO
THE JAPANESE WRITING SYSTEM

First edition compiled by
FLORENCE SAKADE

Third edition revised by
KENNETH HENSHALL, CHRISTOPHER SEELEY & HENK DE GROOT

Fourth edition revised by
JANET IKEDA

TUTTLE Publishing
Tokyo │Rutland, Vermont│ Singapore

"Books to Span the East and West"

Tuttle Publishing was founded in 1832 in the small New England town of Rutland, Vermont [USA]. Our core values remain as strong today as they were then—to publish best-in-class books which bring people together one page at a time. In 1948, we established a publishing outpost in Japan—and Tuttle is now a leader in publishing English-language books about the arts, languages and cultures of Asia. The world has become a much smaller place today and Asia's economic and cultural influence has grown. Yet the need for meaningful dialogue and information about this diverse region has never been greater. Over the past seven decades, Tuttle has published thousands of books on subjects ranging from martial arts and paper crafts to language learning and literature—and our talented authors, illustrators, designers and photographers have won many prestigious awards. We welcome you to explore the wealth of information available on Asia at **www.tuttlepublishing.com**.

Published by Tuttle Publishing, an imprint of Periplus Editions (HK) Ltd.

www.tuttlepublishing.com

Fourth edition © 2013 Periplus Editions (HK) Ltd.
Third edition © 2003 Periplus Editions (HK) Ltd.
Original edition © 1959 by Charles E. Tuttle Co., Inc.

ISBN 978-4-8053-1173-8
ISBN 978-4-8053-885-0 (for sale in Japan only)

28 27 26 25 24
10 9 8 7   2405CM
Printed in China

Distributed by:

Japan
Tuttle Publishing
Yaekari Building, 3rd Floor
5-4-12 Osaki, Shinagawa-ku
Tokyo 141-0032, Japan
Tel: (81) 3 5437-0171; Fax: (81) 3 5437-0755
sales@tuttle.co.jp
www.tuttle.co.jp

North America, Latin America & Europe
Tuttle Publishing
364 Innovation Drive
North Clarendon, VT 05759-9436, USA
Tel: 1 (802) 773-8930; Fax: 1 (802) 773-6993
info@tuttlepublishing.com
www.tuttlepublishing.com

Asia Pacific
Berkeley Books Pte. Ltd.
3 Kallang Sector #04-01
Singapore 349278
Tel: (65) 6741-2178; Fax: (65) 6741-2179
inquiries@periplus.com.sg
www.tuttlepublishing.com

CONTENTS

INTRODUCTION

1 Aim

This newly revised edition is designed for students and others who have at least an elementary knowledge of spoken Japanese and want to acquaint themselves with the Japanese writing system. The most significant revisions are the addition of 196 characters, which were added to the *Jōyō kanji* (General-Use Characters) list in November of 2010. The elimination of 5 seldom-used characters now brings the total of General-Use characters to 2,136. The newly added characters reflect an information age where technology now allows characters to be more widely generated and consumed on screens. New characters reflect prefectural names and major cities and a concern with health and parts of the body. Aficionados of Japanese cuisine and culture will see familiar characters for foods (*mochi, donburi, men, senbei*), plants and Japanese cultural artifacts and customs, in particular inclusion of auspicious characters for tsuru and kame. Previous revisions to the *Jōyō kanji* list had been made in 1981 and 1946.

The highlights of this new edition are the following:

- Radical index for all characters
- Clearly marked characters found on the Kanji List of the AP Japanese Language and Culture Exam (marked with this symbol: ✓)
- Clearly marked characters (marked by level, based on past practice 1, 2, etc.) used for the Japanese Language Proficiency Test (JLPT)

Although proficiency in the Japanese language is not determined by knowing characters alone, this revised edition will provide an excellent study guide for students who wish to increase their reading ability. All characters recommended for the high school National Japanese Exam (NJE) are included.

2 This Book and the Modern Japanese Writing System

2.1 About the Characters Selected

While the *Jōyō kanji* List (hereafter abbreviated to JK List) does not represent an exhaustive list of Chinese characters which the student will encounter in modern Japanese texts, in combination with the two syllabaries (hiragana and katakana) it does nevertheless provide a very sound basis for reading and writing modern Japanese. In Japanese schools, 1,006 of the more commonly used JK List characters are taught in the six years of elementary school, the balance of 1,130 characters being spread out over the intermediate and high school curriculum. The JK List characters also form the basis of character usage in modern newspapers, though sometimes the Japan Newspaper Association chooses to deviate from the List in some ways.

For writing the names of their children, Japanese today can choose from a corpus of characters consisting of the JK List together with a supplementary list of characters for use in given names. The first such name character list, approved in 1951, consisted of 92 characters, but was expanded considerably in 2004. The current Jinmeiyō Kanji list, which is determined by the Ministry of Justice, includes 861 characters. We do not list these here.

This book is divided into two main sections. Section One presents the 1,006 characters designated by the Japanese Ministry of Education, Culture, Sports, Science and Technology (MEXT) to be taught during the six years of elementary school—termed here "Essential Characters." The choice of these characters is the result of extensive research and deliberation by the Ministry. For these characters, the editors of this volume have endeavored to give illustrative character compounds that are in common use.

Section Two of this book sets out the 2,136 characters designated for general everyday use (including the 1,006 characters taught at elementary school). In 1946 the Japanese writing system underwent fairly radical reform in the direction of simplification, but the 1970s onwards saw some movement away from what some saw as an over-simplification, and the trend towards use of a bigger range of Chinese characters has been encouraged by the development and popularity from the mid-1980s of word-processors and computers that can handle conventional Japanese text. Despite this trend, the major impact of the orthographic reforms of the late 1940s has meant that the Japanese writing system of today still remains much simpler than it was before 1946.

2.2 How Characters Are Read in Japanese

Typically, each Chinese character has two types of readings—*on-yomi* and *kun-yomi*. The *on-yomi* (*on* reading, i.e., Sino-Japanese reading) is a reading originally based on the Chinese pronunciation associated with each character, and reflects the fact that the Chinese script was adopted from China the best part of 2,000 years ago, when the Japanese themselves did not have a writing system. Contrasting with the *on-yomi* is the *kun-yomi* (*kun* reading, i.e., native Japanese reading). In some cases, a given Chinese character has several on readings, reflecting different forms of underlying Chinese pronunciation. A given character may also have more than one associated *kun* reading. Context and the use or absence of accompanying kana (*okurigana*) are the pointers as to which reading is appropriate in a given case.

In this book, the majority of the readings set out in the JK List as it appeared in the *Kanpō* (Official Gazette) of 1 October 1981 have been included, but some readings have been excluded, bearing in mind the aim of this book, because they are archaic, obsolescent, or not common (e.g., *nagomu* [to soften] for 和). Also excluded from among the formal readings listed in this book are the sort of common minor—or relatively minor—variations in character readings which are found only in certain environments in compounds. For instance, the character 学 has the *on* reading GAKU, which is truncated to GAK- in the compound 学校 *gakkō* [school, college], the *kun* reading *ame* [rain] of 雨 changes to *ama-* as the first element in compounds such as 雨戸 *amado* [rain-shutters], and the character 合 GŌ is read GAT- in the compound 合点 *gatten* [understanding, consent]. It was considered best for readers of this book to learn such changes gradually as they progress.

In modern Japanese usage there are quite a number of characters which lack either an *on* reading or a *kun* reading. For instance, nowadays the character 糖 [sugar] is employed only for its *on* reading TŌ, while the character 箱 [box] is used only for its *kun* reading *hako*.

2.3 Writing Characters

Firstly, the student should make every effort to practice so as to keep the characters of uniform size in relation to one another. Thus, the 2-stroke character 刀 *katana* should be written within the equal-sized imaginary square or circle as the 15-stroke 論 RON [argument, opinion], and by the same token the element 言 should be written larger when used as an independent character (read GEN, GON, [speech, word]) than when used as a radical / component in a more complex character such as 論 RON above.

Secondly, bear in mind that Chinese characters sometimes consist of just a few strokes, sometimes many, but the characters are always written according to a set stroke order. Listed below are some principles that will be of assistance with regard to priority in the order of strokes.

1. Top to bottom:

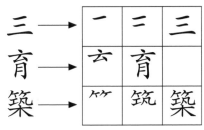

2. Left to right:

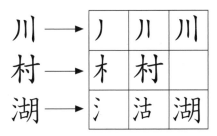

Other rules are:
3. When two or more strokes cross, horizontal strokes usually precede perpendicular ones:

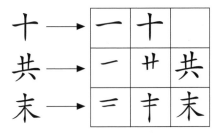

4. Sometimes perpendicular strokes precede horizontal ones:

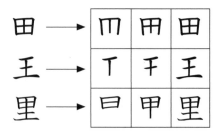

5. Center first, then left and right:

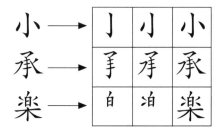

6. Perpendicular line running through center written last:

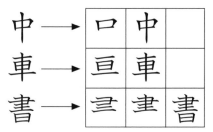

7. Right-to-left diagonal stroke precedes left-to-right:

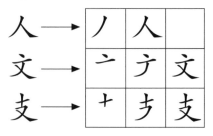

While the above may all seem rather complicated, the student might find solace in the fact that, as noted above, the writing system has been simplified to a considerable extent compared with the past, and has been mastered by many thousands of students having neither native speaker competence in Japanese nor prior background knowledge of the Chinese script.

2.4 Romanization

There are several different systems of representing Japanese using the Roman alphabet. This book employs a slightly modified form of the Hepburn system, this being a system which is widely used and which is based on conventions associated with the spelling of English. The minor modification involves using the letter n rather than m to represent the syllabic nasal ん when the latter occurs immediately before the consonants *m*, *b* or *p* (thus, for instance, *shinbun* [newspaper], not *shimbun*, and *kenpō* [constitution], not *kempō*). Other points to note are:

1. use of a macron to indicate vowel lengthening for *o* and *u*, e.g., *gakkō* [school], *renshū* [practice];
2. use of a hyphen in cases where it is considered that this might facilitate understanding of boundaries between constituent elements in a Japanese word, e.g., *sara-arai* [dishwashing], rather than *saraarai*; and
3. use of the apostrophe ' instead of a hyphen after a syllabic nasal ん, such as *tan'i* [unit] (a word of three short syllables, which in kana would be written たんい) as opposed to *tani* [valley] (a word of two short syllables, written たに in kana).

2.5 Kana Signs and Combinations

The front and back endpapers of this book set out individual symbols in the hiragana and katakana syllabaries, and illustrations of stroke order for each of those symbols. Each of the two syllabaries evolved and became established over a period of many centuries, thereby becoming cemented as integral components in the modern writing system.

Katakana, which are more angular in appearance than hiragana, are today used first and foremost to represent loanwords of European origin, e.g., パン *pan* [bread] and ビール *biiru* [beer]. Hiragana are used widely and variously elsewhere to represent such elements as grammatical particles, inflectional endings of verbs, and frequently to represent in writing words which would otherwise need to be written with intricate or uncommon characters such as those for *ōmu* [parrot] (鸚鵡) or for the ken of *sekken* [soap] (石).

For the convenience of users of this book, the final part consists of an alphabetical index of readings for the 2,136 JK List characters.

3 Layout Details

The 1,006 most essential characters are set out in Section One in accordance with the MEXT's division into six grades. These are in running sequence, but note that the grade divisions are:

1–80	=	Grade One	81–240	=	Grade Two
241–440	=	Grade Three	441–640	=	Grade Four
641–825	=	Grade Five	826–1,006	=	Grade Six

Characters within each grade are set out in the traditional "50 sounds" (*gojūon*) order which is commonly used for reference-type works in Japanese, except that the characters in Grade One alone are ordered on the basis of semantic groupings. Each character is typically accompanied by the on reading, then the kun reading and English meaning(s). The context is the best guide as to which reading is appropriate in a given case.

Also included for each of the 1,006 characters is information regarding the total number of strokes (the stroke count) and the set order to be followed in writing individual strokes. In most cases, three examples of character compounds are provided for each of these Essential characters.

Section Two, which presents the total 2,136 General-Use characters, gives them with their on and/or kun readings, and English meanings, but without illustrative compounds. In many cases, however, compounds containing characters which are among the 1,130 "non-essential" characters may be found among the compounds given for each of the 1,006 characters in Section One. The order adopted for listing the corpus of 2,136 characters is that of stroke count (and, within a given stroke count, by radical). So as to avoid undue repetition, each of the 1,006 Essential characters appearing in Section Two is given with the corresponding reference to Section …One, to which the reader can refer for details. This symbol ▲ marks each of the 196 newest additions to the JK list.

With regard to the typographical conventions employed in giving readings and meanings for characters, these are explained by means of the example below.

見 KEN[1]; *mi(ru)*[2], to see, look[3]

[1] *On* reading in upper case.
[2] *Kun* reading in lower case italics. Parentheses used to indicate end-syllable(s) to be written in kana [(thus, *mi(ru)*, since this word is conventionally written 見る).] Common reading is included though it is not a *kun* reading.
[3] English meaning(s) given in regular lower case.

Also note the use of a comma after a single on-reading to indicate that it can be used as a stand-alone word, e.g., "ZA, seat..." (i.e., "za" exists as a word meaning "seat"), as opposed to "U canopy..." (i.e., "u" does not exist as an independent word).

4 Final Notes
This guide is an ideal way to begin a serious study of the Japanese writing system. Other textbooks should be consulted for studies in vocabulary, grammar and culture. A number of textbooks and reference works are available from Tuttle Publishing.

With each revision this guide continues to provide a useful and comprehensive approach to an ever-growing circle of readers and life-long learners. There are many specialists of Japanese who began their study of Japanese with the first version of this guide and fondly keep that original volume, with its familiar orange and black book jacket, on their shelves. My own well-worn copy reminds me of my very first sensei and the joy that learning and now teaching of Japanese brings.

5 Select Bibliography of Main Works Consulted for This Edition
Note: All the books in Japanese listed below have been published in Tokyo.

Haig, J.H. et al. (ed.), *The New Nelson Japanese-English Character Dictionary*. Charles E. Tuttle, Tokyo, 1997.

Henshall, Kenneth G., *A Guide to Remembering Japanese Characters*. Charles E. Tuttle, Tokyo, 1988.

Maeda, Tomiyoshi. *Jōyō kanji saishin handobukku: nisenjūnen kaitei taiō*. Tōkyō: Meijishoin, 2011.

Sanseidō henshūjo (ed.). *Atarashii kokugo hyōki handobukku*. Tokyo: Sanseidō, 2011.

College Board AP Japanese Language and Culture. http://www.collegeboard.com/student/testing/ap/sub_japaneselang.html

Dictionary.goo.ne.jp. http://dictionary.goo.ne.jp/

Jim Breen's WWWJDIC. http://www.csse.monash.edu.au/~jwb/cgi-bin/wwwjdic.cgi?1C

Jisho.org. http://jisho.org/kanji/radicals/

Kanjijiten.net. http://www.kanjijiten.net/jiten/4151.html#k4155

Japan Ministry of Education, Culture, Sports, Science and Technology. http://www.mext.go.jp/

ACKNOWLEDGMENTS

Many thanks to Professor Janet Ikeda for her careful review of the previous edition's text, and her updates and improvements to allow this book to continue as a core reference for today's learners.

The editors of this revised edition respectfully acknowledge the work of the earlier editions carried out by Florence Sakade and her editorial team, work which has been of assistance to generations of students.

Grateful acknowledgment is also due to Calvert Barksdale, Nancy Goh, Tan Cheng Har, Flavia Hodges, Tan Mike Tze, Nathan Burrows, Neil Chandler, Bruce Penno, Paul Eagle, Shozo Tsuji, Yasuko Tsuji, and Kazuko Seeley.

The 1,006
ESSENTIAL CHARACTERS

一	一			**ICHI, ITSU,** *hito-, hito(tsu),* one 一月 *ichigatsu,* January 一番 *ichiban,* first, best 一冊 *issatsu,* one (book, magazine)
1 1 stroke				☑ 5

二	一	二		**NI,** *futa(tsu),* two 二月 *nigatsu,* February 二か月 *nikagetsu,* two months 二回 *nikai,* twice
2 2 strokes				☑ 5

三	一	二	三	**SAN,** *mi-, mit(tsu),* three 三月 *sangatsu,* March 三人 *sannin,* three people 三日 *mikka,* three days, the third day
3 3 strokes				☑ 5

四	丨	冂	冂	**SHI,** *yon, yo-, yot(tsu), yo(tsu),* four 四月 *shigatsu,* April 四日 *yokka,* four days, the fourth day 四十 *shijū, yonjū,* forty
	冈	四		
4 5 strokes				☑ 5

☑ = AP   # = JLPT

1

五	一	丁	瓦	GO, *itsu(tsu)*, five
	五			五月 *gogatsu*, May 五人 *gonin*, five people 五十 *gojū*, fifty
5 4 strokes				☑ 5

六	丶	二	宀	ROKU, *mut(tsu)*, *mu(tsu)*, six
	六			六月 *rokugatsu*, June 六か月 *rokkagetsu*, six months 六十 *rokujū*, sixty
6 4 strokes				☑ 5

七	一	七		SHICHI, *nana(tsu)*, *nana*, seven
				七月 *shichigatsu*, July 七ヶ月 *nanakagetsu*, seven months 七十 *shichijū*, *nanajū*, seventy
7 2 strokes				☑ 5

八	ノ	八		HACHI, *yat(tsu)*, *ya(tsu)*, eight
				八月 *hachigatsu*, August 八か月 *hachikagetsu*, eight months 八十 *hachijū*, eighty
8 2 strokes				☑ 5

九	ノ	九		KYŪ, KU, *kokono(tsu)*, nine
				九月 *kugatsu*, September 九十 *kujū*, *kyūjū*, ninety 九時 *kuji*, nine o'clock
9 2 strokes				☑ 5

十	一	十		JŪ, *tō*, ten
				十月 *jūgatsu*, October
				十日 *tōka*, ten days, the tenth day
				十回 *jikkai*, ten times
10 **2 strokes**				☑ 5

百	一	一	一	HYAKU, hundred
	万	百	百	二百 *nihyaku*, two hundred 三百 *sanbyaku*, three hundred 百貨店 *hyakkaten*, department store
11 **6 strokes**				☑ 5

千	′	二	千	SEN, *chi*, thousand
				千円 *sen'en*, a thousand yen 三千 *sanzen*, three thousand 五千 *gosen*, five thousand
12 **3 strokes**				☑ 5

日	丨	冂	日	NICHI, JITSU; *hi*, day, sun; ~*ka*, suffix for counting days
	日			日曜日 *nichiyōbi*, Sunday 昨日 *sakujitsu*, *kinō*, yesterday 朝日 *asahi*, morning sun
13 **4 strokes**				☑ 5

月	丿	几	月	GETSU, GATSU; *tsuki*, month, moon
	月			月曜日 *getsuyōbi*, Monday 来月 *raigetsu*, next month 三日月 *mikazuki*, new moon
14 **4 strokes**				☑ 5

3

火	、	丷	少	KA; *hi*, fire 火曜日 *kayōbi, Tuesday* 火ばち *hibachi*, charcoal brazier 火事　*kaji*, fire, conflagration
15 4 strokes	火			☑ 5

水	]	刀	水	SUI; *mizu*, water 大水　*ō-mizu*, flood, inundation 水力　*suiryoku*, water power 水兵　*suihei*, sailor
16 4 strokes	水			☑ 5

木	一	十	才	BOKU, MOKU; *ki*, tree, wood 木曜日 *mokuyōbi, Thursday* 材木　*zaimoku*, lumber 木製　*mokusei*, made of wood
17 4 strokes	木			☑ 5

金	ノ	人	𠆢	KIN, KON, gold; *kane*, money 金曜日 *kin'yōbi, Friday* お金　*o-kane*, money 金魚　*kingyo*, goldfish
	今	全	余	
18 8 strokes	余	金		☑ 5

土	一	十	土	DO, TO; *tsuchi*, earth, soil 土曜日 *doyōbi, Saturday* 土地　*tochi*, ground, plot of land 土人　*dojin*, native
19 3 strokes				☑ 5

年

20
6 strokes

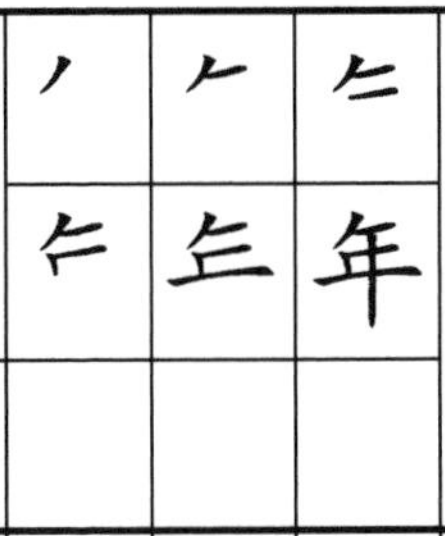

NEN; *toshi*, year

六年生	*rokunensei*, sixth-grade pupil
年寄り	*toshiyori*, old person
青年	*seinen*, youth

✓ 5

左

21
5 strokes

SA; *hidari*, left

左派	*saha*, leftist (political), left wing
左側	*sasoku*, *hidarigawa*, left side
左手	*hidarite*, left hand

✓ 5

右

22
5 strokes

U, YŪ; *migi*, right

左右	*sayū*, left and right
右派	*uha*, right wing (political)
右側	*usoku*, *migigawa*, right side

✓ 5

上

23
3 strokes

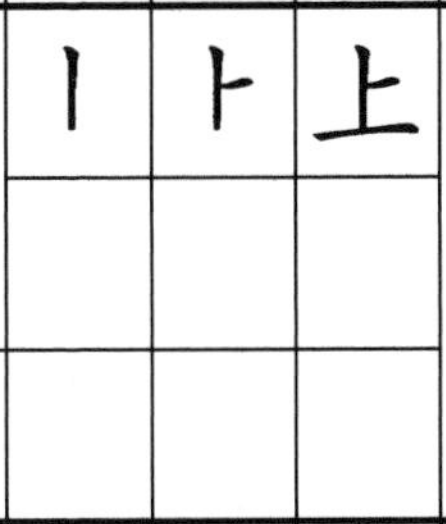

JŌ; *ue*, top, above, on; *kami*, upper; *nobo(ru)*, to go up, to go toward Tōkyō; *a(geru)*, to raise; *a(garu)*, to rise

上流	*jōryū*, upstream, upper class
海上	*kaijō*, on the sea, maritime
川上	*kawakami*, upstream

✓ 5

下

24
3 strokes

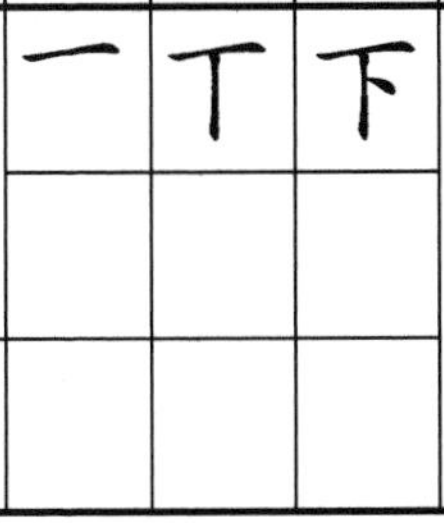

KA, GE; *shita*, bottom, under, beneath; *moto*, base; *shimo*, lower; *kuda(ru)*, to go down, to go away from Tōkyō; *sa(geru)*, to hang (v.t.), to lower; *sa(garu)*, to hang down; *kuda(saru)*, to bestow

川下	*kawashimo*, downstream
下品	*gehin*, vulgar, coarse
地下鉄	*chikatetsu*, subway

✓ 5

大	一	ナ	大	DAI, TAI; ō(kii), big, large, great
				大学　　daigaku, university, college 大変　　taihen, tremendous, serious 大広間 ō-hiroma, grand hall
25 3 strokes				☑ 5

中	ノ	冂	口	CHŪ; naka, middle, within, inside; JŪ, throughout
	中			中学校 chūgakkō, middle school 中心　　chūshin, center, heart (of a 　　　　city, etc.)
26 4 strokes				集中　　shūchū, concentration ☑ 5

小	｣	小	小	SHŌ; ko, o-, chii(sai), small, minor
				小学校 shōgakkō, primary school 小屋　　koya, hut 小説　　shōsetsu, novel (fiction)
27 3 strokes				☑ 5

入	ノ	入		NYŪ; iri, entering, attendance; i(reru), to put in; hai(ru), to enter
				入学　　nyūgaku, entering school 輸入　　yunyū, importation 入口　　iriguchi, entrance
28 2 strokes				☑ 5

出	丨	屮	屮	SHUTSU, SUI; de(ru), to come out, to go out; da(su), to put out, to take out, to bring out, to draw out
	出	出		出発　　shuppatsu, setting out, 　　　　departure, starting
29 5 strokes				出版　　shuppan, publishing 出口　　deguchi, exit　☑ 5

目	丨	冂	月	MOKU, BOKU; *me*, eye; also used as an ordinal suffix
	月	目		横目　*yokome*, side glance 目的　*mokuteki*, purpose 目標　*mokuhyō*, mark, target
30 5 strokes				☑ 4

見	丨	冂	月	KEN; *mi(ru)*, to see, to look; *mi(eru)*, to be visible, to be able to see; *mi(seru)*, to show, to display
	月	目	貝	見事　*migoto*, splendid 見物　*kenbutsu*, sightseeing 見本　*mihon*, sample
31 7 strokes	見			☑ 5

耳	一	厂	下	JI; *mimi*, ear
	耳	耳	耳	早耳　　*hayamimi*, keen of hearing 耳鳴り　*miminari*, ringing in the ears
32 6 strokes				耳が遠い *mimi ga tōi*, deaf　3

音	丶	二	亠	ON, IN; *ne*, *oto*, sound
	立	立	产	音楽　*ongaku*, music 発音　*hatsuon*, pronunciation 母音　*boin*, vowel
33 9 strokes	音	音	音	☑ 4

口	丨	冂	口	KŌ, KU; *kuchi*, mouth
				口ひげ *kuchihige*, mustache 入口　*iriguchi*, entrance 口論　*kōron*, dispute
34 3 strokes				☑ 4

手	一	二	三	SHU; *te*, hand
	手			握手　　*akushu*, handshake 手袋　　*tebukuro*, gloves 手紙　　*tegami*, letter
35 4 strokes				☑ 4

足	ノ	口	口	SOKU; *ashi*, foot, leg; *ta(riru)*, to be sufficient; *ta(su)*, to add, to supplement
	尺	尺	尺	足跡　　*ashi-ato*, footprint 満足　　*manzoku*, satisfaction
36 7 strokes	足			不足　　*fusoku*, insufficiency　☑ 4

立	、	二	立	RITSU, RYŪ; *ta(tsu)*, (v.i.), to stand; *ta(teru)* (v.t.), to erect, to set up
	立	立		独立　　*dokuritsu*, independence 役立つ　*yakudatsu*, useful
37 5 strokes				立場　　*tachiba*, standpoint　☑ 4

力	フ	力		RYOKU, RIKI; *chikara*, strength, power
				力持　　*chikaramochi*, strong 　　　　　person 協力　　*kyōryoku*, co-operation
38 2 strokes				努力　　*doryoku*, endeavor　☑ 4

人	ノ	人		JIN, NIN; *hito*, person
				人類　　*jinrui*, human race 人間　　*ningen*, human being
39 2 strokes				人口　　*jinkō*, population　☑ 5

子	㇇	了	子	SHI, SU; *ko*, child
				子ども *kodomo*, child, children
				原子 *genshi*, atom
				様子 *yōsu*, the state of things, appearance
40 3 strokes				☑ 5

女	く	夕	女	JO, NYO; *me*, female; *onna*, woman, girl
				女中 *jochū*, maid
				少女 *shōjo*, maiden
				女王 *joō*, queen
41 3 strokes				☑ 5

男	丨	冂	冂	DAN, NAN; *otoko*, man, male
	田	田	甲	男性 *dansei*, male sex, male
	男			男子 *danshi*, male, boy
				長男 *chōnan*, eldest son
42 7 strokes				☑ 5

先	ノ	⺧	牛	SEN; *saki*, previous, ahead
	生	歨	先	先生 *sensei*, teacher
				先日 *senjitsu*, the other day
				行き先 *yukisaki*, destination
43 6 strokes				☑ 5

生	ノ	⺧	牛	SEI, SHŌ, birth, life; *u(mareru)*, to be born; *u(mu)*, to give birth; *i(kiru)*, to live; *ki*, pure, genuine; *nama*, raw; *ha(eru)*, to grow, to spring up
	牛	生		一生 *isshō*, one's (whole) life
				生活 *seikatsu*, livelihood
44 5 strokes				大学生 *daigakusei*, college student ☑ 5

学	丶	゛	⺌	GAKU, learning, science; *mana(bu)*, to learn
	⺌	⺍	学	学校　*gakkō*, school 医学　*igaku*, medicine 科学　*kagaku*, science
45 8 strokes	学	学		☑ 5

校	一	十	木	KŌ, school; to correct, to investigate, to compare, to think
	术	杧	栌	校正　*kōsei*, proofreading 校舎　*kōsha*, school building 校友　*kōyū*, alumnus
46 10 strokes	栌	栌	校	☑ 5

王	一	丁	千	Ō, king
	王			王様　*ōsama*, king 王子　*ōji*, prince 王国　*ōkoku*, kingdom, monarchy
47 4 strokes				3

玉	一	丁	千	GYOKU; *tama*, jewel, round object
	王	玉		水玉　*mizutama*, drop of water 目玉　*medama*, eyeball 宝玉　*hōgyoku*, gem
48 5 strokes				2

貝	丨	冂	冃	*kai*, sea shell
	月	目	貝	貝殻　*kaigara*, shell 貝拾い　*kaihiroi*, shell gathering 真珠貝　*shinjugai*, pearl oyster
49 7 strokes	貝			2

円	丨	冂	円
	円		
50 4 strokes			

EN, circle, yen (Japanese monetary unit); *maru(i)*, round

円満   *enman*, perfection, satisfaction
千円札   *sen'ensatsu*, thousand-yen bill
円盤   *enban*, disc   ☑ 5

赤	一	十	土
	夫	赤	赤
	赤		
51 7 strokes			

SEKI, SHAKU; *aka*, *aka(i)*, red; *aka(rameru)* (v.t.), to color up, to add blush; *aka(ramu)*, to turn red, to blush

赤ちゃん   *akachan*, baby, infant
赤十字   *sekijūji*, Red Cross
赤銅   *shakudō*, alloy of copper and gold   ☑ 4

青	一	二	主
	主	青	青
	青	青	
52 8 strokes			

SEI, SHŌ; *ao*, *ao(i)*, blue, green, inexperienced

青年   *seinen*, youth
青白い   *aojiroi*, pale
青空   *aozora*, blue sky   ☑ 4

白	ノ	イ	白
	白	白	
53 5 strokes			

HAKU, BYAKU; *shiro*, *shiro(i)*, white

白人   *hakujin*, Caucasian
白状   *hakujō*, confession
白鳥   *hakuchō*, swan   ☑ 5

夕	ノ	ク	夕
54 3 strokes			

SEKI; *yū*, evening

夕方   *yūgata*, evening
夕飯   *yūhan*, supper
夕風   *yūkaze*, evening breeze   ☑ 4

名	ノ	ク	タ	MEI, MYŌ, name, fame; *na*, name
	タ	名	名	名まえ *namae*, name 有名 *yūmei*, famous, well-known 名人 *meijin*, an expert
55 6 strokes				☑ 5

早	丶	冂	冃	SŌ; *haya*, *haya(i)*, early, fast
	日	旦	早	早口 *haya-kuchi*, quick speaking 早春 *sōshun*, early spring 手早い *tebayai*, quick, nimble
56 6 strokes				☑ 4

草	一	十	艹	SŌ; *kusa*, grass, vegetation
	艹	节	苩	草原 *kusahara, sōgen*, grassy plain 草案 *sōan*, draft (of a manuscript) 草取り *kusatori*, weeding
57 9 strokes	苩	莒	草	3

山	丨	凵	山	SAN; *yama*, mountain
				山道 *sandō, yamamichi*, mountain path 山脈 *sanmyaku*, mountain range 登山 *tozan*, mountain climbing
58 3 strokes				☑ 5

川	丿	川	川	SEN; *kawa*, river
				谷川 *tanigawa*, mountain stream 川端 *kawabata*, riverside 川口 *kawaguchi*, mouth of a river
59 3 strokes				☑ 5

田	丨	冂	冂	DEN; *ta*, rice field
	田	田		田園　*den'en*, fields and gardens, rural districts
60				稲田　*inada*, rice field
5 strokes				田植　*taue*, rice planting　☑ 4

町	丨	冂	冂	CHŌ; *machi*, town
	田	田	田	町外れ *machihazure*, outskirts of a town
61	町			町内　*chōnai*, the neighborhood
7 strokes				町長　*chōchō*, mayor of a town　☑ 4

村	一	十	才	SON; *mura*, village
	木	木	村	村民　*sonmin*, villager
62	村			村長　*sonchō*, village mayor
7 strokes				農村　*nōson*, a farm village　☑ 2

車	一	厂	厅	SHA; *kuruma*, wheel, vehicle
	百	白	亘	自動車　*jidōsha*, automobile
63	車			自転車　*jitensha*, bicycle
7 strokes				発車　*hassha*, departure of a vehicle　☑ 5

林	一	十	才	RIN; *hayashi*, woods
	木	木	村	植林　*shokurin*, reforestation
	村	林		密林　*mitsurin*, thick forest
64				農林　*nōrin*, agriculture and forestry
8 strokes				☑ 2

13

森	一	十	才	SHIN; *mori*, forest, grove
	木	木	本	森林　*shinrin*, forest 森閑　*shinkan*, silent 森厳　*shingen*, solemn, awe- 　　　　inspiring
65 12 strokes	森	森	森	☑ 2

空	、	八	宀	KŪ, *sora*, sky; *a(ku)*, to become empty; *a(keru)*, to vacate; *kara*, emptiness
	宀	穴	空	青空　*aozora*, blue sky 空気　*kūki*, air 空港　*kūkō*, airport
66 8 strokes	空	空		☑ 4

天	一	二	于	TEN, *ame*, sky, heaven
	天			天気　*tenki*, weather 天井　*tenjō*, ceiling 天才　*tensai*, genius
67 4 strokes				☑ 5

気	ノ	⺈	⺌	KI, spirit, energy, mind; KE
	气	气	気	天気　*tenki*, weather 元気　*genki*, good spirits, health 病気　*byōki*, sickness
68 6 strokes				☑ 5

雨	一	厂	冂	U; *ame*, rain
	帀	雨	雨	大雨　*ō-ame*, heavy rain 雨戸　*amado*, rain door, shutter 梅雨　*baiu, tsuyu*, rainy season of 　　　　early summer
69 8 strokes	雨	雨		☑ 5

花	一	十	艹	KA; *hana*, flower
	艹	艼	花	花屋 *hanaya*, flower shop, florist 花瓶 *kabin*, vase 花火 *hanabi*, fireworks
70 **7 strokes**	花			✓ 4

竹	ノ	⺦	⺮	CHIKU; *take*, bamboo
	⺣	竹	竹	竹やぶ *takeyabu*, bamboo grove 竹細工 *takezaiku*, bamboo ware 竹かご *takekago*, bamboo basket
71 **6 strokes**				2

石	一	ア	石	SEKI, KOKU, SHAKU; *ishi*, stone
	石	石		小石 *ko-ishi*, pebble 石炭 *sekitan*, coal 磁石 *jishaku*, magnet
72 **5 strokes**				✓ 3

犬	一	ナ	大	KEN; *inu*, dog
	犬			小犬 *ko-inu*, puppy 番犬 *banken*, watchdog 狂犬病 *kyōkenbyō*, rabies
73 **4 strokes**				✓ 4

虫	丶	口	口	CHŪ; *mushi*, insect, bug, worm
	中	虫	虫	害虫 *gaichū*, harmful insect 虫歯 *mushiba*, decayed tooth 昆虫 *konchū*, insect, bug
74 **6 strokes**				2

糸	ㄥ	ㄠ	ㄠ	SHI; *ito*, thread
	幺	糹	糸	毛糸　　*keito*, woolen yarn 糸口　　*itoguchi*, clue 糸巻　　*itomaki*, spool for thread
75 6 strokes				2

本	一	十	才	HON, book, suffix for counting long, slender objects; *moto*, basis, essence, (tree) root
	木	本		一本　　*ippon*, one (bottle, rod, etc.) 本箱　　*honbako*, bookcase
76 5 strokes				日本　　*Nihon*, *Nippon*, Japan　✓ 5

文	、	二	ナ	BUN, writings, a sentence; MON, old unit of money; *fumi*, letter, book
	文			文化　　*bunka*, culture 文学　　*bungaku*, literature
77 4 strokes				文句　　*monku*, complaint; phrase　✓ 4

字	、	八	宀	JI, letter, mark; *aza*, section (of a village)
	宀	宁	字	字引　　*jibiki*, dictionary 文字　　*moji*, *monji*, letter, character, ideograph
78 6 strokes				数字　　*sūji*, number, numeral　✓ 4

正	一	丁	下	SEI, SHŌ; *tada(shii)*, correct, right; *tada(su)*, to correct, to rectify; *masa(ni)*, surely, truly
	正	正		正直　　*shōjiki*, honesty 正方形　*seihōkei*, square (geometrical figure)
79 5 strokes				正月　　*shōgatsu*, New Year's　✓ 4

16

休	ノ	イ	什	KYŪ; *yasu(mi)*, rest, vacation; *yasu(mu)*, to rest
	什	休	休	休憩 *kyūkei*, rest, intermission 休日 *kyūjitsu*, holiday 休養 *kyūyō*, relaxation, recreation
80 6 strokes				✓ 5

引	⁻	⁼	弓	IN; *hiki*, pulling; *hi(ku)*, to pull, to draw
	引			福引き *fukubiki*, lottery 引用 *in'yō*, quotation, citation 引き立て *hikitate*, favor, patronage
81 4 strokes				✓ 3

羽	フ	ヲ	习	U; *hane*, *ha*, feather, plumage; *-wa*, counter for birds, and rabbits
	羽	羽	羽	羽毛 *umō*, feathers, plumage 一羽 *ichiwa*, one (bird) 羽織 *haori*, haori coat
82 6 strokes				2

雲	一	⼆	于	UN; *kumo*, cloud
	乑	雨	雩	雲状 *unjō*, cloudlike, nebulous 入道雲 *nyūdōgumo*, gigantic clouds 星雲 *seiun*, nebula
	雲	雲	雲	
83 12 strokes				2

園	丨	冂	同	EN; *sono*, garden
	冑	周	周	公園 *kōen*, public park 花園 *hanazono*, flower garden 動物園 *dōbutsu-en*, zoo
	園	園		
84 13 strokes				✓ 3

遠	土	吉	声	**EN, ON**; *tō(i)*, far, distant
	声	声	袁	遠足　　*ensoku*, excursion, long walk
85 13 strokes	袁	遠	遠	遠方　　*enpō*, long distance 永遠　　*eien*, eternity
				☑ 3

何	ノ	イ	仁	**KA**; *nani*, what, how many (interrogative prefix)
	仁	何	何	何人　　*nannin*, how many people? 何時間 *nanjikan*, how much time?
86 7 strokes	何			何時　　*nanji*, what time?
				☑ 5

科	一	二	千	**KA**, course, branch
	禾	禾	禾	学科　　*gakka*, a school subject 教科書　*kyōkasho*, textbook
87 9 strokes	禾	科	科	科学　　*kagaku*, science
				☑ 3

夏	一	一	厂	**KA**; *natsu*, summer
	丙	百	百	夏休み *natsuyasumi*, summer vacation 初夏　　*shoka*, early summer
88 10 strokes	頁	夏	夏	真夏　　*manatsu*, midsummer
				☑ 4

家	、	八	宀	**KA, KE**; *ie, ya*, house
	宀	宀	宁	家主　　*yanushi*, owner of a house, landlord
89 10 strokes	家	家	家	家族　　*kazoku*, family 農家　　*nōka*, farmhouse
				☑ 4

歌	一	可	可	KA; *uta*, song; *uta(u)*, to sing
	可	哥	哥	国歌　　*kokka*, national anthem 歌劇　　*kageki*, opera 歌手　　*kashu*, singer
90 14 strokes	歌	歌	歌	☑ 4

画	一	厂	币	GA, a picture; KAKU, stroke of a Japanese character
	币	雨	雨	図画　　*zuga*, a drawing 映画　　*eiga*, moving picture 計画　　*keikaku*, plan
91 8 strokes	画	画		☑ 4

回	l	冂	冂	KAI, a turn; *mawa(su)*, to turn (v.t.); *mawa(ru)*, to turn (v.i.)
	同	回	回	何回　　*nankai*, how many times? 回転　　*kaiten*, revolution, rotation 回数　　*kaisū*, number of times,
92 6 strokes				frequency 　　　　　　　　　　　　　☑ 3

会	ノ	人	人	KAI, meeting; *a(u)*, to meet; E
	仝	会	会	会場　　*kaijō*, place of meeting, site 会長　　*kaichō*, president (of a 　　　　society), chairman (of a 　　　　committee)
93 6 strokes				会話　　*kaiwa*, conversation 　　　　　　　　　　　　　☑ 4

海	丶	冫	氵	KAI; *umi*, sea, ocean
	氵	汒	汒	海岸　　*kaigan*, seacoast, seaside 海水浴　*kaisuiyoku*, sea bathing 海外　　*kaigai*, overseas, abroad
94 9 strokes	汘	海	海	☑ 4

絵	㇐	幺	糸	KAI; E, picture
	糺	紣	紣	浮世絵 *ukiyoe*, Japanese print 絵葉書 *ehagaki*, picture postcard 挿し絵 *sashie*, illustration
95 12 strokes	給	絵	絵	☑ 3

外	㇒	ク	タ	GAI, GE, outside, foreign; *hoka*, other; *soto*, outside
	列	外		外国　　*gaikoku*, foreign country 外国人 *gaikokujin*, foreigner 外科　　*geka*, surgery
96 5 strokes				☑ 5

角	㇒	ク	⺈	KAKU, angle; *tsuno*, horn of an animal; *kado*, corner
	角	角	角	三角　　*sankaku*, triangle 四角　　*shikaku*, square 角度　　*kakudo*, angle
97 7 strokes	角			2

楽	㇒	亻	白	GAKU, music; RAKU, comfort, ease; *tano(shii)*, pleasant
	白	白	泊	楽しみ *tanoshimi*, pleasure 音楽会 *ongakukai*, concert, musical 気楽　 *kiraku*, ease, comfort
98 13 strokes	洆	淞	楽	☑ 4

活	丶	冫	氵	KATSU, energy
	氵	汇	汗	生活　　*seikatsu*, life 活動　　*katsudō*, activity 活字　　*katsuji*, printer's type
99 9 strokes	汗	活	活	☑ 3

間	ノ	⼝	⼾	KAN, KEN; *aida*, interval, space; *ma*, interval, room, time
	⼾	⼾	門	時間　　*jikan*, time 二時間　*nijikan*, two hours 昼間　　*hiruma*, daytime
100 12 strokes	門	門	間	☑ 5

丸	ノ	九	丸	GAN; *maru*, round (n.); *maru(i)*, round (adj.); -*maru*, suffix in ship names; *maru(meru)*, to make (something) round
				丸薬　　*gan'yaku*, pill 日の丸 *hinomaru*, national flag of 　　　　Japan
101 3 strokes				丸太　　*maruta*, log (of timber)　2

岩	⼁	山	山	GAN; *iwa*, rock, crag
	山	岸	岩	花こう岩 *kakōgan*, granite 岩石　　*ganseki*, rock 岩屋　　*iwaya*, cavern
102 8 strokes	岩	岩		2

顔	立	产	产	GAN; *kao*, face
	彦	彦	彦	顔面　　*ganmen*, face 顔色　　*kao-iro*, complexion 顔付　　*kaotsuki*, face, look, 　　　　countenance
103 18 strokes	彦	顔	顔	☑ 3

汽	丶	丷	氵	KI, steam, vapor
	氵	汽	汽	汽車　　*kisha*, steam-driven train 汽笛　　*kiteki*, steam whistle 汽船　　*kisen*, steamship, steamboat
104 7 strokes	汽			1

記	、	二	言	**KI**, chronicle; *shiru(su)*, to write down
	言	言	訂	日記 *nikki*, diary 記念 *kinen*, remembrance, souvenir
105 10 strokes	記	記		記者 *kisha*, journalist ✓ 3

帰	｜	リ	尸	**KI**; *kae(ru)*, to return, to leave
	尸	尸	尸	帰り道 *kaerimichi*, (on) one's way back 帰化人 *kikajin*, naturalized person
106 10 strokes	帰	帰	帰	帰国 *kikoku*, return to one's native country ✓ 4

弓	ユ	コ	弓	**KYŪ**; *yumi*, bow, archery
				弓道 *kyūdō*, Japanese archery 弓弦 *yumizuru*, bowstring 弓状 *kyūjō*, arch, bow shape
107 3 strokes				1

牛	ノ	⊢	二	**GYŪ**; *ushi*, cow, bull
	牛			小牛 *ko-ushi*, calf 牛乳 *gyūnyū*, milk 牛肉 *gyūniku*, beef
108 4 strokes				✓ 4

魚	ノ	ク	仁	**GYO**; *uo, sakana*, fish
	名	角	角	金魚 *kingyo*, goldfish 魚市場 *uo-ichiba*, fish market 魚釣り *uotsuri*, fishing
109 11 strokes	魚	魚	魚	✓ 4

京	、	二	亠
	古	亩	亨
110 8 strokes	亨	京	

KYŌ, capital; KEI, ten quadrillion

東京　　*Tōkyō*, capital of Japan
京都　　*Kyōto*, ancient capital of Japan
上京　　*jōkyō*, going to Tōkyō

☑ 4

強	ㄱ	ㄱ	弓
	弘	弘	弘
111 11 strokes	殆	強	強

KYŌ, GŌ; *tsuyo(i)*, strong; *tsuyo(meru)* (v.t.), to reinforce, to emphasize; *shi(ite)*, by force; *shii(ru)*, to force, to urge

勉強　　*benkyō*, study
強弱　　*kyōjaku*, strength and weakness
強情　　*gōjō*, obstinacy

☑ 4

教	土	少	老
	孝	孝	孝
112 11 strokes	孝	教	教

KYŌ; *oshi(eru)*, to teach

教室　　*kyōshitsu*, classroom
教育　　*kyōiku*, education
教会　　*kyōkai*, church

☑ 4

近	一	厂	斥
	斤	沂	近
113 7 strokes	近		

KIN; *chika(i)*, near

近道　　*chikamichi*, shortcut
近所　　*kinjo*, neighborhood
最近　　*saikin*, recently

☑ 4

兄	丶	口	口
	尸	兄	
114 5 strokes			

KEI, KYŌ; *ani*, older brother

兄弟　　*kyōdai*, brothers (and sisters)
父兄　　*fukei*, guardians (of pupils)

☑ 4

形	一	二	干	KEI, GYŌ; *katachi*, ~*gata*, shape, form
	开	刑	形	人形　　*ningyō*, doll 長方形　*chōhōkei*, rectangle 半円形　*han'enkei*, semicircle
115 **7 strokes**	形			☑ 3

計	、	二	亖	KEI; *haka(ru)*, to measure; *haka(rau)*, to arrange, to discuss
	言	言	言	合計　　*gōkei*, sum, total 寒暖計　*kandankei*, weather thermometer
116 **9 strokes**	言	言	計	体温計　*taionkei*, clinical thermometer　☑ 4

元	一	二	テ	GEN, GAN; *moto*, beginning, foundation
	元			根元　　*kongen*, *nemoto*, root, origin, source 元来　　*ganrai*, originally, primarily
117 **4 strokes**				元日　　*ganjitsu*, New Year's　☑ 4

言	、	亠	亠	GEN, GON, speech, statement; *koto*, word, speech, expression; *i(u)*, to say
	言	言	言	方言　　*hōgen*, dialect 無言　　*mugon*, silence, muteness
118 **7 strokes**	言			言葉　　*kotoba*, word, language　☑ 4

原	一	厂	厂	GEN, original; *hara*, field, meadow
	厂	厉	盾	原因　　*gen'in*, cause 高原　　*kōgen*, plateau 草原　　*sōgen*, *kusahara*, grassy plain
119 **10 strokes**	原	原	原	3

24

戸	一	ヲ	ヨ	**KO**; *to*, door
	戸			戸外　*kogai*, outdoors 木戸　*kido*, gate, door 江戸　*Edo*, old name for Tōkyō
120 4 strokes				⬜2

古	一	十	十	**KO**; *furu(i)*, old, ancient
	古	古		古代　*kodai*, ancient times 古今　*kokon*, past and present 考古学　*kōkogaku*, archeology
121 5 strokes				✓4

午	ノ	ト	느	**GO**, noon
	午			午前　*gozen*, morning, A.M. 午後　*gogo*, afternoon, P.M. 正午　*shōgo*, noon
122 4 strokes				✓5

後	ノ	ク	彳	**GO, KŌ**; *ushi(ro)*, behind; *nochi*, after; *ato*, the rear, after, the remainder
	彳	彳	彳	食後　*shokugo*, after a meal 最後　*saigo*, last
123 9 strokes	移	移	後	前後　*zengo*, before and after, context ✓5

語	丶	二	言	**GO**, word, speech; *katari*, narration; *kata(ru)*, to tell, to speak
	言	言	訂	外国語　*gaikokugo*, foreign language 英語　*eigo*, English language
124 14 strokes	語	語	語	物語　*monogatari*, tale ✓5

工	一	丁	工	**KŌ, KU**, worker, construction
				工夫 *kōfu*, workman; *kufū*, device
125 3 strokes				工事中 *kōjichū*, under construction
				工学 *kōgaku*, engineering ✓ 4

公	ノ	八	公	**KŌ**; *ōyake*, public
	公			主人公 *shujinkō*, hero, heroine
126 4 strokes				公園 *kōen*, public park
				公転 *kōten*, revolution, turning ✓ 4

広	丶	宀	广	**KŌ**; *hiro(i)*, wide; *hiro(geru)*, to spread (v.t.); *hiro(garu)*, to spread (v.i.); *hiro(maru)*, to be spread
	広	広		広場 *hiroba*, open space, plaza
127 5 strokes				広告 *kōkoku*, advertisement
				広大 *kōdai*, vast ✓ 4

交	丶	宀	六	**KŌ**; *ma(jiru)*, to be mixed; *maji(waru)*, to associate with; *ka(wasu)*, to exchange
	六	疒	交	交際 *kōsai*, intercourse, association
128 6 strokes				交番 *kōban*, police box
				交通 *kōtsū*, traffic 3

光	丨	丬	业	**KŌ**; *hikari*, light, ray; *hika(ru)*, to shine
	业	半	光	光年 *kōnen*, light-year
129 6 strokes				光波 *kōha*, light wave
				観光 *kankō*, sightseeing 3

考 130 6 strokes	一 少	十 芳	土 考	**KŌ**; *kanga(e)*, thought, idea, opinion; *kanga(eru)*, to think 参考 *sankō*, reference 考案 *kōan*, idea, plan, scheme 考査 *kōsa*, examination ☑ 4
行 131 6 strokes	ノ 彳	ク 行	彳 行	**KŌ, GYŌ, AN**; *i(ku)*, *yu(ku)*, to go; *oko(nau)*, to hold, to conduct 行列 *gyōretsu*, procession, queue 急行 *kyūkō*, express 銀行 *ginkō*, bank ☑ 5
高 132 10 strokes	丶 亠 口	亠 高 	亠 高 	**KŌ**; *taka(i)*, high, costly; *taka(maru)*, to rise, to be elevated; *taka(meru)*, to lift, to boost 高等学校 *kōtōgakkō*, high school 最高 *saikō*, highest 高台 *takadai*, elevated land ☑ 5
黄 133 11 strokes	一 艹 苗	廿 苎 苗	廿 苎 黄	**KŌ, Ō**; *ki*, yellow 黄色 *ki-iro*, yellow 黄金 *ōgon*, gold 黄熱病 *ōnetsubyō*, yellow fever 2
合 134 6 strokes	ノ 个	人 合	亼 合	**GŌ**; *a(u)*, to be together, to fit; *a(waseru)*, to join, to combine 合図 *aizu*, signal, sign 都合 *tsugō*, circumstances, convenience 組合 *kumiai*, union ☑ 3

谷	ノ	ハ	ゾ	KOKU; *tani*, valley
	父	谷	谷	谷間 *tanima*, valley 谷底 *tanizoko*, bottom of a ravine 渓谷 *keikoku*, gorge
135 7 strokes	谷			2

国	l	冂	冂	KOKU; *kuni*, country
	冂	用	囯	国語 *kokugo*, national language (Japanese) 国会 *kokkai*, the National Diet 全国 *zenkoku*, national
136 8 strokes	国	国		✓ 5

黒	ヽ	冂	日	KOKU; *kuro*, *kuro(i)*, black
	甲	里	里	黒人 *kokujin*, negro 黒板 *kokuban*, blackboard 暗黒 *ankoku*, darkness, blackness
137 11 strokes	黒	黒	黒	✓ 4

今	ノ	人	仝	KON, KIN; *ima*, now, the present
	今			今月 *kongetsu*, this month 今度 *kondo*, next time 今夜 *kon'ya*, tonight
138 4 strokes				✓ 5

才	一	寸	才	SAI, talent, suffix for counting age
				十六才 *jūroku-sai*, sixteen years old 天才 *tensai*, genius 才能 *sainō*, talent
139 3 strokes				3

細	く	幺	幺	SAI; *hoso(i)*, slender, narrow; *koma(kai)*, minute, fine, detailed
	糸	糸	紅	細道　　*hosomichi*, narrow road 細工　　*saiku*, work, craftsmanship 細菌　　*saikin*, bacillus, germ
140 11 strokes	細	細	細	2

作	ノ	イ	イ	SAKU, SA; *tsuku(ru)*, to make
	仁	竹	作	作文　　*sakubun*, (literary) composition 名作　　*meisaku*, masterpiece 作曲　　*sakkyoku*, musical composition
141 7 strokes	作			✓ 4

算	ノ	ゝ	ゲ	SAN, reckoning
	竹	竹	笞	算数　　*sansū*, arithmetic, calculation 計算　　*keisan*, computation, figuring 予算　　*yosan*, budget
142 14 strokes	笪	算	算	2

止	丨	ト	止	SHI; *to(maru)*, to stop (v.i.); *to(meru)*, to bring to a stop; *tome*, stop
	止			中止　　*chūshi*, discontinuation 禁止　　*kinshi*, prohibition 通行止　*tsūkōdome*, suspension of traffic
143 4 strokes				✓ 4

市	、	二	广	SHI, city; *ichi*, market
	亣	市		市役所　*shiyakusho*, city office 市場　　*ichiba, shijō*, market 都市　　*toshi*, cities
144 5 strokes				✓ 3

矢	ノ	㇏	二	SHI; *ya*, arrow
	矢	矢		矢印　　*yajirushi*, arrow(-sign) 弓矢　　*yumiya*, bow and arrow 一矢　　*isshi*, retort, shot in return
145 5 strokes				1

姉	く	女	女	SHI; *ane*, elder sister
	女	女	女	姉妹　　*shimai, ane-imōto*, sisters 姉娘　　*anemusume*, elder daughter 姉婿　　*anemuko*, elder sister's 　　　　husband
146 8 strokes	姉	姉		✓ 4

思	丨	冂	田	SHI; *omo(u)*, to think, to recall
	田	田	田	思想　　*shisō*, thought, idea 不思議　*fushigi*, strange 思い出　*omoide*, remembrance, 　　　　recollection
147 9 strokes	思	思	思	✓ 4

紙	幺	幺	糸	SHI; *kami*, paper
	糸	糸	糸	ボール紙　*bōrugami*, cardboard 表紙　　*hyōshi*, cover, binding 紙くず　*kamikuzu*, wastepaper
148 10 strokes	紙	紙	紙	✓ 4

寺	一	十	土	JI; *tera*, temple
	土	寺	寺	寺院　　*ji-in*, Buddhist temple 山寺　　*yamadera*, mountain 　　　　temple 寺子屋　*terakoya*, small private 　　　　school in Edo era
149 6 strokes				✓ 2

自	´	⺈	冂	JI, SHI; *mizuka(ra)*, self, in person
	冃	自	自	自分　　*jibun*, self 自信　　*jishin*, confidence 自由　　*jiyū*, freedom
150 6 strokes			☑ 4	

時	丨	刀	日	JI; *toki*, time
	旷	旷	旷	時々　　*tokidoki*, sometimes 時計　　*tokei*, watch, clock 時代　　*jidai*, period, epoch
151 10 strokes	旷	時	時　　☑ 5	

室	丶	丷	宀	SHITSU, room; *muro*, storeroom, cave
	宀	宏	宏	教室　　*kyōshitsu*, classroom 室内　　*shitsunai*, indoors 温室　　*onshitsu*, hothouse,
152 9 strokes	宏	室	室	greenhouse　　☑ 4

社	丶	⺀	⺭	SHA, a company; *yashiro*, Shintō shrine
	⺭	⺭	社	社会　　*shakai*, society, the world, 　　　　 the community 会社　　*kaisha*, (business) company
153 7 strokes	社			神社　　*jinja*, shrine　　☑ 4

弱	⁊	彐	弓	JAKU; *yowa(i)*, weak; *yowa(ru)*, to grow weak, to be perplexed; *yowa(meru)* (v.t.), to weaken
	弓	弖	引	弱虫　　*yowamushi*, weakling 弱音　　*yowane*, complaints
154 10 strokes	弓	弱	弱	貧弱　　*hinjaku*, scantiness, 　　　　 meagerness　　 2

31

首	丶	丷	丷	SHU; *kubi*, neck
	丷	产	首	首輪　*kubiwa*, collar (dog) 手首　*tekubi*, wrist 首府　*shufu*, capital
155 9 strokes	首	首	首	3

秋	一	二	千	SHŪ; *aki*, fall, autumn
	千	禾	禾	初秋　*shoshū*, early autumn 秋風　*akikaze*, autumn breeze 秋分　*shūbun*, autumnal equinox
156 9 strokes	利	秋	秋	✓ 4

週	丿	冂	月	SHŪ, week
	用	用	周	週刊誌 *shūkanshi*, weekly magazine 来週　*raishū*, next week 今週　*konshū*, this week
157 11 strokes	周	调	週	✓ 4

春	一	二	三	SHUN; *haru*, spring
	三	夫	未	春風　*harukaze*, spring breeze 青春　*seishun*, springtime of life 晩春　*banshun*, late spring
158 9 strokes	春	春	春	✓ 4

書	丁	二	ヨ	SHO; *ka(ku)*, to write
	三	聿	書	辞書　*jisho*, dictionary 書物　*shomotsu*, book, volume 教科書 *kyōkasho*, textbook
159 10 strokes	書	書	書	✓ 5

少	ノ	小	小	SHŌ; *suko(shi)*, *suku(nai)*, few, little, scarce
	少			少年 *shōnen*, boy, lad 多少 *tashō*, more or less, somewhat 少佐 *shōsa*, major (army), lieutenant commander (navy)
160 4 strokes				☑ 4

場	一	十	土	JŌ; *ba*, place
	𡈽	𡈽	𡈽	工場 *kōjō*, *kōba*, factory 場所 *basho*, place 仕事場 *shigotoba*, place of work
161 12 strokes	場	場	場	☑ 4

色	ノ	ク	ク	SHOKU, SHIKI; *iro*, color
	名	岳	色	顔色 *kao-iro*, complexion 天然色 *tennenshoku*, natural color, technicolor 色彩 *shikisai*, color, hue
162 6 strokes				☑ 4

食	ノ	入	八	SHOKU, food; *ta(beru)*, to eat; *ku(u)*, to eat
	今	今	宣	食物 *shokumotsu*, food, edibles 食堂 *shokudō*, dining hall 食事 *shokuji*, a meal
163 9 strokes	食	食	食	☑ 5

心	丶	心	心	SHIN; *kokoro*, spirit, heart, mind
	心			心持ち *kokoromochi*, mood, feeling, sensation 真心 *magokoro*, sincerity, devotion 一心 *isshin*, whole-heartedness
164 4 strokes				☑ 4

新	、	亠	立	SHIN; *atara(shii)*, new; *ara(tani)*, newly, afresh; *nii-*, first, new
	辛	亲	亲	新聞　　*shinbun*, newspaper 新年　　*shinnen*, the New Year 新学期　*shingakki*, new school term
165 13 strokes	新	新	新	☑ 4

親	立	亲	亲	SHIN; *oya*, parent; *shita(shimu)*, to make friends with, to take kindly to; *shita(shii)*, intimate, familiar
	新	新	親	両親　　*ryōshin*, parents 親切　　*shinsetsu*, kindness 親類　　*shinrui*, relative, relation
166 16 strokes	親	親	親	☑ 4

図	丨	冂	冂	ZU, drawing, plan; TO; *haka(ru)*, to devise
	冈	汉	図	図画　　*zuga*, drawing, a picture 地図　　*chizu*, map 図書館　*toshokan*, library
167 7 strokes	図			☑ 4

数	丷	米	米	SŪ; *kazu*, number; *kazo(eru)*, to count
	娄	娄	娄	数字　　*sūji*, figure, numeral 数学　　*sūgaku*, mathematics 人数　　*ninzū*, the number of people
168 13 strokes	数	数	数	☑ 3

西	一	厂	冂	SEI, SAI; *nishi*, west
	丙	西	西	西洋　　　*seiyō*, the West, the Occident 大西洋　*Taiseiyō*, Atlantic Ocean 東西　　　*tōzai*, east and west, Orient and Occident
169 6 strokes				☑ 5

声	一	十	士	SEI, SHŌ; *koe*, voice
	吉	吉	吉	泣き声 *nakigoe*, crying voice 音声学 *onseigaku*, phonetics 声帯 *seitai*, the vocal cords
170 **7 strokes**	声			3

星	丶	口	曰	SEI, JŌ; *hoshi*, star
	曰	尸	尸	星座 *seiza*, constellation 火星 *kasei*, Mars 明星 *myōjō*, Venus
171 **9 strokes**	早	昇	星	2

晴	l	冂	月	SEI; *ha(re)*, fine weather; *ha(reru)*, to clear (weather), to be dispelled; *ha(rasu)*, to clear away, to dispel (doubts)
	日	日一	日十	秋晴れ *akibare*, clear autumn weather
172 **12 strokes**	日キ	晴	晴	晴れ着 *haregi*, one's best clothes 晴天 *seiten*, fine weather ✓ 3

切	一	七	切	SETSU, SAI; *ki(ru)*, to cut; *ki(reru)*, to be sharp, to snap, to break, to run out, to expire
	切			一切れ *hitokire*, one slice 親切 *shinsetsu*, kindness
173 **4 strokes**				一切 *issai*, all, everything ✓ 4

雪	一	冖	冖	SETSU; *yuki*, snow
	帀	雨	雨	雪だるま *yukidaruma*, snowman 雪解け *yukidoke*, thaw 積雪 *sekisetsu*, snowdrift
174 **11 strokes**	雪	雪	雪	✓ 3

船	ノ	力	角
	角	舟	舟

SEN; *fune, funa*, boat, ship

渡し船　*watashi-bune*, ferry
船員　　*sen'in*, sailor
汽船　　*kisen*, steamboat, steamship

175 11 strokes	船	船	船

3

線	く	幺	糸
	糸'	約	約

SEN, line, track, wire, string

地平線　*chiheisen*, horizon (on land)
光線　　*kōsen*, light, beam, ray
直線　　*chokusen*, straight line

176 15 strokes	線	線	線

✓ 2

前	丶	ᨆ	丷
	广	疒	前

ZEN; *mae*, before, in front of, previous

午前　　*gozen*, morning, A.M.
前後　　*zengo*, before and after, context
以前　　*izen*, ago, since, before

177 9 strokes	前	前	前

✓ 5

組	㇀	幺	幺
	糸	糽	紀

SO; *kumi*, class, group, set; *ku(mu)*, to join, to unite

組み立て *kumitate*, construction, structure
一組　　*hitokumi*, one set, one class
番組　　*bangumi*, program

178 11 strokes	紀	組	組

✓ 3

走	一	十	土
	キ	キ	走

SŌ; *hashi(ru)*, to run

競走　　*kyōsō*, race, running match
走り書き *hashirigaki*, hasty writing
走り去る *hashirisaru*, to run away

179 7 strokes	走		

✓ 4

多	ノ	ク	タ	TA; ō(i), many, much, abundant
	夕	多	多	多数　*tasū*, large number 多分　*tabun*, perhaps 多量　*taryō*, great quantity
180 6 strokes				☑ 4

太	一	ナ	大	TAI, TA; *futo(i)*, big, deep (voice), bold (lines), shameless; *futo(ru)*, to grow fat
	太			太陽　*taiyō*, sun 丸太　*maruta*, log
181 4 strokes				太平洋 *Taiheiyō*, Pacific Ocean ☑ 3

体	ノ	イ	仁	TAI, TEI, body; *karada*, the body, health
	什	付	休	体育　*tai-iku*, physical education 団体　*dantai*, a group 車体　*shatai*, body of a vehicle
182 7 strokes	体			☑ 4

台	∠	ム	仁	DAI, TAI; a stand
	台	台		台風　*taifū*, typhoon 舞台　*butai*, stage 燈台　*tōdai*, lighthouse
183 5 strokes				☑ 4

地	一	十	土	CHI, JI, earth, ground
	圠	地	地	地上　*chijō*, on the ground 地下　*chika*, underground 地面　*jimen*, surface of the earth
184 6 strokes				☑ 4

池	、	＼	⅓	CHI; *ike*, pond, lake
	氵	汁	池	電池　　*denchi*, electric cell, battery
185 6 strokes				池畔　　*chihan*, side of a pond, around a pond
				用水池　*yōsuichi*, reservoir
				✓ 2

知	ノ	ヒ	ヒ	CHI; *shi(ru)*, to know; *shi(raseru)*, to inform
	チ	矢	知	知識　　*chishiki*, knowledge
186 8 strokes	知	知		知人　　*chijin*, an acquaintance
				承知　　*shōchi*, assent, agreement
				✓ 4

茶	一	十	艹	CHA, SA, tea, tea plant
	ザ	艼	苂	茶色　　*cha-iro*, light brown
187 9 strokes	苂	茶	茶	茶の湯　*cha-no-yu*, tea ceremony
				茶わん　*chawan*, teacup, rice bowl
				✓ 4

昼	﹁	コ	尸	CHŪ; *hiru*, noon, daytime
	尺	尺	尽	昼間　　*hiruma*, daytime
188 9 strokes	尽	昼	昼	昼夜　　*chūya*, day and night
				昼食　　*chūshoku*, noon meal, lunch
				✓ 4

長	｜	厂	F	CHŌ, head of an institution or organization; *naga(i)*, long
	F	乤	長	細長い　*hosonagai*, long and narrow
189 8 strokes	長	長		長ぐつ　*nagagutsu*, boots
				校長　　*kōchō*, principal of a school
				✓ 5

38

鳥	'	イ	户	CHŌ; *tori*, bird
	户	户	自	鳥類　　*chōrui*, birds (as a species) 小鳥　　*kotori*, small bird 渡り鳥　*wataridori*, migratory bird
190 11 strokes	鳥	鳥	鳥	☑ 4

朝	一	十	十	CHŌ; *asa*, morning
	古	吉	吉	朝刊　　*chōkan*, morning paper 朝食　　*chōshoku*, breakfast 毎朝　　*mai-asa*, every morning
191 12 strokes	直	卓	朝	☑ 4

直	一	十	宀	CHOKU, upright, honest, cheap; JIKI, direct; *tada(chini)*, immediately; *nao(su)*, to repair, to put right, to convert; *nao(ru)*, to be repaired, to change for the better
	市	市	直	
192 8 strokes	直	直		直角　　*chokkaku*, right angle 正直　　*shōjiki*, honesty 素直　　*sunao*, gentle, obedient　3

通	⁊	⁊	⁊	TSŪ; *tō(ru)*, to go along, to pass; *tō(su)*, to let pass, to continue; *kayo(u)*, to go back and forth, to commute
	冎	吊	甬	
193 10 strokes	通	通	通	大通り　*ō-dōri*, main street 通信　　*tsūshin*, correspondence, communication 通訳　　*tsūyaku*, interpreter　☑ 4

弟	丶	⼢	丷	TEI, DAI; *otōto*, younger brother
	弟	弟	弟	兄弟　　*kyōdai*, brothers 弟妹　　*teimai*, younger brothers and sisters
194 7 strokes	弟			☑ 4

39

店	、	一	广	**TEN**; *mise*, store
	广	庁	庐	店番　*miseban*, tending a store 商店　*shōten*, store (shop) 売店　*baiten*, stand, stall
195 **8 strokes**	店	店		☑ 4

点	⌐	├	上	**TEN**, point, marks, dot
	占	占	点	点数　*tensū*, merit marks 点字　*tenji*, braille points 決勝点 *kesshōten*, goal
196 **9 strokes**	点	点	点	☑ 3

電	一	二	干	**DEN**, lightning, electricity
	雨	雨	雪	電気　*denki*, electricity 電話　*denwa*, telephone 電報　*denpō*, telegram
197 **13 strokes**	雪	雷	電	☑ 5

刀	コ	刀		**TŌ**; *katana*, sword
				小刀　*kogatana*, pocketknife 大刀　*daitō*, long sword 軍刀　*guntō*, sabre
198 **2 strokes**				1

冬	ノ	ク	夂	**TŌ**; *fuyu*, winter
	冬	冬		冬休み *fuyuyasumi*, winter vacation 冬眠　*tōmin*, hibernation 冬期　*tōki*, winter season
199 **5 strokes**				☑ 4

当 200 6 strokes	丶	丷	丷	TŌ; *a(taru)*, to hit, to be equal to, to win (v.i.); *a(teru)*, to hit, to apply, to guess (v.t.)
	꼭	当	当	見当 *kentō*, guess 手当 *teate*, treatment, allowance 当然 *tōzen*, justly, naturally
				③

東 201 8 strokes	一	厂	戸	TŌ; *higashi*, east
	戸	百	申	東側 *higashigawa*, east side 東洋 *tōyō*, the East, the Orient 北東 *hokutō*, northeast
	東	東		✓ ⑤

答 202 12 strokes	ノ	⺊	⺮	TŌ; *kota(e)*, answer; *kota(eru)*, to answer
	⺮	竹	竻	答案 *tōan*, examination paper 問答 *mondō*, questions and answers
	筓	笒	答	解答 *kaitō*, answer, solution ✓ ④

頭 203 16 strokes	一	日	戸	TŌ, ZU; *atama*, head, top, brain; *kashira*, head, top, leader
	豆	豆	豆	先頭 *sentō*, leader, head 教頭 *kyōtō*, head teacher 頭痛 *zutsū*, headache
	豇	頭	頭	✓ ③

同 204 6 strokes	丨	冂	冂	DŌ; *ona(ji)*, same
	同	同	同	同時 *dōji*, the same time 同情 *dōjō*, sympathy 一同 *ichidō*, all (of us, them), all the persons concerned
				✓ ④

41

道	、	゛	立	DŌ; *michi*, road, path
	ソ	产	首	水道　　*suidō*, waterworks 道具　　*dōgu*, tool 鉄道　　*tetsudō*, railroad
205 12 strokes	首	渞	道	☑ 4

読	、	二	言	DOKU, TOKU; *yo(mu)*, to read
	言	計	計	読者　　*dokusha*, reader (person) 読書　　*dokusho*, reading 読み返す *yomikaesu*, to reread
206 14 strokes	詰	読	読	☑ 5

内	一	冂	内	NAI, DAI; *uchi*, inside, home, within, during, among, between
	内			案内　　*annai*, guidance, invitation 内海　　*uchiumi*, *naikai*, inland sea 内容　　*naiyō*, contents
207 4 strokes				☑ 3

南	一	十	十	NAN; *minami*, south
	内	内	南	南部　　*nanbu*, southern part 南極　　*Nankyoku*, South Pole 西南　　*seinan*, southwest
208 9 strokes	南	南	南	☑ 5

肉	一	冂	内	NIKU, meat, flesh
	内	肉	肉	牛肉　　*gyūniku*, beef 筋肉　　*kinniku*, muscles 肉屋　　*nikuya*, butcher, butcher shop
209 6 strokes				☑ 5

馬	一	厂	厂	BA; *uma*, horse
	厅	馬	馬	馬車　　　*basha*, carriage 競馬場 *keibajō*, race track
210 10 strokes	馬	馬	馬	3

売	一	十	士	BAI; *u(ri)*, sale; *u(ru)*, to sell
	产	声	壳	売り出し *uridashi*, opening sale, 　　　　　bargain sale 商売　　　*shōbai*, business 発売　　　*hatsubai*, sale
211 7 strokes	売			✓ 4

買	丶	冖	冂	BAI; *ka(u)*, to buy, to purchase
	罒	罒	罒	売買　　　*baibai*, purchase and sale, 　　　　　buying and selling 買い物 *kaimono*, shopping 買い手 *kaite*, buyer
212 12 strokes	冒	買		✓ 4

麦	一	十	主	BAKU; *mugi*, barley, wheat
	主	丰	麦	麦わら *mugiwara*, (barley) straw 麦刈り *mugikari*, mowing barley 小麦　　　*komugi*, wheat
213 7 strokes	麦			2

半	丶	⸝⸜	丷	HAN; *naka(ba)*, half
	兰	半		半分　　　*hanbun*, half 一時半 *ichiji-han*, one-thirty, half- 　　　　　past one 半島　　　*hantō*, peninsula
214 5 strokes				✓ 5

番	一	⺈	⿰	BAN, number, guard, order, (one's) turn
	二	平	采	番組　*bangumi*, program 交番　*kōban*, police-box 順番　*junban*, order, one's turn
215 12 strokes	釆	番	番	☑ 3

父	⼃	八	分	FU; *chichi*, father
	父			父兄会 *fukeikai*, parents' association 祖父　*sofu*, grandfather 父母　*fubo*, parents
216 4 strokes				☑ 5

風	⼃	几	凡	FŪ; *kaze*, wind
	凡	凨	凨	風景　*fūkei*, scenery 台風　*taifū*, typhoon 南風　*minamikaze*, south wind
217 9 strokes	風	風	風	☑ 4

分	⼃	八	分	BUN, BU, part, share; FUN, a minute; *wa(keru)* (v.t.), to divide; *wa(kareru)*, to be separated, to branch off; *wa(karu)*, to know, to understand
	分			自分　*jibun*, self 二分　*nifun*, two minutes 十分　*jippun*, ten minutes
218 4 strokes				☑ 5

聞	⼁	⼕	⼕	BUN; *ki(ku)*, to hear, to listen to, to ask, to obey; *ki(koeru)*, to be heard
	⺕	⺕	門	新聞　*shinbun*, newspaper 新聞社 *shinbunsha*, newspaper office
219 14 strokes	門	門	聞	見聞　*kenbun*, information, experience　☑ 5

44

米	、	⸌⸍	丷	BEI, America, rice; MAI, rice; *kome*, rice
	半	米	米	米国 *Beikoku*, America, the United States
220 6 strokes				米作 *beisaku*, rice-growing (crop) 白米 *hakumai*, polished rice 3

歩	ノ	⺊	⺊	HO, BU; *ayu(mu)*, *aru(ku)*, to walk, to step
	止	止	歩	第一歩 *dai-ippo*, the first step 進歩 *shinpo*, progress
221 8 strokes	歩	歩		散歩 *sanpo*, a walk, a stroll ✓ 4

母	⺄	母	母	BO; *haha*, mother
	母	母		母の日 *Haha-no-hi*, Mother's Day 母国 *bokoku*, mother country
222 5 strokes				母親 *haha-oya*, mother ✓ 5

方	⺀	亠	方	HŌ, direction, side; *kata [gata]*, side, way of ~ing, person
	方			両方 *ryōhō*, both sides 作り方 *tsukurikata*, way of making
223 4 strokes				夕方 *yūgata*, evening ✓ 4

北	ー	十	土	HOKU; *kita*, north
	土	北		北極 *Hokkyoku*, North Pole 南北 *nanboku*, north and south
224 5 strokes				北風 *kitakaze*, north wind ✓ 5

毎	ノ	ｰ	仁	MAI, every (prefix)
	勺	勾	毎	毎日　*mainichi*, every day
				毎朝　*mai-asa*, every morning
				毎週　*maishū*, every week
225 6 strokes				☑ 5

妹	く	女	女	MAI; *imōto*, younger sister
	女	女=	奸	弟妹　*teimai*, younger brothers and sisters
226 8 strokes	奸	妹		姉妹　*shimai*, sisters
				☑ 4

万	一	丁	万	MAN, ten thousand; BAN
				万年筆 *mannenhitsu*, fountain pen
				万一　*man'ichi*, if by any chance
				万国　*bankoku*, all countries
227 3 strokes				☑ 5

明	｜	冂	日	MEI, MYŌ, bright; *aka(rui)*, light, bright; *aki(raka)*, bright; *a(keru)*, to dawn, to break (day); *a(kasu)*, to disclose (a secret), to pass the night
	日	日)	明	
228 8 strokes	明	明		夜明け *yoake*, dawn 説明　*setsumei*, explanation 発明　*hatsumei*, invention ☑ 4

鳴	口	口ʾ	叮	MEI; *na(ku)*, to sing (birds), to cry (animals), to howl (animals), to chirp (insects); *na(ru)* (v.i.), to ring, to sound; *na(rasu)* (v.t.), to ring (a bell), to sound (a drum), to complain, to be famous
	叭	叭	咆	
229 14 strokes	咱	鳴	鳴	鳴き声 *nakigoe*, cry (of animals) 悲鳴　*himei*, scream, cry of distress 鳴動　*meidō*, rumbling 3

毛	ノ	二	三	MŌ; *ke*, hair
	毛			毛糸　*keito*, woolen thread, yarn 毛虫　*kemushi*, caterpillar 毛布　*mōfu*, blanket
230 4 strokes				2

門	丨	冂	尸	MON; *kado*, gate
	尸	尸	門	校門　*kōmon*, school gate 専門　*senmon*, specialty 門口　*kadoguchi*, door, entrance
231 8 strokes	門	門		✓ 2

夜	丶	二	广	YA; *yo*, *yoru*, evening, night
	疒	疒	夜	夜中　*yonaka*, midnight 十五夜　*jūgoya*, night of the full 　　　moon 今夜　*kon'ya*, tonight
232 8 strokes	疒	夜		✓ 4

野	丶	口	日	YA; *no*, field, plain
	甲	里	野	野原　*nohara*, field 野球　*yakyū*, baseball 野外　*yagai*, outdoors
233 11 strokes	野	野	野	✓ 4

友	一	ナ	方	YŪ; *tomo*, friend
	友			友だち *tomodachi*, friend 友人　*yūjin*, friend 友情　*yūjō*, friendship
234 4 strokes				✓ 5

用	ノ	刀	月	YŌ, business; *mochi(iru)*, to use
	月	用		用意 *yōi*, preparation 用心 *yōjin*, heed, care, caution 用事 *yōji*, business
235 5 strokes				✓ 4

曜	l	⼧	日	YŌ, term used for days of the week
	日	日⼋	日⼘	木曜日 *mokuyōbi*, Thursday 土曜日 *doyōbi*, Saturday 水曜日 *suiyōbi*, Wednesday
236 18 strokes	日⼘	日⿂	曜	✓ 4

来	一	宀	冖	RAI; *ku(ru)*, to come; *kita(ru)*, to arrive, next; *kita(su)*, to cause, to induce
	立	平	来	来年 *rainen*, next year 以来 *irai*, since, from that time 将来 *shōrai*, the future
237 7 strokes	来			✓ 5

里	⼁	冂	日	RI, Japanese linear unit (2.44 miles); *sato* village, country, one's native home (usually as viewed by a woman married into another family)
	日	甲	甲	郷里 *kyōri*, one's native place, home 村里 *murazato*, village
238 7 strokes	里			一里 *ichiri*, one *ri* 1

理	一	丁	干	RI, reason, logic
	王	玑	珇	理解 *rikai*, understanding 整理 *seiri*, arrangement, adjustment 料理 *ryōri*, cooking
239 11 strokes	珇	理	理	✓ 4

話	、	二	三	WA; *hanashi*, story; *hana(su)*, to speak
	言	言	言	世話　*sewa*, aid 電話　*denwa*, telephone 会話　*kaiwa*, conversation
240 13 strokes	言	訐	話	☑ 5

悪	一	一	一	AKU, badness, evil; *waru(i)*, bad, evil
	口	亜	亜	悪口　*warukuchi*, evil talk, gossip 悪人　*akunin*, bad man, villain 悪路　*akuro*, bad road
241 11 strokes	亜	悪		☑ 4

安	、	ハ	宀	AN; *yasu(i)*, cheap, inexpensive
	宀	安	安	安心　*anshin*, peace of mind 安全　*anzen*, safe 不安　*fuan*, uneasiness
242 6 strokes				☑ 4

暗	丨	冂	日	AN; *kura(i)*, dark
	日	日'	旷	真っ暗 *makkura*, pitch dark 暗号　*angō*, code, cryptograph 暗記　*anki*, memorization
243 13 strokes	旷	暗	暗	☑ 3

医	一	丆	丆	I, to heal, to cure
	医	医	矢	医者　*isha*, physician, doctor 医学　*igaku*, medical science 医院　*i-in*, medical practitioner's office
244 7 strokes	医			☑ 4

委	丿	二	千
	千	禾	禾
245 8 strokes	委	委	

I; *yuda(neru)*, to entrust with

委員　　*i-in*, committee, delegate
委員長　*i-inchō*, chairman of a committee
委任　　*i-nin*, charge, trust, commission

2

意	丶	亠	立
	立	音	音
246 13 strokes	音	音	意

I, mind, heart, attention, care

注意　*chūi*, care, attention
意見　*iken*, opinion, admonition
意味　*imi*, meaning

☑ 4

育	丶	亠	去
	云	产	育
247 8 strokes	育	育	

IKU; *haguku(mu)*, brood over (one's chicks), *soda(teru)*, to bring up, to educate, to raise; *soda(tsu)*, to grow up

教育　*kyōiku*, education
体育　*tai-iku*, physical education
育児　*ikuji*, upbringing of a child

☑ 3

員	丶	冂	口
	尸	吊	目
248 10 strokes	冒	員	員

IN, member, official, personnel

満員　*man'in*, no vacancy, full house
一員　*ichi-in*, (one) member
職員　*shokuin*, staff, personnel

☑ 4

院	フ	子	阝
	阝'	阝'	阝宀
249 10 strokes	陀	陀	院

IN, temple, academy, board, suffix for "institution"

病院　*byōin*, hospital
美容院　*biyōin*, beauty shop
下院　*ka-in*, House of Representatives, Lower House

☑ 4

飲	ノ	今	含	IN; *no(mu)*, to drink 飲料水 *inryōsui* drinking water 飲み水 *nomimizu*, drinking water 飲み物 *nomimono*, drinks
	飣	飣	飣	
250 12 strokes	飮	飮	飲	☑ 4
運	`	冖	冖	UN, luck; *hako(bu)*, to carry, to transport 運良く *un'yoku*, luckily 運動 *undō*, exercise, motion 運命 *unmei*, fate
	冒	宣	軍	
251 12 strokes	軍	運	運	☑ 4
泳	`	:	シ	EI; *oyo(gu)*, to swim 水泳 *suiei*, swimming 平泳ぎ *hira-oyogi*, breast stroke 水泳大会 *suiei taikai*, swimming meet
	氵	汀	氾	
252 8 strokes	氾	泳		☑ 3
駅	l	厂	Π	EKI, station 駅前 *ekimae*, in front of the station 駅長 *ekichō*, station master 駅員 *eki-in*, station employee
	馬	馬	馬	
253 14 strokes	馿	駅	駅	☑ 4
央	`	冂	凸	Ō, center, middle 中央 *chūō*, center 中央線 *Chūō-sen*, the Chūō Line (electric railway in Tōkyō) 震央 *shin'ō*, the epicenter, the center of an earthquake
	央	央		
254 5 strokes				2

51

横	木	杧	栏
	栉	梻	横
255 15 strokes	横	横	横

Ō; *yoko*, the side, the width

横書き *yokogaki*, writing from left to right
横断 *ōdan*, crossing, intersection
横顔 *yokogao*, side view of a person's face, profile

✓ 3

屋	⌐	⊐	尸
	尸	尸	层
256 9 strokes	居	屋	屋

OKU, house; *ya*, shop, business

屋根 *yane*, roof
時計屋 *tokeiya*, watch shop
屋上 *okujō*, housetop, roof

✓ 4

温	シ	シ	氵
	沪	沪	泪
257 12 strokes	温	温	温

ON; warm; *atata(kai)*, warm (to the touch); *atata(maru)*, to warm oneself; *atata(meru)*, to heat

温度 *ondo*, temperature
温泉 *onsen*, hot spring
体温 *taion*, body temperature

✓ 2

化	ノ	イ	イ
	化		
258 4 strokes			

KA, influence; KE; *ba(keru)*, to take the form of; *ba(kasu)*, to bewitch

変化 *henka*, change, variation, alteration
化学 *kagaku*, chemistry
化粧 *keshō*, make-up

✓ 3

荷	一	サ	ヰ
	芢	芢	荐
259 10 strokes	荷	荷	荷

KA; *ni*, a load, burden

荷物 *nimotsu*, baggage
荷船 *nibune*, freighter
荷作り *nizukuri*, packing

✓ 2

界

260
9 strokes

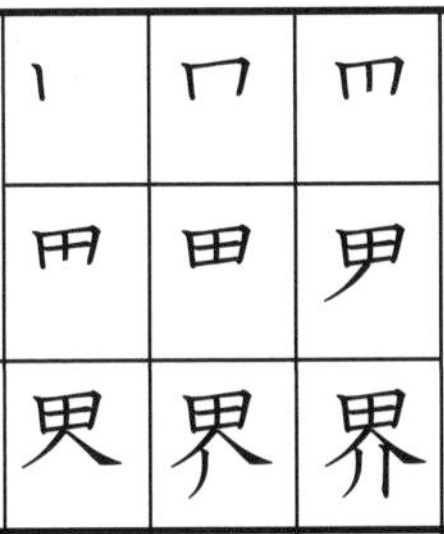

KAI, world

世界 *sekai*, world
世界一 *sekai-ichi*, best in the world
限界 *genkai*, boundary, limits

✓ 4

開

261
12 strokes

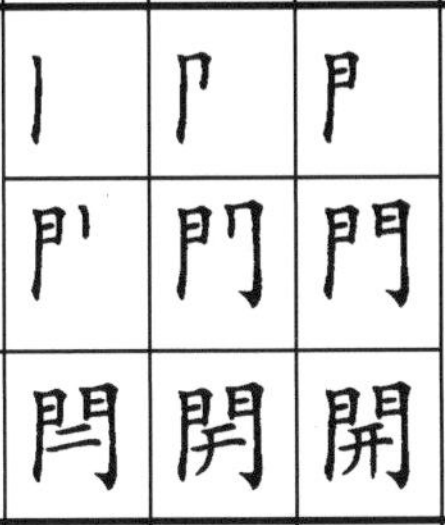

KAI; *hira(ku)*, to open (v.t. & i.); *a(keru)* (v.t.), to open; *hira(keru)*, to be civilized, to open; *a(ku)* (v.i.) to be open

開会 *kaikai*, opening a meeting
満開 *mankai*, full bloom
開発 *kaihatsu*, development, exploitation

✓ 4

階

262
12 strokes

KAI, story of a building, floor, grade

階段 *kaidan*, stairs, stairway
階級 *kaikyū*, class, caste
三階 *sangai*, 3rd floor

✓ 2

寒

263
12 strokes

KAN, the coldest season of the year; *samu(i)*, cold

極寒 *gokkan*, bitter cold
寒中 *kanchū*, cold season
寒流 *kanryū*, cold current

✓ 3

感

264
13 strokes

KAN, feeling, thought

感想 *kansō*, thoughts, impressions
感心 *kanshin*, admiration
感覚 *kankaku*, sensation

3

| 漢 | 氵 氵 氵
氵 氵 氵
氵 氵 漢 | KAN, China; ~kan, suffix for "man"

漢字　　*kanji*, Chinese character
漢文　　*kanbun*, Chinese
　　　　composition
悪漢　　*akkan*, villain, crook |
| 265
13 strokes | | ☑ 4 |

| 館 | ノ 个 卩
亼 亽 𠁥
𩙿 𩚋 館 | KAN, building, hall; *yakata*,
mansion

図書館 *toshokan*, library
映画館 *eigakan*, movie theater
旅館　*ryokan*, inn, hotel |
| 266
16 strokes | | ☑ 4 |

| 岸 | ᷅ 屮 山
屮 尸 尸
岸 岸 | GAN; *kishi*, bank, shore

海岸　　*kaigan*, seashore
岸壁　　*ganpeki*, quay, wharf
川岸　　*kawagishi*, riverbank |
| 267
8 strokes | | 2 |

| 起 | 土 キ 丰
走 走 起
起 起 | KI; *o(kiru)*, to rise, to get up;
o(kosu), to raise, to awaken (v.t.);
o(koru), to occur, to develop

早起き *hayaoki*, early rising
起原　*kigen*, origin
起重機 *kijūki*, crane, derrick |
| 268
10 strokes | | ☑ 4 |

| 期 | 一 十 廿
甘 甘 其
其 期 期 | KI, GO, period, term

学期　　*gakki*, school term
期待　　*kitai*, expectation
時期　　*jiki*, the times, season |
| 269
12 strokes | | ☑ 3 |

54

客	丶	丷	宀	KYAKU, KAKU, guest, visitor, customer
	宀	岁	安	お客さん *o-kyaku-san*, guest 客車　　*kyakusha*, railroad passenger car
270 9 strokes	宏	客	客	客船　　*kyakusen*, passenger boat 3

究	丶	丷	宀	KYŪ, study; *kiwa(meru)*, to study thoroughly
	宀	宂	空	研究　*kenkyū*, research 研究会 *kenkyūkai*, research society 研究家 *kenkyūka*, researcher
271 7 strokes	究			✓ 4

急	ノ	ク	⼅	KYŪ; *iso(gu)*, to hurry
	乌	刍	刍	急病　*kyūbyō*, sudden illness 急行　*kyūkō*, express 大急ぎ *ō-isogi*, great haste
272 9 strokes	急	急	急	✓ 4

級	㇑	纟	幺	KYŪ, rank, grade
	糸	糹	糸	学級　　*gakkyū*, school class 上級　　*jōkyū*, high class 同級生 *dōkyūsei*, classmate
273 9 strokes	糾	級	級	1

宮	丶	丷	宀	KYŪ, GŪ, KU; *miya*, shrine, prince (of the blood)
	宀	宀	宮	宮殿　*kyūden*, palace 神宮　*jingū*, Shintō shrine 宮様　*miya-sama*, royal prince
274 10 strokes				1

球	一	王	王	KYŪ, sphere, globe; *tama*, ball
	玎	刲	玣	野球 *yakyū*, baseball 地球 *chikyū*, the earth, the globe 電球 *denkyū*, electric light bulb
275 11 strokes	球	球	球	[3]

去	一	十	土	KYO, KO, past; *sa(ru)*, to leave, to depart
	去	去		去年 *kyonen*, last year 過去 *kako*, the past, past tense
276 5 strokes				☑[4]

橋	木	朾	杯	KYŌ; *hashi*, bridge
	扩	杝	枦	桟橋 *sanbashi*, pier 土橋 *dobashi*, earthen bridge 鉄橋 *tekkyō*, iron bridge
277 16 strokes	橋	橋	橋	☑[2]

業	丶	丷	丷	GYŌ, occupation, business, industry, studies; GŌ, karma; *waza*, act, deed
	业	业	业	職業 *shokugyō*, occupation, profession 産業 *sangyō*, industry
278 13 strokes	誉	睾	業	工業 *kōgyō*, industry, manu-facturing industry ☑[4]

曲	丨	冂	巾	KYOKU, melody; *ma(garu)*, to bend, to twist, to turn, (v.i.); *ma(geru)*, to bend, to twist, to turn (v.t.)
	曲	曲	曲	曲線 *kyokusen*, curved line 作曲 *sakkyoku*, musical composition
279 6 strokes				曲がり道 *magarimichi*, crooked road, winding lane [3]

局	⁻	⁻	尸	KYOKU, bureau, board, office, department
	尸	局	局	放送局 *hōsōkyoku*, broadcasting station 編集局 *henshūkyoku*, editorial department
280 7 strokes	局			郵便局 *yūbinkyoku*, post office ☑ 3

銀	ノ	^	乍	GIN, silver
	牟	金	釘	銀行　*ginkō*, bank 銀色　*gin'iro*, silver color 銀貨　*ginka*, silver coin
281 14 strokes	鈤	銀	銀	4

区	⁻	フ	又	KU, ward, section
	区			区別　*kubetsu*, distinction, classification 地区　*chiku*, area
282 4 strokes				区画　*kukaku*, boundary, block, division 2

苦	一	十	艹	KU, pain, anxiety; *kuru(shii)*, painful; *niga(i)*, bitter
	芏	芏	芐	苦労　*kurō*, troubles, toil 苦心　*kushin*, pains, hard work
283 8 strokes	苦	苦		苦戦　*kusen*, hard fighting 3

具	l	冂	月	GU, tool, utensil; ingredients
	目	目	且	道具　*dōgu*, tool, utensil, instrument 具合　*guai*, condition, state
284 8 strokes	具	具		具体的 *gutaiteki*, concrete, definite 3

君	フ	ヨ	尹	KUN, Mister, Master; *kimi*, you (familiar form)
	尹	尹	君	佐藤君 *Satō-kun*, Mr. Satō 貴君 *kikun*, you (lit., masc.) 諸君 *shokun*, gentlemen, ladies
285 7 strokes	君			and gentlemen, you 〔3〕

係	ノ	イ	イ	KEI; *kakari*, charge, duty, in charge (of); *kaka(ru)*, to affect, to concern
	伫	佟	伝	係員 *kakari-in*, clerk in charge 関係 *kankei*, relation, connection, participation, implication
286 9 strokes	侲	倸	係	記録係 *kirokugakari*, person in charge of records, recorder 〔✓〕〔3〕

軽	厂	戸	亘	KEI; *karu*, *karu(i)*, light (in weight), slight, easy; *karo(yaka)*, airy, light
	車	軒	軡	軽卒 *keisotsu*, rashness, hastiness 軽音楽 *kei-ongaku*, light music 気軽 *kigaru*, light-hearted
287 12 strokes	軽	軽	軽	〔✓〕〔2〕

血	ノ	イ	冇	KETSU; *chi*, blood
	冇	血	血	血液 *ketsueki*, blood 出血 *shukketsu*, bleeding, hemorrhage
288 6 strokes				血管 *kekkan*, blood vessel 〔2〕

決	ヽ	⠘	シ	KETSU; *ki(maru)*, to be decided; *ki(meru)*, to decide
	汀	江	沖	決心 *kesshin*, making up one's mind 決定 *kettei*, decision
289 7 strokes	決			解決 *kaiketsu*, solution 〔✓〕〔3〕

58

研 290 9 strokes	一 丁 石 石 矿 研	KEN, study; *to(gu)*, to sharpen, to wash (rice) 研究　　*kenkyū*, study, research 研究室　*kenkyūshitsu*, laboratory 研究所　*kenkyūjo*, research institute　　4
県 291 9 strokes	丨 冂 日 目 県 県	KEN, prefecture 県道　　*kendō*, prefectural road 県庁　　*kenchō*, prefectural office 県知事　*kenchiji*, prefectural governor　　2
庫 292 10 strokes	丶 亠 广 庐 唐 庫	KO, warehouse 書庫　　*shoko*, library 倉庫　　*sōko*, warehouse 冷蔵庫　*reizōko*, icebox, refrigerator　　2
湖 293 12 strokes	丶 氵 湖 湖	KO; *mizu-umi*, lake 湖水　　*kosui*, lake 湖岸　　*kogan*, shore of a lake 湖畔　　*kohan*, border of a lake　　2
向 294 6 strokes	丿 白 向 向	KŌ; *mu(ku)*, to turn toward, to be suited for; *mu(kau)*, to face, to head for; *mu(kō)*, the opposite side, beyond 向こう　　*mukō*, opposite 向こう側　*mukōgawa*, opposite side 方向　　　*hōkō*, direction, course　　✓ 3

幸	一	十	土	KŌ; *saiwa(i)*, blessings, good luck, happiness, fortune; *sachi*, happiness, luck; *shiawa(se)*, happiness, good fortune
	圭	赱	壵	
295 8 strokes	壵	幸		不幸　*fukō*, unhappiness, misfortune 幸福　*kōfuku*, happiness 幸運　*kōun*, good fortune　　3

港	氵	汁	沪	KŌ; *minato*, harbor
	泔	洰	洪	港町　*minatomachi*, port town 入港　*nyūkō*, entry into port 空港　*kūkō*, airport
296 12 strokes	洪	港	港	✓ 3

号	丶	口	口	GŌ, number, issue (of a magazine)
	曱	号		番号　*bangō*, number 記号　*kigō*, symbol 信号　*shingō*, signal, code
297 5 strokes				✓ 3

根	一	十	木	KON, root (math.), perseverance; *ne*, root
	朾	朾	朾	根気　*konki*, patience, perseverance
298 10 strokes	柙	根	根	大根　*daikon*, giant white radish 根本　*konpon*, basis　　2

祭	ノ	ク	タ	SAI; *matsu(ri)*, festival; *matsu(ru)*, to deify, to worship as a god, to offer prayers for the sake of
	タ	タフ	奴	
299 11 strokes	怒	祭	祭	村祭り　*muramatsuri*, village festival 祭日　*saijitsu*, national holiday 文化祭　*bunkasai*, cultural festival ✓ 2

皿	丶	口	皿	*sara*, plate, dish, bowl
	皿	皿		皿洗い　　　*sara-arai*, dishwashing
				皿洗い機　*sara-araiki*, dishwasher
300				灰皿　　　　*haizara*, ashtray
5 strokes				2

仕	ノ	イ	仁	SHI, JI, work; *tsuka(eru)*, to serve
	什	仕		仕事　　*shigoto*, work
				給仕　　*kyūji*, office boy, waiter
301				仕方　　*shikata*, way of doing
5 strokes				✓ 4

死	一	厂	歹	SHI, death; *shi(nu)*, to die
	歹	死	死	死体　　*shitai*, corpse
				死傷者　*shishōsha*, dead and injured,
				casualties
302				必死　　*hisshi*, certain death,
6 strokes				desperation
				4

使	ノ	イ	仁	SHI; *tsuka(u)*, to use
	伩	佢	佢	使い　　*tsukai*, errand, messenger
				使命　　*shimei*, mission, errand
	伊	使		使用　　*shiyō*, use
303				
8 strokes				✓ 4

始	く	女	女	SHI; *haji(maru)*, to begin (v.i.);
				haji(meru), to begin (v.t.)
	姒	妈	女	
				開始　　*kaishi*, commencement, start
	始	始		始末　　*shimatsu*, circumstances, the
304				particulars; management
8 strokes				始業　　*shigyō*, beginning of work
				or class　　　✓ 4

指	一	十	扌	SHI; *yubi*, finger; *sa(su)*, to point at, to indicate
	扌	北	拼	親指　　*oyayubi*, thumb 指輪　　*yubiwa*, ring 指揮者　*shikisha*, conductor, commander
305 9 strokes	指	指	指	☑ 3

歯	丨	卜	止	SHI; *ha*, tooth
	止	华	华	虫歯　　*mushiba*, decayed tooth 歯医者　*ha-isha*, dentist 歯車　　*haguruma*, gear, cogwheel
306 12 strokes	柴	歯	歯	3

詩	丶	二	三	SHI, poetry, poem
	言	言	計	詩人　　*shijin*, poet 詩集　　*shishū*, anthology of poetry 叙事詩　*jojishi*, epic poem
307 13 strokes	詰	詩	詩	1

次	丶	冫	ソ	JI, SHI; *tsugi*, next; *tsu(gu)*, to rank next to
	沙	次	次	次第　　*shidai*, order, reason, as soon as 次官　　*jikan*, vice-minister 目次　　*mokuji*, table of contents
308 6 strokes				☑ 3

事	一	一	二	JI; *koto*, thing, action, affair, fact
	三	三	写	仕事　　*shigoto*, work 用事　　*yōji*, business 大事　　*daiji*, great matter, serious affair, importance
309 8 strokes	写	事		☑ 4

持	一	十	才	JI; *mo(chi)*, durability; *mo(tsu)*, to have, to hold
	扌	扩	扗	気持　　*kimochi*, feeling 持参　　*jisan*, bringing 支持　　*shiji*, support
310 9 strokes	扗	持	持	✓ 4

式	一	二	弌	SHIKI, ceremony, form, model; ~*shiki*, ~-style (suffix for "style", "type")
	弍	式	式	式場　　*shikijō*, ceremonial hall 卒業式 *sotsugyō-shiki*, graduation
311 6 strokes				ceremony, commencement 旧式　　*kyūshiki*, old-style ✓ 3

実	、	丷	宀	JITSU, reality; *mi*, nut, fruit; *mino(ru)*, to bear fruit
	宀	宁	宇	実際　　*jissai*, actual state, reality 真実　　*shinjitsu*, truth 果実　　*kajitsu*, fruit
312 8 strokes	宲	実		✓ 3

写	一	冖	写	SHA; *utsu(su)*, to copy, to imitate, to take (a photograph); *utsu(ru)*, to be photographed, to be projected
	写	写		写真　　*shashin*, photograph 写生　　*shasei*, sketch, drawing
313 5 strokes				from nature 映写　　*eisha*, projection ✓ 4

者	一	十	土	SHA; *mono*, person
	耂	者	者	若者　　*wakamono*, young man 医者　　*isha*, doctor 学者　　*gakusha*, scholar
314 8 strokes	者	者		✓ 4

主	、	二	宁	SHU, SU; *nushi*, master, owner; *omo*, main, foremost
	宇	主		主人　　　*shujin*, master 民主主義 *minshushugi*, democracy 持主　　　*mochinushi*, owner
315 5 strokes				☑ 4

守	、	宀	宀	SHU, SU; *mamo(ru)*, to protect, to guard, to defend, to obey (the law), to keep (a promise); *mori*, *mo(ri)*, nursemaid, baby-sitter
	宀	守	守	お守り　*o-mamori*, amulet, charm 留守　　*rusu*, absence
316 6 strokes				保守　　*hoshu*, conservatism　3

取	一	厂	F	SHU; *to(ru)*, to take
	F	E	耳	取り出す *toridasu*, to take out 取材　　*shuzai*, choice of subject 取扱い　*toriatsukai*, treatment, handling
317 8 strokes	取	取		☑ 3

酒	、	冫	汀	SHU; *saka-*, *sake*, rice wine, liquor
	汀	沥	洒	ぶどう酒 *budōshu*, wine 酒飲み　*sakenomi*, drinker 酒屋　　*sakaya*, liquor shop
318 10 strokes	酒	酒		☑ 3

受	一	⺈	⺈	JU; *u(keru)*, to receive; *u(karu)*, to pass (an exam)
	爫	爫	严	受持　　*ukemochi*, charge, matter in hand 受付　　*uketsuke*, receptionist, information desk
319 8 strokes	受	受		受話機 *juwaki*, telephone receiver ☑ 3

64

州 320 6 strokes	`	リ	少
	州	州	州

SHŪ, province, state (U.S.A.); *su*, shallows, a sandbank

本州　*Honshū* (main island of Japan)
九州　*Kyūshū* (Japan's third largest island)
ユタ州　*Yuta-shū*, State of Utah ☑ 2

拾 321 9 strokes	一	十	扌
	扌	扒	扖
	扗	拾	拾

SHŪ; JŪ, ten (used in legal documents); *hiro(u)*, to pick up

拾い物　*hiroimono*, something picked up, windfall, bargain
命拾い　*inochibiroi*, narrow escape (from death)
拾弐円　*jūni-en*, 12 yen ☐ 2

終 322 11 strokes	∠	幺	幺
	糸	糸	終
	終	終	終

SHŪ; *o(wari)*, end; *o(waru)*, to come to an end; *o(eru)*, to finish

終戦　*shūsen*, end of a war
終業　*shūgyō*, end of work
最終　*saishū*, the last ☑ 4

習 323 11 strokes	フ	ヲ	ヨ
	习	羽	羽
	習	習	習

SHŪ; *nara(u)*, to learn, to study

練習　*renshū*, practice
習字　*shūji*, penmanship
習慣　*shūkan*, habit, custom ☑ 4

集 324 12 strokes	ノ	イ	亻
	亻	什	住
	隹	隹	集

SHŪ; *atsu(meru)*, to collect (v.t.); *atsu(maru)*, to gather together (v.i.); *tsudo(u)*, to meet, to gather

編集　*henshū*, editing
詩集　*shishū*, anthology of poems
文集　*bunshū*, literary anthology ☑ 4

住	ノ	イ	イ	JŪ, dwelling; *su(mu)*, to dwell, to live; *su(mai)*, dwelling
	仁	什	住	住所 *jūsho*, address 衣食住 *i-shoku-jū*, necessities of life (clothing, food, shelter)
325 7 strokes	住			住宅 *jūtaku*, dwelling, living quarters ☑ 4

重	一	二	宀	JŪ, CHŌ; *omo(i)*, heavy; *kasa(neru)*, to pile (things) up; *kasa(naru)*, to be piled up; ~*e*, ~fold
	盲	盲	盲	体重 *taijū*, weight (of the body) 厳重 *genjū*, strictness
326 9 strokes	重	重	重	二重 *futae*, *nijū*, duplicate, double, twofold ☑ 4

宿	、	丶	宀	SHUKU; *yado*, inn; *yado(ru)*, to lodge at; *yado(su)*, to provide shelter
	宀	宀	宀	宿屋 *yadoya*, inn 宿題 *shukudai*, homework 下宿 *geshuku*, boardinghouse
327 11 strokes	疒	宿	宿	☑ 3

所	一	ヲ	ヨ	SHO; *tokoro*, place
	戸	尸	所	台所 *daidokoro*, kitchen 場所 *basho*, place 近所 *kinjo*, neighborhood
328 8 strokes	所	所		☑ 3

暑	、	冂	曰	SHO; *atsu(i)*, hot
	日	昆	昇	残暑 *zansho*, lingering summer heat 避暑 *hisho*, summering, going to a summer resort
329 12 strokes	昇	暑	暑	暑中 *shochū*, midsummer ☑ 1

助 330 7 strokes	丨 冂 月 月 且 助 助	JO; *tasu(karu)*, to be aided, to be rescued; *tasu(keru)*, to aid, to rescue; ~*suke*, suffix for masculine names 助手 *joshu*, assistant 補助 *hojo*, assistance 助力 *joryoku*, help, aid <div align="right">3</div>
昭 331 9 strokes	丨 冂 日 日 町 町 昭 昭 昭	SHŌ, bright 昭和 *Shōwa*, Emperor Hirohito or his reign (1926–1989) <div align="right">1</div>
消 332 10 strokes	氵 氵 氵 氵 氵 消 消 消	SHŌ; *ki(eru)*, to vanish, to go out, to melt away; *ke(su)*, to extinguish, to switch off, to put out (a light) 消しゴム *keshigomu*, eraser 消防 *shōbō*, fire fighting 消毒 *shōdoku*, disinfection <div align="right">3</div>
商 333 11 strokes	丶 亠 六 六 产 产 产 商 商	SHŌ; *akina(u)*, to sell, to deal in 商人 *shōnin*, merchant 商売 *shōbai*, business, trade, transaction 商業 *shōgyō*, commerce, trade <div align="right">✓ 3</div>
章 334 11 strokes	亠 立 产 音 音 音 童 章	SHŌ, chapter 文章 *bunshō*, sentence 記章 *kishō*, medal, badge 勲章 *kunshō*, decoration, order (for honors) <div align="right">2</div>

勝 335 12 strokes	月 胖 朕	月 胖 勝	胩 朕 勝	SHŌ; *ka(tsu)*, to win; *masa(ru)*, to excel 勝負 *shōbu*, victory or defeat, match 勝敗 *shōhai*, the outcome (of a battle) 勝手 *katte*, selfish, willful 3
乗 336 9 strokes	一 乍 垂	二 乕 垂	三 乗 乗	JŌ; *no(ru)*, to ride; *no(seru)*, to give a ride to, to place upon 乗り物 *norimono*, vehicle 乗客 *jōkyaku*, passenger 遠乗り *tōnori*, a long ride ✓ 3
植 337 12 strokes	一 才 枯	十 杧 植	才 村 植	SHOKU; *u(eru)*, to plant, to set up (type); *u(waru)*, to be planted 植物 *shokubutsu*, plant, vetegation 植民地 *shokuminchi*, colony 田植え *taue*, rice planting 2
申 338 5 strokes	丶 曰	冂 申	曰	SHIN; *mō(su)*, to say 申し込み *mōshikomi*, application, proposal 申告 *shinkoku*, report, filing a return 申し合わせ *mōshiawase*, arrangement 3
身 339 7 strokes	丶 身 身	亠 身	冂 身	SHIN; *mi*, body 身体 *shintai*, body 身長 *shinchō*, height (of the body) 身分 *mibun*, social position ✓ 3

神 340 9 strokes	丶	ラ	ネ
	ネ	礻	初
	初	神	神

SHIN, JIN; *kami*, god

神経質 *shinkeishitsu*, nervous temperament
精神 *seishin*, soul, spirit
神様 *kamisama*, god

☑ 3

真 341 10 strokes	一	十	宀
	市	古	直
	直	真	真

SHIN; *ma*, truth, reality

写真機 *shashinki*, camera
真夏 *manatsu*, midsummer

4

深 342 11 strokes	丶	冫	氵
	沪	沪	泙
	沪	深	深

SHIN; *fuka(i)*, deep, profound, thick (fog), close (connection); *fuka(sa)*, depth, profundity; *fuka(meru)* (v.t.), to make deeper, to intensify

深夜 *shin'ya*, midnight
深呼吸 *shinkokyū*, deep breath
深刻 *shinkoku*, serious, significant

3

進 343 11 strokes	ノ	イ	亻
	什	隹	隹
	淮	進	進

SHIN; *susu(mu)*, to advance, to proceed; *susu(meru)* (v.t.), to move forward, to stimulate

進行 *shinkō*, progress, advance
進級 *shinkyū*, promotion
行進 *kōshin*, march, parade

☑ 3

世 344 5 strokes	一	十	廿
	世	世	

SEI; *yo*, world, age, reign

世界 *sekai*, the world
世紀 *seiki*, century
世間 *seken*, the world, society, life

☑ 4

69

整	一	己	丰	SEI; *totono(eru)*, to put in order, to get ready; *totono(u)*, to be ready
	圭	束	剌	整理 *seiri*, adjustment, arrangement, reorganization
345 16 strokes	剌	敕	整	整備 *seibi*, adjustment, complete equipment, consolidation [1]

昔	一	十	廿	SEKI, SHAKU; *mukashi*, in the past, olden times
	𠀋	芐	芐	昔話 *mukashibanashi*, old tale, folklore
346 8 strokes	昔	昔		今昔 *konjaku*, past and present 大昔 *ōmukashi*, high antiquity, in the remote past ☑[3]

全	ノ	人	今	ZEN, whole; *matta(ku)*, *sube(te)*, entirely, all
	今	全	全	全体 *zentai*, the whole 全部 *zenbu*, all, the whole 完全 *kanzen*, perfect
347 6 strokes				☑[3]

相	一	十	才	SŌ, appearance, aspect, phase; SHŌ, minister of state; *ai-*, each other, mutual
	木	利	机	相談 *sōdan*, consultation, talk 相手 *aite*, companion, the other party
348 9 strokes	杣	相	相	首相 *shushō*, prime minister ☑[3]

送	、	゛	゛	SŌ; *oku(ru)*, to send
	゛	芊	关	放送 *hōsō*, broadcast 輸送 *yusō*, transportation 送金 *sōkin*, sending money
349 9 strokes	关	送	送	☑[4]

70

想	一	十	才	**SŌ, idea, thought**
	木	机	相	想像　*sōzō*, imagination 理想　*risō*, ideal 予想　*yosō*, expectation
350 13 strokes	相	想	想	3

息	⸌	⸜	白	**SOKU, son; *iki*, breath**
	自	自	自	ため息　*tameiki*, sigh 休息　*kyūsoku*, rest 消息　*shōsoku*, news, letter, 　　circumstances
351 10 strokes	息	息	息	3

速	一	⸜	曰	**SOKU; *haya(i)*, speedy, quick; *haya(maru)* (v.i.) quicken, speed up; *haya(meru)* (v.t.), to hasten, to accelerate; *sumi(yaka)*, speedy, prompt**
	束	束	束	速度　*sokudo*, speed 速記　*sokki*, stenography, shorthand
352 10 strokes	凍	凍	速	速達　*sokutatsu*, express 　　mail, special delivery　✓ 3

族	亠	方	方	**ZOKU, family, tribe, clan**
	方	扩	扩	家族　*kazoku*, family, household 民族　*minzoku*, race, people, 　　nation 水族館　*suizokukan*, aquarium
353 11 strokes	扩	族	族	✓ 4

他	ノ	イ	仆	**TA; *hoka*, other**
	仲	他		他国　*takoku*, other countries 他人　*tanin*, other people, stranger その他　*sonota*, the others, the rest; 　　and so forth
354 5 strokes				3

打	一	十	扌	DA; u(tsu), to strike, to beat
	扌	打		舌打ち shita-uchi, smacking one's lips, click of the tongue
355 5 strokes				打者 dasha, batter, hitter 三塁打 sanrui-da, three-base hit ☑ 3

対	、	ニ	ゔ	TAI, opposite, against; TSUI, pair, set
	文	文	対	反対 hantai, opposition, opposite, objection, reverse 対面 taimen, interview, confrontation
356 7 strokes	対			二対一 ni-tai-ichi, (score of) 2 to 1 ☑ 3

待	ノ	ク	彳	TAI; ma(tsu), to wait for
	彳	彳	往	待合室 machiaishitsu, waiting room 接待 settai, reception 招待 shōtai, invitation
357 9 strokes	往	待	待	☑ 4

代	ノ	イ	仁	DAI, generation, price; ka(eru), to substitute, to use instead; ka(waru), to take the place of, to relieve; yo, generation, era, reign
	代	代		
358 5 strokes				時代 jidai, period, era, age 現代 gendai, the present age 代表 daihyō, representative 4

第	ノ	㇑	㇏	DAI, grade, prefix for ordinal numbers
	竹	竺	竻	第一回 dai-ikkai, the first time 及第 kyūdai, passing an examination
359 11 strokes	笋	第	第	落第 rakudai, failure (in an examination), rejection ☑ 1

題	日	旦	早	**DAI**, subject, topic, theme, title (of book, story, etc.)
	早	是	是	問題 *mondai*, question, problem 話題 *wadai*, topic of conversation 宿題 *shukudai*, homework
360 18 strokes	是	是	題	☑ 4

炭	⼂	屮	山	**TAN**; *sumi*, charcoal
	屵	岸	岸	炭坑 *tankō*, coal mine 石炭 *sekitan*, coal 木炭 *mokutan*, charcoal
361 9 strokes	炭	炭	炭	2

短	⼃	㇏	㇏	**TAN**, shortness, defect; *mijika(i)*, short, brief
	⽮	矢	矢	短気 *tanki*, quick temper 最短 *saitan*, shortest 長短 *chōtan*, long and short,
362 12 strokes	矩	短	短	merits and demerits ☑ 2

談	⼂	二	言	**DAN**, talk
	言	言	言	相談 *sōdan*, consultation 談話 *danwa*, conversation, talk 歓談 *kandan*, pleasant chat
363 15 strokes	談	談	談	3

着	⼂	⼆	丷	**CHAKU**; *ki(ru)*, to wear; *tsu(ku)*, to reach, to arrive; *ki(seru)*, to dress, to plate
	并	羊	羊	着物 *kimono*, Japanese robe 一着 *itchaku*, first arrival, a suit
364 12 strokes	羊	着	着	(of clothes) 上着 *uwagi*, coat　☑ 4

73

注	`	`	`	CHŪ; *soso(gu)*, to pour, to concentrate on
	`	`	`	注意 *chūi*, attention, care, warning, advice
365 8 strokes	汁	注		注目 *chūmoku*, attention, observation
				注文 *chūmon*, order, request, demand ☑ 4
柱	一	十	才	CHŪ; *hashira*, post, pillar
	木	术	杧	帆柱 *hobashira*, mast
				柱時計 *hashiradokei*, wall clock
366 9 strokes	杧	柱	柱	電柱 *denchū*, telegraph (electric) pole
				2
丁	一	丁		CHŌ, Japanese linear unit (120 yds.), division of a ward or town, leaf of a book; TEI, "D" grade
				横丁 *yokochō*, side street, alleyway
367 2 strokes				丁度 *chōdo*, exactly, just
				丁寧 *teinei*, politeness 1
帳	`	冂	巾	CHŌ, curtain, register
	巾	帄	帐	帳面 *chōmen*, notebook, account book
				手帳 *techō*, memo book, notebook
368 11 strokes	帐	帳	帳	日記帳 *nikkichō*, diary
				1
調	言	言	訂	CHŌ; *shira(be)*, melody, inspection; *shira(beru)*, to investigate, to examine, to inspect; *totono(u)*, to be prepared, to be arranged, to be settled
	訂	訂	訶	調子 *chōshi*, tune, key, rhythm, tone, way, condition
369 15 strokes	調	調		調査 *chōsa*, investigation, examination
				調節 *chōsetsu*, adjustment ☑ 3

追	´	イ	亇	TSUI; o(u), to run after, to drive away
	自	白	自	追いかける　oikakeru, to chase 追求　　　　tsuikyū, pursuit 追放　　　　tsuihō, banishment,
370 9 strokes	⺍自	辶白	追	exile, purge ③

定	丶	丷	宀	TEI, JŌ; sada(meru), to fix, to decide, to establish; sada(ka), certain; sada(maru), to be decided, to be settled
	宀	宁	宇	定員　　tei-in, regular staff, full 　　　　number of personnel 定期　　teiki, fixed period or term, 　　　　regularity; prefix for "regular"
371 8 strokes	定	定		予定　　yotei, previous arrangement, 　　　　program, schedule　✓ ③

庭	丶	亠	广	TEI; niwa, garden
	广	庁	庄	庭園　　teien, garden 校庭　　kōtei, school playground 家庭　　katei, home
372 10 strokes	庄	庭	庭	✓ ③

笛	ノ	ヒ	ケ	TEKI; fue, flute, whistle
	ケケ	竹	竺	警笛　　keiteki, alarm whistle, 　　　　warning horn 汽笛　　kiteki, steam whistle, siren 口笛　　kuchibue, whistling
373 11 strokes	笁	笛	笛	①

鉄	ノ	ト	午	TETSU, iron, steel
	金	金	釒	鉄道　　tetsudō, railroad 地下鉄　chikatetsu, subway 鉄橋　　tekkyō, iron bridge, railway 　　　　bridge
374 13 strokes	釪	鉄	鉄	②

75

転	一	曰	亘	TEN, to turn round, to change, to fall, to tumble; *koro(gasu)*, to knock down, to roll over; *koro(garu)*, to tumble; to lie down; *koro(geru)*, to roll over; *koro(bu)*, to tumble, to fall down
	車	転	転	転校　　*tenkō*, change of schools 転任　　*tennin*, change of post 運転　　*unten*, driving, working, operation
375 11 strokes	転	転		✓ 4

都	土	⺧	耂	TO, TSU; *miyako*, capital, metropolis
	者	者	者	都会　　*tokai*, city 首都　　*shuto*, capital 都合　　*tsugō*, circumstances, conditions
376 11 strokes	者˺	者˹	都	✓ 3

度	丶	亠	广	DO, TO, TAKU, degree, time, times; *tabi*, occasion, counter for number of times
	广	庐	庐	一度　　*ichido*, once 速度　　*sokudo*, speed 程度　　*teido*, degree, level, extent
377 9 strokes	庐	度	度	✓ 4

投	一	扌	扌	TŌ; *na(geru)*, to throw, to give up
	扌	抈	投	投票　　*tōhyō*, voting 投資　　*tōshi*, investment 投書　　*tōsho*, contribution (to a magazine, newspaper, etc)
378 7 strokes	投			3

豆	一	丆	戸	TŌ, ZU; *mame*, peas, beans; *mame-*, baby/miniature
	戸	戸	豆	豆腐　　*tōfu*, bean-curd 大豆　　*daizu*, soy beans 豆本　　*mamehon*, miniature book
379 7 strokes	豆			1

島	イ	ヤ	ヤ	TŌ; *shima*, island
	戶	皀	鳥	半島 *hantō*, peninsula 群島 *guntō*, group of islands 島国 *shimaguni*, island country
380 10 strokes	鳥	島	島	☑ 2

湯	、	氵	氵	TŌ; *yu*, hot water
	沪	沪	沪	湯気 *yuge*, steam 湯船 *yubune*, bathtub 熱湯 *nettō*, boiling water
381 12 strokes	湯	湯	湯	2

登	ᄀ	ㄅ	ㄗ	TŌ, TO; *nobo(ri)*, climbing (n.); *nobo(ru)*, to climb
	癶	癶	癶	登山 *tozan*, mountain climbing 登校 *tōkō*, attending school 木登り *ki-nobori*, tree climbing
382 12 strokes	咎	登	登	☑ 3

等	ノ	亠	ケ	TŌ, class, quality; *hito(shii)*, like, equal
	竹	竺	笁	上等 *jōtō*, high-class, very good, superior 一等 *ittō*, first class, most, best
383 12 strokes	笁	等	等	高等学校 *kōtōgakkō*, senior high school 3

動	二	旨	重	DŌ; *ugo(ku)*, to move
	重	重	重	動物 *dōbutsu*, animal 自動車 *jidōsha*, automobile 運動 *undō*, motion, physical exercise, athletic sports
384 11 strokes	動			☑ 4

童	ヽ	亠	立	DŌ; *warabe*, child
	立	立	音	児童　*jidō*, child, boys and girls 童話　*dōwa*, nursery tale 童謡　*dōyō*, nursery song
385 12 strokes	音	童	童	[2]
農	冂	曲	曲	NŌ, farming
	曲	芦	農	農場　*nōjō*, farm 農業　*nōgyō*, agriculture 農家　*nōka*, farmhouse
386 13 strokes	農	農	農	[2]
波	ヽ	丶丶	氵	HA; *nami*, wave
	氵	沪	沪	大波　　ō-*nami*, big wave 防波堤　*bōhatei*, breakwater 電波　　*denpa*, electric wave
387 8 strokes	波	波		[2]
配	一	冂	西	HAI; *kuba(ru)*, to distribute, to deliver
	西	酉	酉	配給　*haikyū*, ration, distribution (of food or goods) 配達　*haitatsu*, delivery 心配　*shinpai*, worry
388 10 strokes	酉′	酉′	配	☑ [3]
倍	ノ	イ	イ	BAI, two times, double; suffix denoting "times"
	什	件	佇	数倍　*sūbai*, several times 何倍　*nanbai*, how many times? 倍率　*bairitsu*, magnifying power
389 10 strokes	倍	倍	倍	[2]

箱	⟋	⟍	⟍	*hako*, box, case
	竹	竹	竹	下駄箱 *getabako*, shoe cabinet
				郵便箱 *yūbinbako*, mailbox, postbox
390 15 strokes	箱	箱	箱	箱庭 *hakoniwa*, miniature garden [3]

畑	丶	丷	少	*hata*, *hatake*, field, farm, cultivated field
	火	灯	灯	田畑 *tahata*/*denpata*, fields
				麦畑 *mugibatake*, wheat (barley) field
391 9 strokes	畑	畑	畑	花畑 *hanabatake*, flower garden [3]

発	⁊	⁊	⁊	HATSU, to expose, to open, to shoot, to happen
	癶	癶	癶	発音 *hatsuon*, pronunciation
				発表 *happyō*, announcement
				出発 *shuppatsu*, departure
392 9 strokes	癶	発	発	☑ [4]

反	一	厂	厉	HAN, antithesis, anti-; HON, TAN, unit of measure (for land and cloth); *so(ru)* (v.i.), to curve; *so(rasu)* (v.t.), to bend (something)
	反			反対 *hantai*, opposition, contrast
393 4 strokes				反省 *hansei*, self-examination
				反射 *hansha*, reflection ☑ [3]

坂	一	十	土	HAN; *saka*, slope, hill
	圠	圹	坈	坂道 *sakamichi*, sloping road
				上り坂 *noborizaka*, ascent, uphill road
394 7 strokes	坂			急坂 *kyūhan*, steep slope [2]

板	一	十	才	HAN; *ita*, board (of wood)
	木	杧	杫	板の間 *ita-no-ma*, wooden floor 掲示板 *keijiban*, notice-board 看板 *kanban*, poster, signboard, shingle
395 8 strokes	朸	板		2

皮	ノ	厂	广	HI; *kawa*, skin, leather
	皮	皮		毛皮 *kegawa*, fur 皮肉 *hiniku*, irony 皮膚 *hifu*, skin
396 5 strokes				2

悲	ノ	ナ	ヲ	HI; *kana(shii)*; sad, *kana(shimu)*, to be sad
	ヲ	刲	非	悲劇 *higeki*, tragedy, tragic event 悲壮 *hisō*, pathetic 慈悲 *jihi*, mercy
397 12 strokes	非	非	悲	3

美	丶	䒑	丷	BI, beauty; *utsuku(shii)*, beautiful
	半	羊	羊	美術 *bijutsu*, fine arts 美人 *bijin*, a beauty, pretty girl, beautiful woman 美術館 *bijutsukan*, art museum
398 9 strokes	羊	美	美	✓ 3

鼻	⼍	门	自	BI; *hana*, nose
	自	鳥	畠	鼻先 *hanasaki*, tip of one's nose, under one's very nose 鼻紙 *hanagami*, paper handkerchief
399 14 strokes	畠	鼻	鼻	鼻血 *hanaji*, nosebleed ✓ 2

筆	ノ	⺮	⺮	HITSU; *fude*, writing brush
	⺮	⺮	⺮	万年筆 *mannenhitsu*, fountain pen 鉛筆 *enpitsu*, pencil 筆者 *hissha*, writer
400 12 strokes	筆	筆	筆	2

氷	丨	丨	刂	HYŌ; *kōri*, ice
	氷	氷		氷すべり *kōrisuberi*, ice skating 氷山 *hyōzan*, iceberg 砕氷船 *saihyōsen*, icebreaker
401 5 strokes				✓ 2

表	一	十	丰	HYŌ, list, table, schedule; *omote*, the outside, surface; *ara(wasu)*, to show, to indicate, to expose, to express, to represent
	圭	表	表	表紙 *hyōshi*, cover of a book 表面 *hyōmen*, surface
402 8 strokes	表	表		時間表 *jikanhyō*, schedule, timetable ✓ 3

秒	ノ	二	千	BYŌ, second (unit of time)
	千	禾	利	秒針 *byōshin*, second hand 一秒 *ichibyō*, one second 数秒 *sūbyō*, several seconds
403 9 strokes	利	秒	秒	2

病	丶	广	广	BYŌ; *yamai*, illness; *ya(mu)*, to fall ill
	疒	疒	疒	病気 *byōki*, illness, sickness 病院 *byōin*, hospital 病人 *byōnin*, sick person
404 10 strokes	病	病	病	✓ 4

81

品	丶	口	口	HIN, elegance, dignity; *shina*, goods
	口	무	무	品物　*shinamono*, article, goods 手品　*tejina*, jugglery, sleight of hand 作品　*sakuhin*, work, works
405 9 strokes	무	品	品	☑ 4
負	ノ	ク	ケ	FU; *o(u)*, to bear, to owe; *ma(keru)*, to be defeated, to reduce a price; *ma(kasu)*, to defeat
	角	角	角	勝負　*shōbu*, victory or defeat, game 負傷　*fushō*, wound 背負う　*se-ou*, to carry on one's back
406 9 strokes	負	負	負	3
部	丶	二	亠	BU, department, copy, part
	立	立	音	全部　*zenbu*, all, whole 東部　*tōbu*, eastern part 部分　*bubun*, part
407 11 strokes	咅	部	部	☑ 3
服	ノ	刀	月	FUKU, dress, European clothes
	月	月	肝	洋服　*yōfuku*, European clothes 礼服　*reifuku*, full dress 制服　*seifuku*, uniform
408 8 strokes	服	服		☑ 4
福	丶	ラ	ネ	FUKU, good fortune
	ネ	ネ	ネ	幸福　*kōfuku*, happiness 福の神　*fuku-no-kami*, God of Wealth 祝福　*shukufuku*, blessing
409 13 strokes	福	福	福	3

物	ノ	ト	牛
	牛	牜	牣
410 8 strokes	物	物	

BUTSU, MOTSU; *mono*, thing, article, object

食べ物　*tabemono*, food
名物　　*meibutsu*, noted product, special product
貨物　　*kamotsu*, freight

☑ 4

平	一	一	二
	平	平	
411 5 strokes			

HEI, BYŌ; *tai(ra)*, evenness, flatness; *hira(tai)*, even, level, simple

平和　　*heiwa*, peace
平気　　*heiki*, calmness, indifference
平等　　*byōdō*, equality

☑ 3

返	一	厂	反
	反	反	返
412 7 strokes	返		

HEN; *kae(su)*, to return, to give back

返事　　　*henji*, answer
繰り返す　*kurikaesu*, to repeat
恩返し　　*ongaeshi*, repayment of a favor, returning a favor

3

勉	ノ	ク	ケ
	台	台	台
413 10 strokes	争	免	勉

BEN, to exert oneself, to make efforts

勉強　　*benkyō*, study
勤勉　　*kinben*, diligence
勉強家　*benkyōka*, studious person

☑ 4

放	、	二	亠
	方	方	放
414 8 strokes	放	放	

HŌ; *hana(su)*, to let go, to release; *hana(tsu)*, to set free, to send forth, to shoot; *hō(ru)*, to throw

放送　　*hōsō*, broadcasting
放課後　*hōkago*, after school
開放　　*kaihō*, freedom, opening

3

味	丶	﹍	口	MI; *aji*, taste, relish, experience; *aji(wau)*, to savor, to appreciate
	口一	口二	叶	無味　*mumi*, tastelessness 味方　*mikata*, friend, ally 興味　*kyōmi*, interest, enjoyment
415 8 strokes	咪	味		☑ 4

命	ノ	人	人	MEI, order, command; MYŌ; *inochi*, life
	仒	合	合	命令　*meirei*, order, command 使命　*shimei*, mission 生命　*seimei*, life, soul
416 8 strokes	合	命		3

面	一	﹁	厂	MEN, side, phase, mask; *omote*, face, outside, front, surface; *omo* (lit.), face, surface; *tsura*, face
	厇	而	而	表面　*hyōmen*, surface 正面　*shōmen*, the front 場面　*bamen*, scene
417 9 strokes	而	面	面	☑ 3

問	l	冂	冂	MON; *to(u)*, to ask, to question, to care, to accuse; *to(i)*, *ton*, question, inquiry
	門	門	門	問題　*mondai*, problem, issue, trouble
418 11 strokes	門	門	問	学問　*gakumon*, learning 疑問　*gimon*, doubt, question ☑ 4

役	ノ	ク	彳	YAKU, office, duty, role, use, service; EKI (lit.), war
	彳	役	役	役所　*yakusho*, public office 役人　*yakunin*, government official 役者　*yakusha*, actor, actress
419 7 strokes	役			3

薬	一	十	艹	YAKU; *kusuri*, medicine, chemicals
	苩	苩	苩	薬学　*yakugaku*, pharmacy (study) 火薬　*kayaku*, gunpowder 薬局　*yakkyoku*, pharmacy,
420 16 strokes	菏	薴	薬	pharmacist's office ☑ 3

由	丨	冂	巾	YU, YŪ; *yoshi*, a reason, significance
	由	由		自由　*jiyū*, liberty, freedom 不自由 *fujiyū*, inconvenience, 　　　　discomfort
421 5 strokes				理由　*riyū*, reason ☑ 3

油	丶	冫	氵	YU; *abura*, oil
	氵	汩	沖	油絵　*abura-e*, oil painting 石油　*sekiyu*, petroleum 油田　*yuden*, oil field
422 8 strokes	油	油		2

有	一	ナ	オ	YŪ, U; *a(ru)*, to exist, to have, to measure, to have experience, to happen, to consist of
	冇	有	有	有名　*yūmei*, fame, well-known 有益　*yūeki*, benefit, profit
423 6 strokes				有志　*yūshi*, volunteer ☑ 4

遊	丶	亠	亍	YŪ; *aso(bu)*, to play, to be idle
	方	方	方	遊星　*yūsei*, planet 遊戯　*yūgi*, game, sports, 　　　　children's play
424 12 strokes	斿	游	遊	遊覧　*yūran*, excursion, 　　　　sightseeing ☑ 3

85

予	ﾌ	マ	丑	YO, previous
	予			予防　yobō, prevention
				予定　yotei, previous arrangement, schedule
				予想　yosō, anticipation
425 4 strokes				✓ 3

羊	`	` `	丷	YŌ; hitsuji, sheep, ram, ewe
	丷	兰	羊	羊毛　yōmō, wool
				羊皮　yōhi, sheepskin
				子羊　kohitsuji, a lamb
426 6 strokes				1

洋	`	:	氵	YŌ, ocean
	氵	汀	沪	西洋　seiyō, the West, the Occident
	泮	洋	洋	洋間　yōma, Western-style room
				洋服　yōfuku, Western-style clothes
				太平洋 Taiheiyō, Pacific Ocean
427 9 strokes				✓ 4

葉	一	十	艹	YŌ; ha, leaves, foliage
	艹	苧	苗	葉緑素 yōryokuso, chlorophyll
	荤	荘	葉	落ち葉 ochiba, fallen leaves
				葉巻　hamaki, cigar
428 12 strokes				3

陽	ﾌ	ﾖ	阝	YŌ, positive, male principle in nature
	阝日	阻	阴	太陽　taiyō, sun
	陽	陽	陽	太陽系 taiyōkei, solar system
				陽気　yōki, season, weather, cheerfulness
429 12 strokes				3

様	木	栏	栏	YŌ, way, style, manner; *sama*, Mr., Mrs., Miss, etc. (polite suffix for personal names); state, way, form, condition
	栏	样	栲	
430 14 strokes	栲	様	様	神様　　*kamisama*, god 様子　　*yōsu*, appearance, manner, state　　☑ 3
落	一	十	艹	RAKU; *o(chiru)*, to fall (v.i.), to be omitted, to be inferior to; *o(tosu)*, to omit, to make worse, to let drop, to lose
	艹	艻	芐	
431 12 strokes	茐	茨	落	落第　　*rakudai*, failure (in an examination), rejection 落成　　*rakusei*, completion (building, etc.)　☑ 3
流	丶	氵	氵	RYŪ, RU; *naga(re)*, stream, current, flow; *naga(reru)*, to flow (v.i.); *naga(su)*, to set afloat, to wash away, to pour (v.t.)
	氵	汻	汯	
432 10 strokes	泸	済	流	流れ星 *nagareboshi*, shooting star 流行　*ryūkō*, fashion, vogue 電流　*denryū*, electric current　3
旅	㇐	方	方	RYO; *tabi*, travel, journey
	方	方'	放	旅人　　*tabibito*, traveler 旅行　　*ryokō*, trip, travel 旅館　　*ryokan*, inn, hotel
433 10 strokes	放	旅	旅	☑ 4
両	一	一	冂	RYŌ, old Japanese monetary unit; two, both
	丙	両	両	両手　*ryōte*, both hands 両方　*ryōhō*, both, both sides 両親　*ryōshin*, parents, father and mother
434 6 strokes				☑ 3

87

緑	糸	幻	糹
	糸	絈	絈
435 14 strokes	絈	綠	緑

RYOKU, ROKU; *midori*, green

新緑　　*shinryoku*, fresh verdure
緑地　　*ryokuchi*, green tract of land
緑色　　*midori-iro*, green (color)

2

礼	丶	ラ	ネ
	ネ	礼	
436 5 strokes			

REI, salutation, courtesy, bow, thanks

礼儀　　*reigi*, courtesy, manners, etiquette
無礼　　*burei*, impoliteness, discourtesy
失礼　　*shitsurei*, discourtesy, rudeness

✓ 3

列	一	フ	歹
	歹	列	列
437 6 strokes			

RETSU, row, line

行列　　*gyōretsu*, row, procession
列車　　*ressha*, train
整列　　*seiretsu*, standing in a row

3

練	糸	幻	紀
	約	絈	絹
438 14 strokes	紳	練	練

REN; *ne(ru)*, to polish (one's style), to discipline (one's mind), to parade, to knead (a dough)

練習　　*renshū*, practice
熟練　　*jukuren*, skill, dexterity
訓練　　*kunren*, drill, training

✓ 2

路	口	卩	甼
	足	足	趴
439 13 strokes	趴	跋	路

RO, road, route, path; ~*ji*, suffix denoting "way"

道路　　*dōro*, road
線路　　*senro*, railway track
航路　　*kōro*, sea route

3

和 440 8 strokes	一 禾 和	二 禾 和	千 禾	WA, harmony, peace, Japan; *yawa(ragu)*, to soften, to calm down (v.i.); *nago(yaka)*, calm, harmonious 平和　*heiwa*, peace 和服　*wafuku*, Japanese clothes, kimono 調和　*chōwa*, harmony　☑ 3
愛 441 13 strokes	一 宀 愛	冖 严 愛	冖 恶 愛	AI, love; *ai(suru)*, to love 愛情　*aijō*, love, affection 愛国心　*aikokushin*, patriotism 愛児　*aiji*, one's beloved child　3
案 442 10 strokes	丶 宀 安	八 安 宰	宀 安 案	AN, plan, idea; *an(jiru)*, to be anxious about, to be concerned about 案外　*angai*, unexpectedly 案内　*annai*, guide, guidance 名案　*meian*, good idea, good plan　1
以 443 5 strokes	丨 以	丄 以	丛	I, with, through, on account of 以上　*ijō*, above, more than 以外　*igai*, besides, outside of 以前　*izen*, before, formerly　☑ 4
衣 444 6 strokes	丶 衣	亠 衣	亠 衣	I; *koromo*, clothes, garment, priest's robe 衣類　*irui*, clothing 衣食住　*i-shoku-jū*, necessities of life (clothing, food, shelter) 衣替え　*koromogae*, change of dress　2

位	ノ	イ	イ
	仁	仁	付
445 **7 strokes**	位		

I; *kurai*, rank, position, grade; about (approximately)

地位	*chi-i*, rank, social standing
位置	*ichi*, location, situation
学位	*gaku-i*, academic degree

[3]

囲	|	冂	冂
	月	用	囲
446 **7 strokes**	囲		

I; *kako(mu)*, *kako(u)*, to surround, to enclose, to besiege

胸囲	*kyōi*, girth of the chest, chest measurement
周囲	*shūi*, circumference, surroundings
範囲	*han'i*, extent, sphere, limits

[2]

胃	\	冂	冂
	四	田	胃
447 **9 strokes**	胃	胃	胃

I, stomach

胃袋	*ibukuro*, stomach
胃病	*ibyō*, stomach trouble
胃腸	*i-chō*, stomach and intestines

[2]

印	´	イ	イ
	白	臼	印
448 **6 strokes**			

IN, seal, stamp; *shirushi*, sign, symbol, trace

印刷	*insatsu*, printing
矢印	*yajirushi*, arrow sign
目印	*mejirushi*, mark

[2]

英	一	十	艹
	艹	苎	苎
449 **8 strokes**	英	英	

EI, England, excellent

英語	*eigo*, English language
英雄	*eiyū*, hero
日英	*Nichi-Ei*, Japan and England

☑ [4]

栄	、	゛	゛	EI, honor; *saka(e)*; *ha(e)*, prosperity; *saka(eru)*, to prosper; *ha(eru)*, to excel, to shine
	゛	゛	゛	光栄　*kōei*, honor 繁栄　*han'ei*, prosperity 栄養　*eiyō*, nutrition
450 9 strokes	学	栄	栄	2

塩	土	扌	扩	EN; *shio*, salt
	坫	坫	垆	塩水　*shiomizu*, salt water 塩田　*enden*, salt bed 食塩　*shokuen*, table salt
451 13 strokes	塩	塩	塩	2

億	ノ	イ	亻	OKU, one hundred million
	仟	倍	倍	二十億年　*nijūoku-nen*, two billion 　　　　　years 数億円　*sūoku-en*, several 　　　　　hundred million yen
452 15 strokes	億	億	億	2

加	フ	カ	加	KA; *kuwa(eru)*, to add, to join, to increase (v.t.); *kuwa(waru)*, to join, to enter (v.i.)
	加	加		参加　*sanka*, participation 加入　*kanyū*, entrance, joining 増加　*zōka*, increase
453 5 strokes				3

果	丶	冂	日	KA, fruit, result; *ha(te)*, end, result; *ha(tasu)*, to carry out, to realize, to fulfill; *ha(teru)*, to end, to die
	日	旦	甲	結果　*kekka*, result, effect 効果　*kōka*, effect 果実　*kajitsu*, fruit
454 8 strokes	果	果		3

貨 455 11 strokes	ノ 化 皆	イ 代 貨	イ 皆 貨	KA, freight; goods, property 百貨店 *hyakkaten*, department store 銀貨 *ginka*, silver coin 雑貨 *zakka*, miscellaneous goods, sundries <div align="right">5</div>
課 456 15 strokes	` 訂 訂	冖 訂 評	言 訂 課	KA, section, lesson 課外 *kagai*, extra-curricular 課題 *kadai*, theme, homework 学課 *gakka*, lesson <div align="right">2</div>
芽 457 8 strokes	一 廿 芽	十 芦 芽	艹 芒	GA; *me*, bud, sprout, shoot 木の芽 *ki-no-me*, leaf bud 新芽 *shinme*, sprout, bud, shoot 芽生え *mebae*, bud, sprout <div align="right">1</div>
改 458 7 strokes	⼁ 己 改	コ 卍	己 改	KAI; *arata(meru)*, to change, to reform, to revise; *arata(maru)*, to be reformed 改良 *kairyō*, improvement 改心 *kaishin*, conversion, reform 改札口 *kaisatsuguchi*, ticket gate <div align="right">2</div>
械 459 11 strokes	十 朾 械	木 杓 械	朾 梆 械	KAI, shackles 機械 *kikai*, machine 器械 *kikai*, instrument, apparatus <div align="right">2</div>

92

害	、	ハ	宀	GAI, harm, calamity
	宀	中	宔	害虫　　*gaichū*, harmful insect 損害　　*songai*, loss, damage 障害　　*shōgai*, obstacle, hindrance
460 10 strokes	宝	害		3

街	ノ	ク	彳	GAI, KAI; *machi*, street, town, quarters
	彳	彺	彺	商店街　*shōtengai*, shopping centre 市街　　*shigai*, the streets; city, town
461 12 strokes	徍	街	街	街道　　*kaidō*, highway, route 1

各	ノ	ク	夂	KAKU; *ono-ono*, each, every
	冬	各	各	各地　　*kakuchi*, every place 各人　　*kakujin*, each person 各駅　　*kaku-eki*, each station
462 6 strokes				2

覚	、	゛	゛゛	KAKU; *obo(eru)*, to remember, to understand; *sa(masu)*, to awake (v.t.); *sa(meru)*, to wake up (v.i.)
	⺍	⺍	尚	覚え書　*oboegaki*, memorandum note 感覚　　*kankaku*, sensation, sense, feeling
463 12 strokes	尚	覚	覚	自覚　　*jikaku*, consciousness, self-consciousness　3

完	、	ハ	宀	KAN, end, completion
	宀	宀	宇	完全　　*kanzen*, perfection 完成　　*kansei*, completion 完結　　*kanketsu*, completion, finish, termination
464 7 strokes	完			3

93

官	`	˙	宀
	宀	宁	宁
465 8 strokes	官	官	

KAN, government, government position

官庁	*kanchō*, government office
裁判官	*saibankan*, judge
警官	*keikan*, policeman, police officer

3

管	ノ	ト	ベ
	ベケ	竹	竺
466 14 strokes	竺	管	管

KAN, to control, to administer; *kuda*, tube, pipe

鉄管	*tekkan*, iron pipe (tube)
血管	*kekkan*, blood vessel
管理	*kanri*, administration, control, charge

2

関	l	⺆	門
	門	門	閂
467 14 strokes	閂	関	関

KAN; *seki*, barrier; *kan(suru)*, *kaka(waru)*, to relate to

関心	*kanshin*, concern, interest
玄関	*genkan*, entrance hall, entrance
機関車	*kikansha*, engine, locomotive

✓ 3

観	ノ	⺍	午
	午	午	午
468 18 strokes	奔	雈	観

KAN, to look at carefully, to show

観光	*kankō*, sightseeing
観察	*kansatsu*, observation
観測	*kansoku*, observation, survey

3

願	一	厂	厂
	盾	原	原
469 19 strokes	原	原	願

GAN; *nega(i)*, wish, petition, request; *nega(u)*, to ask, to request, to wish, to beg

願書	*gansho*, written application
志願	*shigan*, volunteering, desire, application

✓ 3

94

希	ノ	メ	㇒
	产	产	希
470 7 strokes	希		

KI, rare; desire

希望　　*kibō*, hope, desire
希望者　*kibōsha*, aspirant, applicant
希薄　　*kihaku*, thin, weak, sparse

②

季	一	二	千
	禾	禾	禾
471 8 strokes	季	季	

KI, season

季節　*kisetsu*, season
四季　*shiki*, the four seasons
雨季　*uki*, rainy season

②

紀	㇑	幺	幺
	糸	糸	糸
472 9 strokes	紀	紀	紀

KI, history, chronicle

世紀　　　*seiki*, century, period
二十世紀　*nijisseiki*, twentieth
　　　　　century
紀元　　　*kigen*, era, epoch

①

喜	一	十	士
	吉	吉	吉
473 12 strokes	壴	喜	

KI; *yoroko(bi)*, joy, happy event, congratulation; *yoroko(bu)*, to rejoice, to be glad

大喜び　*ō-yorokobi*, great joy, great
　　　　delight
喜劇　　*kigeki*, comedy
歓喜　　*kanki*, joy, ecstasy ③

旗	疒	疒	旂
	旂	旂	旂
474 14 strokes	旗	旗	旗

KI; *hata*, flag

国旗　　*kokki*, national flag
校旗　　*kōki*, school flag
星条旗　*seijōki*, the Stars and Stripes

①

器	口	吅	吅	KI; *utsuwa*, vessel, utensil, capacity, caliber
	罒	哭	哭	食器　　*shokki*, tableware 陶器　　*tōki*, pottery, ceramics 洗面器　*senmenki*, wash basin
475 15 strokes	器			1
機	木	杓	栐	KI; *hata*, loom
	栐	栐	栐	機械　　*kikai*, machine, mechanism 機会　　*kikai*, opportunity, chance 危機　　*kiki*, crisis, emergency
476 16 strokes	機	機	機	✓ 3
議	言	訁	詳	GI, discussion
	詳	詳	詳	会議　　*kaigi*, conference 議論　　*giron*, argument, discussion 議会　　*gikai*, Diet
477 20 strokes	議			3
求	一	寸	寸	KYŪ; *moto(me)*, request, demand; *moto(meru)*, to request, to search for, to buy, to wish for
	才	求	求	求人　　*kyūjin*, offer of a job 請求　　*seikyū*, demand 求職　　*kyūshoku*, seeking 　　　　　employment
478 7 strokes	求			3
泣	丶	冫	氵	KYŪ; *na(ku)*, to cry, weep, sob
	氵	泣	泣	泣き声　*nakigoe*, crying, sobbing 泣き虫　*nakimushi*, crybaby 感泣　　*kankyū*, weeping with 　　　　　emotion
479 8 strokes	泣	泣		✓ 1

救 480 11 strokes	一	十	才	KYŪ; *suku(i)*, rescue, help; *suku(u)*, to rescue, to help
	求	求	求	救済 *kyūsai*, relief
	救	救	救	救助 *kyūjo*, rescue
				救急車 *kyūkyūsha*, ambulance ☐1

給 481 12 strokes	ム	ム	幺	KYU, to supply
	幺	糸	糸	給料 *kyūryō*, pay, salary
	糸	給	給	供給 *kyōkyū*, supply
				月給 *gekkyū*, monthly salary ☐3

挙 482 10 strokes	丶	⌣	⌣	KYO, to conduct, to perform; *a(geru)*, *a(garu)* (v.i), to raise, to hold (a function)
	⌣	⌣	兴	選挙 *senkyo*, election
	兴	挙	挙	挙行 *kyokō*, performance
				挙手 *kyoshu*, raising one's hand, a show of hands ☐1

漁 483 14 strokes	氵	氵	氵	GYO; RYŌ, fishing
	沪	渔	渔	漁船 *gyosen*, fishing boat
	漁	漁	漁	漁業 *gyogyō*, fishing industry
				漁師 *ryōshi*, fisherman ☐2

共 484 6 strokes	一	十	廾	KYŌ; *tomo*, both, as well as, together
	土	共	共	共通 *kyōtsū*, commonness
				共和国 *kyōwakoku*, republic
				共産党 *kyōsantō*, Communist Party ☐3

97

協 485 8 strokes	一 十 忄 忄 协 协 协 協	KYŌ, to be in harmony 協力　*kyōryoku*, cooperation 協会　*kyōkai*, society, association 協議　*kyōgi*, conference, consultation　2
鏡 486 19 strokes	金 鏟 鏱 鏱 鏱 鏱 鏱 鏱 鏱 鏡	KYŌ; *kagami*, mirror 鏡台　*kyōdai*, dressing table, mirror stand 双眼鏡　*sōgankyō*, binoculars 顕微鏡　*kenbikyō*, microscope　1
競 487 20 strokes	立 音 竞 竞 竞 競 竞 競	KYŌ, KEI; *kiso(u)*, to rival, to compete; *se(ru)*, to bid, to compete for 競争　*kyōsō*, competition 競技　*kyōgi*, match, tournament, sporting events 競馬　*keiba*, horse race　2
極 488 12 strokes	才 杠 杠 柯 極 極 極	KYOKU, terrestrial poles, magnetic poles, zenith; GOKU, very, extremely; *kiwa(maru)* (v.i.), to reach an end, an extreme; *kiwa(mi)*, apex 極端　*kyokutan*, extremity 北極　*hokkyoku*, North Pole 至極　*shigoku*, very, quite　2
訓 489 10 strokes	丶 亠 亖 言 言 言 訂 訓 訓	KUN, precept, Japanese rendering of a Chinese character (i.e., "kun" reading) 教訓　*kyōkun*, teachings, lesson 訓練　*kunren*, training, drill 訓辞　*kunji*, address of instructions　2

軍	`	⼍	⼌
	⼐	冟	冒
490 9 strokes	宣	軍	

GUN, army, military authorities

軍備　　*gunbi*, armaments
軍隊　　*guntai*, troops, army
軍艦　　*gunkan*, warship

2

郡	⼋	⼆	⼲
	尹	君	君ˊ
491 10 strokes	君阝	郡	

GUN, county, district

郡部　　*gunbu*, rural district,
　　　　counties
郡長　　*gunchō*, head of a county

1

径	`	⼃	彳
	彳ˊ	彳又	彳又
492 8 strokes	径	径	

KEI; path, course, direct

径路　　　*keiro*, course, path
直径　　　*chokkei*, diameter
直情径行　*chokujōkeikō*,
　　　　　impulsiveness

1

型	⼀	⼆	干
	开	刑	刑
493 9 strokes	刑	型	型

KEI; *kata*, type, model, mold,
conventionality

模型　　*mokei*, model
小型　　*kogata*, small size
大型　　*ō-gata*, large size

2

景	`	⼌	⽇
	⽇	昌	旦
494 12 strokes	暑	景	景

KEI, KE, view, scene

風景　　　*fūkei*, scenery, view
不景気　　*fukeiki*, bad times,
　　　　　depression
光景　　　*kōkei*, spectacle, scene

3

芸 495 7 strokes	一	十	サ
	サ	芸	芸
	芸		

GEI, arts, accomplishments

芸術　*geijutsu*, art
民芸　*mingei*, folk art
芸者　*geisha*, Japanese singing and dancing girl

2

欠 496 4 strokes	ノ	⺁	欠
	欠		

KETSU, lack, absence; *ka(keru)*, to be broken off, to lack (v.i.); *ka(ku)*, to lack, to want (v.t.)

欠点　*ketten*, fault
欠席　*kesseki*, absence
欠乏　*ketsubō*, shortage

3

結 497 12 strokes	㇑	幺	幺
	糸	糸	糸
	紆	紆	結

KETSU; *musu(bi)*, end, knot; *musu(bu)*, to tie, to bind, to conclude, to link; *yu(u)*, to dress (the hair); *yu(waeru)*, to fasten, to bind

結果　*kekka*, result
結婚　*kekkon*, marriage
連結　*renketsu*, coupling, connection, linking

☑ 1

建 498 9 strokes	㇕	㇕	㇕
	㇕	冃	聿
	彗	建	建

KEN, KON; *ta(teru)*, to build, to establish; *ta(tsu)*, to be built; ~*date*, ~-storied building

建物　*tatemono*, a building
建築　*kenchiku*, construction, architecture, building
二階建　*nikaidate*, two-storied building

4

健 499 11 strokes	亻	亻	亻
	仴	仴	仴
	律	健	健

KEN; *suko(yaka)*, healthy, sound

強健　*kyōken*, robust
保健　*hoken*, (preservation of) health
健全　*kenzen*, healthy, sound

1

100

験	ー	厂	厂	KEN, GEN, effect; to examine
	馬	馬	駅	実験 *jikken*, experiment 経験 *keiken*, experience 試験 *shiken*, examination, experiment
500 18 strokes	駘	驗	験	☑ 4

固	一	冂	冃	KO; *kata(meru)*, to harden, to make hard (v.t.); *kata(maru)*, to become hard; *kata(i)*, hard, firm
	円	円	固	固有 *koyū*, peculiar, one's own 固体 *kotai*, a solid (body) 強固 *kyōko*, firmness, solidity, stability
501 8 strokes	固	固		2

功	一	T	工	KŌ, merits, effect, service; KU
	巧	功		成功 *seikō*, success 功績 *kōseki*, meritorious deed 功労 *kōrō*, service
502 5 strokes				1

好	く	女	女	KŌ; *kono(mu)*, *su(ku)*, to like, love; *su(ki)*, fond of, like
	奵	好	好	好意 *kōi*, goodwill, kindness 好き嫌い *sukikirai*, likes and dislikes 好き好む *sukikonomu*, like, prefer
503 6 strokes				☑ 3

候	ノ	イ	亻	KŌ, season, sign; to inquire after
	广	俨	俨	気候 *kikō*, climate, weather 天候 *tenkō*, weather 候補 *kōho*, candidacy, candidate
504 10 strokes	佢	候	候	3

101

航	丿	ノ	凢
	舟	舟	舟

KŌ, to sail on the water

航海　　*kōkai*, voyage, navigation
航路　　*kōro*, sea route, air route
航空　　*kōkū*, aviation, air voyage

505 10 strokes	舟	舟	航

2

康	丶	亠	广
	庁	庐	庐

KŌ, to enjoy

健康　　　*kenkō*, health, good health
不健康　*fukenkō*, bad health

506 11 strokes	庚	庚	康

1

告	丿	广	牛
	生	生	告

KOKU; *tsu(geru)*, to tell, to inform

報告　　*hōkoku*, report
広告　　*kōkoku*, advertisement
忠告　　*chūkoku*, advice

507 7 strokes	告		

3

差	丶	丷	丷
	丬	羊	羊

SA, difference, remainder (math.); *sa(su)*, to thrust, to insert

差別　　*sabetsu*, distinction, discrimination
大差　　*taisa*, great difference
差出人 *sashidashinin*, sender, addresser

508 10 strokes	羊	美	差

3

菜	一	十	艹
	艹	芯	苹

SAI; *na*, greens, rape (vegetable)

野菜　　*yasai*, vegetables
菜の花 *na-no-hana*, rape blossoms
菜園　　*saien*, vegetable garden

509 11 strokes	芝	菜	

2

102

最	丶	冂	日
	旦	몯	咼
510 12 strokes	咼	咼	最

SAI, prefix for forming superlatives; *motto(mo)*, most

最初　　*saisho*, the first, beginning
最後　　*saigo*, the last
最善　　*saizen*, the best

☑ 3

材	一	十	才
	才	朴	村
511 7 strokes	材		

ZAI, material (for work), timber, ability, talent

木材　　*mokuzai*, lumber, wood
材料　　*zairyō*, raw material, ingredients
人材　　*jinzai*, capable man

2

昨	丨	冂	日
	日	旷	昨
512 9 strokes	昨	昨	昨

SAKU, yesterday, ancient times

昨日　　*sakujitsu*, yesterday
昨年　　*sakunen*, last year
昨夜　　*sakuya*, last night

☑ 3

札	一	十	才
	才	札	
513 5 strokes			

SATSU, paper money; *fuda*, label, namecard, tag, placard; bid

札入れ　*satsu-ire*, wallet
名札　　*nafuda*, nameplate, name-tag
入札　　*nyūsatsu*, bid, bidding

2

刷	フ	コ	尸
	尸	月	吊
514 8 strokes	刷	刷	

SATSU; *su(ru)*, to print; *~zuri*, suffix for "printing"

印刷　　　*insatsu*, printing
校正刷り　*kōseizuri*, proofs (printing)
謄写版刷り　*tōshaban-zuri*, mimeographed copy

2

殺	ノ	メ	乄	SATSU, SAI, SETSU; *koro(su)*, to kill
	杀	杀	朮	
515 10 strokes	殺	殺	殺	殺人 *satsujin*, homicide, murder 殺風景 *sappūkei*, tasteless, dreary 自殺 *jisatsu*, suicide
				3

察	丶	丷	宀	SATSU; *sas(suru)*, to guess, to perceive, to sympathize with
	宀	灾	灾	
516 14 strokes	袋	窣	察	観察 *kansatsu*, observation 視察 *shisatsu*, inspection 警察 *keisatsu*, police
				3

参	ム	厶	厶	SAN, three (used in legal papers); *mai(ru)*, to go, to come, to surrender, to be nonplussed, to visit for worship
	夲	矢	矣	
517 8 strokes	参	参		参加 *sanka*, participation 参観 *sankan*, visit 参考書 *sankōsho*, reference book
				3

産	丶	亠	亠	SAN, childbearing, product, fortune; *u(mu)*, to give birth to, to produce; *u(mareru)*, to be born; *ubu*, birthing, bearing
	立	立	产	
518 11 strokes	产	产	産	産物 *sanbutsu*, products 産地 *sanchi*, place of production 産業 *sangyō*, industry
				3

散	一	十	卄	SAN; *chi(ru)*, to fall (leaves), to be scattered (v.i.); *chi(rasu)*, to scatter, to disperse (v.t.); *chi(rakaru)*, to be in order; *chi(rakasu)*, to scatter
	廿	昔	背	
519 12 strokes	散	散	散	散歩 *sanpo*, walk, stroll 解散 *kaisan*, breakup, dissolution 胃散 *isan*, medical powder for the stomach
				3

残 520 10 strokes	一 歹 残	フ 歹 残	歹 歼 残	ZAN; *noko(ri)*, remainder; *noko(ru)*, to be left over, to remain; *noko(su)*, to leave, to save 残念　　*zannen*, regret, disappointment 残金　　*zankin*, balance, money left over 残り物　*nokorimono*, remains, left-overs ✓ 3
士 521 3 strokes	一	十	士	SHI, man, figure, samurai 武士　　*bushi*, samurai 紳士　　*shinshi*, gentleman 勇士　　*yūshi*, brave man, hero 1
氏 522 4 strokes	′ 氏	ピ	⼾	SHI, Mister (used as suffix); *uji*, family name, lineage 氏名　　　　*shimei*, full name 氏族制度　*shizoku-seido*, the clan or the family system 諸氏　　　　*shoshi*, Messrs., gentlemen 1
史 523 5 strokes	丶 史	口 史	口	SHI, annals, history, chronicles 歴史　*rekishi*, history 女史　*joshi*, Madame, Mrs., Miss 史上　*shijō*, in history, in the annals 2
司 524 5 strokes	フ 司	ヨ 司	司	SHI, to rule, to manage 司会者 *shikaisha*, master of ceremonies, moderator, chairman 司令　*shirei*, order, command 司令部 *shireibu*, headquarters 1

105

試	言	言	言	SHI; kokoro(mi), trial, test; kokoro(miru), to try; tame(su), to try, to test
	言	言	試	試験 shiken, examination 試運転 shi-unten, test driving, trial run
525 13 strokes	試			試合 shiai, match, contest ☑ 4

児	丨	丨丨	丨冂	JI, NI, infant, child
	旧	旧	児	児童 jidō, child, boys and girls, juvenile 孤児 koji, orphan
526 7 strokes	児			小児まひ shōni-mahi, infantile paralysis ☐ 2

治	丶	丶丶	氵	JI, CHI; osa(meru), to rule over; osa(maru), to be peaceful; nao(ru) (v.i.), to heal; nao(su) (v.t.), to cure
	汃	汕	治	政治 seiji, politics, administration 自治 jichi, self-government
527 8 strokes	治	治		治療 chiryō, medical treatment ☑ 3

辞	丿	二	千	JI, word, speech; ji(suru), to resign, to take one's leave, to decline; ya(meru), to retire, to quit
	舌	舌	舌	辞書 jisho, dictionary 辞職 jishoku, resignation
528 13 strokes	辞	辞	辞	祝辞 shukuji, congratulatory address ☑ 3

失	丿	二	二	SHITSU; ushina(u), to lose, to miss
		生	失	失礼 shitsurei, impoliteness 失敗 shippai, failure 失望 shitsubō, despair, disappointment
529 5 strokes				☑ 3

借 530 10 strokes	ノ 什 佳	イ 伊 借	仁 佳 借	SHAKU; *ka(ri)*, borrowing, debt; *ka(riru)*, to borrow, to rent, to substitute temporarily, to obtain (help) 借金 *shakkin*, debt, loan 借り物 *karimono*, borrowed thing 拝借 *haishaku*, loan, borrowing [4]
種 531 14 strokes	ノ 禾 稍	二 禾 種	千 利 種	SHU, kind, sort; *tane*, seed 種まき *tanemaki*, sowing seed 種類 *shurui*, sort, kind 人種 *jinshu*, human race [3]
周 532 8 strokes	ノ 用 周	几 円 周	月 円	SHŪ, circumference; to go round; *mawa(ri)*, border, periphery 周囲 *shūi*, circumference, surroundings 周辺 *shūhen*, outskirts 一周 *isshū*, one round [2]
祝 533 9 strokes	、 ネ 初	ラ ネ 初	オ 初 祝	SHUKU; SHŪ; *iwa(i)*, celebration; *iwa(u)*, to celebrate 祝賀 *shukuga*, celebration 祝福 *shukufuku*, blessing 祝日 *shukujitsu*, festival day [2]
順 534 12 strokes	ノ 川 順	川 川 順	川 順 順	JUN, order, turn 順序 *junjo*, order, procedure, method 順番 *junban*, order, turn 順調 *junchō*, normal condition, smooth progress [2]

107

初	`、`	`ラ`	`ネ`	SHO; *hatsu*, *hajime(te)*, first; *ui*, *haji(me)*, beginning, first time; *-so(meru)*, to begin-
	`ネ`	`ネ`	`初`	初秋 *shoshū*, early autumn 初雪 *hatsuyuki*, first snow of the year
535 7 strokes	`初`			初期 *shoki*, first stage　☑3

松	`一`	`十`	`才`	SHŌ; *matsu*, pine
	`木`	`松`	`松`	松葉 *matsuba*, pine needles 松林 *matsubayashi*, pine forest 松竹梅 *shōchikubai*, pine-bamboo-plum decorations
536 8 strokes	`松`	`松`		1

笑	`ノ`	`ヒ`	`ケ`	SHŌ; *wara(u)*, to laugh, smile; *e(mu)*, to smile, beam
	`竹`	`竹`	`竺`	大笑い *ōwarai*, loud laughter 苦笑 *kushō*, forced laugh 微笑 *bishō/hohoemi*, smile
537 10 strokes	`竺`	`笑`	`笑`	☑3

唱	`丶`	`冂`	`口`	SHŌ; *tona(eru)*, to chant, to recite, to say
	`叮`	`叮`	`叩`	独唱 *dokushō*, vocal solo 合唱 *gasshō*, chorus 唱歌 *shōka*, song, singing
538 11 strokes	`唱`	`唱`	`唱`	1

焼	`火`	`火`	`灯`	SHŌ; *ya(ku)*, to burn, to bake, to grill, to toast (v.t.), to burn with jealousy; *ya(keru)*, to be burned, to be roasted, to be jealous of
	`炉`	`炉`	`焼`	夕焼け *yūyake*, evening glow, sunset colors
539 12 strokes	`焼`	`焼`	`焼`	焼失 *shōshitsu*, destruction by fire　2

108

象	⼃	⼌	⼩	SHŌ, image; ZŌ, elephant
	乎	乎	乎	対象　　*taishō*, object 印象　　*inshō*, impression 象げ　　*zōge*, ivory
540 12 strokes	乎	象	象	②

照	丨	冂	日	SHŌ; *te(rasu)*, to shine on, to compare with, to shed light on; *te(ru)*, to shine; *te(reru)*, to be shy, to be embarrassed
	日	町	昭	日照り　*hideri*, drought 照明　　*shōmei*, illumination
541 13 strokes	昭	照	照	対照　　*taishō*, contrast　②

賞	⼀	⼩	⼩⼩	SHŌ, prize
	⼩⼩	丷	尚	賞品　　*shōhin*, prize (thing) 賞金　　*shōkin*, prize (money) 鑑賞　　*kanshō*, appreciation
542 15 strokes	営	賞	賞	②

臣	丨	厂	厂	SHIN, JIN, retainer, subject
	臣	臣	臣	大臣　　*daijin*, cabinet minister 忠臣　　*chūshin*, loyal retainer
543 7 strokes	臣			②

信	⼃	⼇	亻	SHIN, sincerity, trust, faith; *shin(jiru)*, to believe, to trust, to believe in
	亻	信	信	信用　　*shin'yō*, trust, confidence, belief, credit
544 9 strokes	信	信	信	信号　　*shingō*, signal 通信　　*tsūshin*, communication ✓ ③

成	ノ	厂	厉	SEI, JŌ; *na(ru)*, to become, to be completed, to consist of, to come to, to succeed; to come, to go (honorific); *na(su)*, to do, to perform
	成	成	成	成長　　*seichō*, growth 完成　　*kansei*, completion 賛成　　*sansei*, agreement, approval
545 6 strokes				✓ 3

省	ノ	ハ	小	SEI, to look; *habu(ku)*, to omit, to cut down; *kaeri(miru)*, to reflect upon (oneself); SHŌ, suffix for "government department"
	少	半	省	省略　　*shōryaku*, omission 外務省　*Gaimushō*, Ministry of 　　　　Foreign Affairs (Japan)
546 9 strokes	省	省	省	反省　　*hansei*, self-examination　 2

清	シ	シ	汁	SEI; *kiyo(i)*, *kiyo(raka)*, pure, clear; *kiyo(meru)* (v.t.), *kiyo(maru)* (v.i.), to cleanse, purge, to exorcize
	沣	沣	清	清潔　　*seiketsu*, cleanliness 清書　　*seisho*, fair copy 血清　　*kessei*, (blood) serum
547 11 strokes	清	清	清	2

静	十	主	青	SEI, JŌ; *shizu*, *shizu(ka)*, quiet, silent, peaceful; *shizu(maru)*, to become quiet; *shizu(meru)*, to make calm, to soothe
	青	青	靜	静止　　*seishi*, stillness, standstill 静物　　*seibutsu*, still life 安静　　*ansei*, complete rest
548 14 strokes	静	静	静	✓ 3

席	、	二	广	SEKI, seat, place
	广	庐	庐	出席　　*shusseki*, attendance, 　　　　presence 欠席　　*kesseki*, absence 座席　　*zaseki*, seat
549 10 strokes	庐	席	席	3

110

積 550 16 strokes	禾 秂 積	利 耒 積	秆 秄	SEKI, product (math.); *tsumo(ri)*, intention; *tsu(mu)*, to pile up, to load, to accumulate (v.t.); *tsumo(ru)*, to be piled up 面積 *menseki*, area 積極的 *sekkyokuteki*, positive, active, progressive 積荷 *tsumini*, cargo, a load ③
折 551 7 strokes	一 扌 折	十 扌	才 折	SETSU; *ori*, *o(ru)*, to break, to fold, to bend; *o(reru)*, to break, to be broken 曲折 *kyokusetsu*, winding, complications 折(り)合(い) *oriai*, mutual relations, compromise 折(り)目 *orime*, crease 屈折 *kussetsu*, inflection ③
節 552 13 strokes	ノ 竹 節	亻 竺 節	𠂉 竻 節	SETSU, SECHI, paragraph, season, time; *fushi*, joint, knot, tune 節約 *setsuyaku*, economy, frugality 調節 *chōsetsu*, regulation, control 使節 *shisetsu*, delegate, envoy ✓ ①
説 553 14 strokes	丶 言 誩	言 訁 説	言 訜	SETSU, opinion, theory; ZEI; *to(ku)*, to explain, to persuade, to preach 説明 *setsumei*, explanation 伝説 *densetsu*, legend 社説 *shasetsu*, editorial ✓ ③
浅 554 9 strokes	丶 氵 浅	冫 浅	氵 浅	SEN; *asa(i)*, shallow 浅見 *senken*, superficial view 浅薄 *senpaku*, superficial 遠浅 *tōasa*, shoaling beach, shallowness extending far from shore ②

戦	⺍	当	当	SEN; *ikusa, tataka(i)*, fight, war, struggle; *takaka(u)*, to fight, to make war, to struggle, to compete in games
	単	単	戦	戦争　　*sensō*, war 終戦　　*shūsen*, end of a war 戦場　　*senjō*, battlefield
555 13 strokes	戦	戦		3

選	⁷	㇈	己	SEN; *era(bu)*, to choose, to select
	己己	己己	巽	選挙　　*senkyo*, election 選手　　*senshu*, player, champion 当選　　*tōsen*, victory in an election
556 15 strokes	巽	選	選	✓ 3

然	ノ	ク	タ	ZEN, NEN, yes, but, however
	タ	夕ケ	然	自然　　*shizen*, nature 当然　　*tōzen*, natural, just, as a matter of course 天然　　*tennen*, nature
557 12 strokes	然	然	然	✓ 3

争	ノ	⺈	々	SŌ; *araso(i)*, quarrel, dispute, competition; *araso(u)*, to struggle, to dispute, to quarrel
	刍	刍	争	競争　　　*kyōsō*, competition 言い争う *ii-arasou*, to quarrel 争奪戦　 *sōdatsusen*, scramble, contest, challenge
558 6 strokes				3

倉	ノ	入	亼	SŌ; *kura*, warehouse
	今	今	合	倉庫　　*sōko*, warehouse 船倉　　*sensō*, hold (of a ship) 米倉　　*komegura*, rice granary
559 10 strokes	倉	倉	倉	1

巣 560 11 strokes	丶	丷	丷
	产	当	当
	単	単	巣

SŌ; *su*, nest, den, breeding place

巣箱　*subako*, nesting box
巣立つ　*sudatsu*, to leave the nest, home
営巣　*eisō*, nest building

☐1

束 561 7 strokes	一	一	一
	一	申	束
	束		

SOKU; *taba*, bundle, bunch; bind

約束　*yakusoku*, appointment; promise
束縛　*sokubaku*, restriction, restraint
花束　*hanataba*, bouquet, bunch of flowers

☐3

側 562 11 strokes	ノ	イ	们
	佀	佀	俱
	俱	側	側

SOKU; *gawa*, side

内側　*uchigawa*, the inside
右側　*migigawa*, *usoku*, right side
側面　*sokumen*, the side

✓ 3

続 563 13 strokes	糸	糸	糸
	紵	紵	続
	続	続	

ZOKU; *tsuzu(ki)*, continuation, sequel, range; *tsuzu(ku)*, to continue, to follow, to last (v.i.); *tsuzu(keru)*, to continue, to resume (v.t.)

続出　*zokushutsu*, successive occurrence
手続　*tetsuzuki*, procedure
相続　*sōzoku*, inheritance

✓ 3

卒 564 8 strokes	丶	亠	广
	六	六	衣
	衣	卒	

SOTSU, a private, common soldier; to finish

卒業　*sotsugyō*, graduation
卒業生　*sotsugyōsei*, graduate
兵卒　*heisotsu*, private (soldier)

✓ 2

孫	⁷	了	孑	SON; *mago*, grandchild
	孑	矜	猝	子孫　　*shison*, descendants
565 10 strokes	猝	孫	孫	孫請け　*mago-uke*, sub-sub 　　　　　contractor 曾孫　　*sōson*, *himago*, great grand 　　　　　child　　　　　　　　　　 ☐2

帯	一	十	卅	TAI; *obi*, girdle; *o(biru)*, to wear
	卅	世	典	地帯　　*chitai*, zone 熱帯　　*nettai*, torrid zone, tropics
566 10 strokes	帯	帯	帯	帯封　　*obifū*, half wrapper 　　　　　　　　　　　　　　　　 ☐2

隊	⁷	⁷	⻖	TAI, a party, a corps, band, unit
	⻖	⻖	阼	兵隊　　*heitai*, soldier 楽隊　　*gakutai*, band (musical)
567 12 strokes	防	隊	隊	隊長　　*taichō*, captain, commander, 　　　　　leader 　　　　　　　　　　　　　　　　 ☐1

達	土	去	去	TATSU; *tas(suru)*, to arrive, to reach, to attain (one's object)
	圭	幸	查	発達　　*hattatsu*, development 配達　　*haitatsu*, delivery
568 12 strokes	幸	達	達	達人　　*tatsujin*, an expert 　　　　　　　　　　　　　　 ☑ ☐3

単	丶	丷	丷	TAN, single
	丷	当	当	単純　　*tanjun*, simple 簡単　　*kantan*, simple, easy
569 9 strokes	当	単	単	単価　　*tanka*, unit price 　　　　　　　　　　　　　　 ☑ ☐3

114

置	丶	冖	罒
	罒	罒	罒
570 13 strokes	罘	置	置

CHI; *o(ku)*, to put, to place

位置　*ichi*, position
置物　*okimono*, ornament (for a *tokonoma*)
物置　*mono-oki*, storeroom

✓ 3

仲	ノ	イ	亻
	伀	仲	仲
571 6 strokes			

CHŪ; *naka*, relationship

仲がいい　*naka ga ii*, to be on good terms with
仲間　*nakama*, workmate, colleague, associate
仲裁　*chūsai*, mediation

2

貯	冂	目	貝
	貝	貝'	貝'
572 12 strokes	貯	貯	貯

CHO, to store, to save

貯水地　*chosuichi*, reservoir
貯蔵　*chozō*, storage
貯金　*chokin*, savings

2

兆	ノ	ノ	㇇
	兆	兆	兆
573 6 strokes			

CHŌ, trillion (U.S.), sign; *kiza(shi)*, sign, omen; *kiza(su)*, to show signs

兆候　*chōkō*, sign, omen
二兆円　*nichōen*, two trillion yen
前兆　*zenchō*, omen, portent

2

腸	ノ	刀	月
	肥	胆	腴
574 13 strokes	腸	腸	腸

CHŌ, the intestines

盲腸　*mōchō*, (vermiform) appendix
大腸　*daichō*, large intestine
腸カタル　*chōkataru*, intestinal catarrh

1

115

低	ノ	イ	仁
	仁	佢	低
575 7 strokes	低		

TEI; *hiku(i)*, low, short; *hiku(meru)* (v.t.), *hiku(maru)* (v.i.), to lessen

低気圧 *tei-kiatsu*, low atmospheric pressure
低空　*teikū*, low altitude
低地　*teichi*, low ground

✓ 2

底	、	亠	广
	广	庐	庄
576 8 strokes	底	底	

TEI; *soko*, bottom, depth

谷底　*tanizoko*, bottom of a ravine
海底　*kaitei*, bottom of the sea
徹底的 *tetteiteki*, thoroughgoing, out-and-out

2

停	ノ	イ	仁
	仁	佇	信
577 11 strokes	停	停	停

TEI, to stop

停止　*teishi*, stop, suspension
停電　*teiden*, electricity stoppage
停留所 *teiryūjo*, stopping place, streetcar (bus) stop

2

的	ノ	イ	白
	白	白	白
578 8 strokes	的	的	

TEKI, like, similar, suffix for forming adjectives from nouns; *mato*, mark, target

目的　*mokuteki*, purpose
世界的 *sekaiteki*, international, world-wide
社会的 *shakaiteki*, social

✓ 3

典	丶	冂	巾
	巾	曲	曲
579 8 strokes	典	典	

TEN, ceremony, celebration

辞典　*jiten*, dictionary
古典　*koten*, classics
祭典　*saiten*, festival, rite

1

116

伝	ノ	イ	仁
	仁	仁	伝

DEN; *tsuta(eru)* to report, to impart, to transmit; *tsuta(waru)*, to be reported, imparted, transmitted, *tsuta(u)*, to follow along

伝記　*denki*, biography
伝染病 *densenbyō*, epidemic
宣伝　*senden*, propaganda　✓ ③

580
6 strokes

徒	ノ	ク	彳
	彳	徃	徍
	徒	徒	

TO, companion

生徒　　*seito*, pupil, student
徒歩　　*toho*, going on foot
徒競走 *tokyōsō*, running match

581
10 strokes　③

努	く	タ	女
	如	奴	努
	努		

DO; *tsuto(meru)*, to make efforts

努力　　*doryoku*, effort
努力家 *doryokuka*, hard worker

582
7 strokes　③

灯	ヽ	⺍	少
	火	灯	灯

TŌ, *hi*, light, lamp

電灯　　　*dentō*, electric light
安全灯　 *anzentō*, safety lamp
懐中電灯 *kaichūdentō*, flashlight, electric torch

583
6 strokes　②

堂	ヽ	⺌	⺍
	𭕄	当	当
	尚	堂	堂

DŌ, temple, hall

食堂　　　　*shokudō*, dining room, eating house
公会堂　　 *kōkaidō*, town hall, public hall
国会議事堂 *Kokkai-gijidō*, the Diet Building　④

584
11 strokes

117

働 585 13 strokes	ノ 侜 働	イ 侸 働	侸 偅	DŌ; *hatara(ki)*, work (n.); *hatara(ku)*, to work, to do (evil), to come into play 労働者 *rōdōsha*, laborer 働き手 *hatarakite*, bread winner, worker 働き者 *hatarakimono*, hard worker ☑3
特 586 10 strokes	ノ 牛 牻	⺦ 牛 特	牛 牻 特	TOKU, special 特別 *tokubetsu*, special, particular 特長 *tokuchō*, strong point 特急 *tokkyū*, limited express ☑4
得 587 11 strokes	ノ 徂 得	⺈ 徂	彳 得	TOKU, profit, benefit, advantage; *e(ru)*, to get, to obtain; *-u(ru)*, to be able to 得意 *tokui*, proud satisfaction; customer; one's forte 納得 *nattoku*, understanding, compliance 得点 *tokuten*, score (in a game) 3
毒 588 8 strokes	一 主 毒	十 毒 毒	≠ 青	DOKU, poison 気の毒 *ki-no-doku*, sorry, pitiful 毒草 *dokusō*, poisonous herb 中毒 *chūdoku*, poisoning 2
熱 589 15 strokes	土 坴 執	⺶ 刲 熱	夫 執 熱	NETSU, heat, fever, craze, zeal; *nes(suru)*, to heat, to become hot; *atsu(i)*, hot 熱病 *netsubyō*, fever 熱心 *nesshin*, zeal 熱帯 *nettai*, tropical zone ☑3

念	ノ	人	𠆢	NEN, thought, feeling, desire
	今	今	今	記念 *kinen*, commemoration
				残念 *zannen*, regret, disappointment
590	念	念		念願 *nengan*, one's heart's desire
8 strokes				3

敗	丨	冂	目	HAI; *yabu(reru)*, to be defeated
	貝	貝	貝	敗戦 *haisen*, lost battle
				腐敗 *fuhai*, putrefaction, corruption
591	敗	敗	敗	失敗 *shippai*, failure
11 strokes				3

梅	木	朾	杧	BAI; *ume*, plum, plum tree
	柠	柘	梅	梅雨 *baiu/tsuyu*, rainy season
				梅酒 *umeshu*, plum brandy
592	梅			梅干し *umeboshi*, pickled plums
10 strokes				1

博	一	十	忄	HAKU, BAKU, learned; to spread; abundant
	恒	博	博	博士 *hakushi*, doctor (degree)
				博物館 *hakubutsukan*, museum
593	博	博		博覧会 *hakurankai*, exposition
12 strokes				1

飯	ノ	𠆢	仐	HAN; *meshi*, boiled rice, a meal
	食	食	食	朝飯 *asahan*, *asameshi*, breakfast
				昼飯 *hirumeshi*, lunch
594	飰	飯	飯	夕飯 *yūhan*, *yūmeshi*, supper
12 strokes				✓ 4

飛	て	て	飞	HI; *to(bu)*, to fly; *to(basu)*, to let fly, to launch
	飞	飞	飛	飛び込む *tobikomu*, to jump in, to dive into, to rush in 飛行機 *hikōki*, airplane
595 9 strokes	飛	飛	飛	飛行場 *hikōjō*, airport ✓ 3

費	一	二	弖	HI; (v.i.), (v.t.), to spend, to consume, to squander
	弗	弗	費	費用 *hiyō*, expense 旅費 *ryohi*, traveling expenses
596 12 strokes	費			出費 *shuppi*, expenditure 3

必	、	ソ	义	HITSU; *kanara(zu)*, without fail, by all means, invariably, necessarily
	必	必		必要 *hitsuyō*, need 必死 *hisshi*, inevitable death, desperation
597 5 strokes				必勝 *hisshō*, sure victory ✓ 3

票	一	一	二	HYŌ, vote
	西	西	西	投票 *tōhyō*, voting 伝票 *denpyō*, chit
598 11 strokes	票	票	票	五十票 *gojippyō*, fifty votes 1

標	一	十	才	HYŌ, mark, sign; to write down, to express
	標	標	標	標本 *hyōhon*, specimen 標語 *hyōgo*, motto
599 15 strokes	標	標	標	目標 *mokuhyō*, mark, object 1

120

不	一	フ	不	FU, dis-, in-, un-, mal-, ill-
	不			不自由 *fujiyū*, inconvenience, want 不平 *fuhei*, discontent, complaint 不幸 *fukō*, misfortune, unhappiness, death
600 4 strokes				☑ 4

夫	一	二	夫	FU, FŪ; husband
	夫			工夫 *kōfu*, laborer, workman; *kufū*, device 夫婦 *fūfu*, husband and wife 夫人 *fujin*, married lady, Mrs.
601 4 strokes				☑ 3

付	ノ	イ	仁	FU; *tsu(ku)*, to adhere, to stick (v.i.); *tsu(keru)*, to attach, to stick (v.t.)
	付	付		付近 *fukin*, neighborhood 寄付 *kifu*, contribution 受付 *uketsuke*, acceptance, information office
602 5 strokes				☑ 3

府	、	亠	广	FU, urban prefecture, center
	广	庁	庁	政府 *seifu*, government 首府 *shufu*, capital 府県 *fuken*, prefectures
603 8 strokes	府	府		2

副	一	百	戸	FUKU, vice-, sub-, secondary
	畐	畐	畐	副詞 *fukushi*, adverb 副会長 *fukukaichō*, vice-president (of a society) 副業 *fukugyō*, side job
604 11 strokes	畐	副	副	2

121

粉	、	⸜	⏦	FUN; *kona*, *ko*, powder 火の粉 *hi-no-ko*, spark 小麦粉 *komugiko*, wheat flour 製粉　*seifun*, milling (flour)
	丬	米	米	
605 10 strokes	粎	粉	粉	[2]

兵	⸍	⼁	⼷	HEI, soldier; HYŌ 兵隊　*heitai*, soldier 兵器　*heiki*, arms 兵士　*heishi*, soldier
	斤	丘	兵	
606 7 strokes	兵			[2]

別	丶	口	口	BETSU, distinction, exception; different, particular; *waka(reru)*, to part (from) 特別　*tokubetsu*, special 別問題 *betsumondai*, another 　　　question 別れ　*wakare*, parting, 　　　separation
	弓	別	別	
607 7 strokes	別			✓ [4]

辺	フ	刀	刀	HEN, -*be*, side, neighborhood; *atari*, vicinity 底辺　*teihen*, the base (geom.) 周辺　*shūhen*, outskirts 近辺　*kinpen*, neighborhood
	辺	辺		
608 5 strokes				[2]

変	丶	亠	亠	HEN, odd; disturbance, accident, change; *ka(waru)*, to change, to be uncommon, to move (v.i.); *ka(eru)*, to change, to reform 変化　*henka*, change, variety, 　　　conjugation 大変　*taihen*, serious, great, 　　　terrible
	亣	亦	亦	
609 9 strokes	亦	変	変	✓ [3]

便 610 9 strokes	ノ イ 仁 仁 仁 佢 佢 便 便	**BEN**, convenience, bodily waste; **BIN**, mail; *tayo(ri)*, tidings, communication, a letter 便利　*benri*, convenience 便所　*benjo*, toilet 航空便 *kōkūbin*, air mail ✓ 3
包 611 5 strokes	ノ 勹 匀 匀 包	**HŌ**; *tsutsu(mu)*, to wrap, to cover 小包　*kozutsumi*, postal package 包み紙 *tsutsumigami*, wrapping paper 包囲　*hōi*, encirclement 2
法 612 8 strokes	丶 丶 氵 氵 汁 汁 法 法	**HŌ**, **HA(T)**, **HO(T)**, law, doctrine, reason, method 方法　*hōhō*, way, method 法律　*hōritsu*, law 文法　*bunpō*, grammar ✓ 3
望 613 11 strokes	丶 亠 亡 亡刀 亡月 亡月 望 望 望	**BŌ**, **MŌ**; *nozo(mi)*, desire, wish; *nozo(mu)*, to desire, to expect, to see 失望　*shitsubō*, disappointment 希望　*kibō*, hope, wish 絶望　*zetsubō*, despair 3
牧 614 8 strokes	ノ 宀 牛 牛 牛 牜 牧 牧	**BOKU**; *maki*, pasture 牧場　*bokujō*, makiba, stock farm 牧草　*bokusō*, grass 放牧　*hōboku*, grazing 1

123

末	一	二	十	MATSU; *sue*, end, future, youngest child, trifle
	末	末		末っ子 *suekko*, youngest child 月末 *getsumatsu*, end of the month
615 5 strokes				始末 *shimatsu*, management, circumstances ☑ 3

満	氵	氵	汁	MAN, fullness; *mi(chiru)*, to rise (tide), to wax (moon); *mi(tasu)*, to fill, to meet (a requirement)
	洪	洪	洪	満員 *man'in*, filled to capacity 満月 *mangetsu*, full moon
616 12 strokes	満	満	満	満七歳 *man-shichisai*, full seven years old 3

未	一	二	十	MI, yet, never, till now, un-
	未	未		未来 *mirai*, future 未開 *mikai*, uncivilized, uncultivated
617 5 strokes				未知 *michi*, unknown, strange ☑ 3

脈	丿	刀	月	MYAKU, pulse, hope, range
	肝	肝	肝	山脈 *sanmyaku*, mountain range 静脈 *jōmyaku*, (blood) vein 鉱脈 *kōmyaku*, vein of ore
618 10 strokes	脈	脈	脈	1

民	乛	コ	尸	MIN; *tami*, people, subjects
	尺	民		市民 *shimin*, townsman 国民 *kokumin*, nation 民族 *minzoku*, race
619 5 strokes				3

124

無 620 12 strokes	ノ	ト	仁
	仁	血	無
	無	無	無

MU, BU; *na(shi)* (lit.), *na(i)*, to be non-existent, not to have, to be missing, to lack, to be deceased

無理　*muri*, unreasonable, compulsory, impossible, excessive
無線　*musen*, wireless (radio)
無事　*buji*, safe, peaceful, well

☑ ③

約 621 9 strokes	㇑	㇑	幺
	糹	糹	糸
	糽	約	約

YAKU, promise, abridgment; approximately, about (prefix)

約束　*yakusoku*, promise, appointment, regulation
予約　*yoyaku*, subscription, pre-engagement
約四十分　*yaku-yonjippun*, about forty minutes

③

勇 622 9 strokes	㇇	マ	甼
	厼	甬	甬
	甬	勇	勇

YŪ; *isa(mashii)*, *isa(mu)*, brave

勇気　*yūki*, courage
勇士　*yūshi*, brave man
勇敢　*yūkan*, bravery

②

要 623 9 strokes	一	㇑	一
	襾	西	西
	要	要	要

YŌ; the main point, necessity; *yō(suru)*, to require, to need; *i(ru)*, to need, to be required; *kaname*, the pivot, the mainpoint

必要　*hitsuyō*, necessity, need
要求　*yōkyū*, request, demand
重要　*jūyō*, important

☑ ③

養 624 15 strokes	丶	㇌	丷
	产	羊	羊
	美	養	養

YŌ; *yashina(u)*, to bring up, to support, to recuperate, to cultivate

教養　*kyōyō*, culture
養成　*yōsei*, training
養殖　*yōshoku*, raising, culture

①

125

浴	`	⠈	氵	YOKU; *a(biru)*, to bathe oneself in (water, the sun); *a(biseru)*, to pour (liquid) on, to shower with (abuse)
	氵	汀	汀	水浴び *mizu-abi*, bathing 入浴 *nyūyoku*, taking a bath 日光浴 *nikkō-yoku*, sun bath
625 10 strokes	浴	浴	浴	2

利	⠐	⠓	千	RI, advantage, profit, interest (on money); *ki(ku)*, to function well
	禾	禾	利	利用 *riyō*, utilization 利益 *rieki*, gains, benefit 権利 *kenri*, a right, a claim
626 7 strokes	利			✓ 3

陸	⠁	了	阝	RIKU, land
	阝-	阝+	陆	大陸 *tairiku*, continent 上陸 *jōriku*, landing 着陸 *chakuriku*, landing (of an airplane)
627 11 strokes	陆	陆	陸	2

良	⠄	⠕	⠅	RYŌ; *yo(i)*, good, well, fine, right, satisfactory
	⠅	自	良	改良 *kairyō*, improvement 良心 *ryōshin*, conscience 最良 *sairyō*, the best, the ideal
628 7 strokes	良			2

料	`	⠘	⠜	RYŌ, charge, materials
	半	米	米	原料 *genryō*, raw material 料理 *ryōri*, cooking 料金 *ryōkin*, charge
629 10 strokes	米	米一	料	✓ 4

量	丶	口	日	RYŌ, quantity, measure; *haka(ru)*, to weigh, to measure
	日	旦	昌	雨量　　*uryō*, rainfall 重量　　*jūryō*, weight 分量　　*bunryō*, quantity
630 12 strokes	를	量	量	2

輪	車	車	軐	RIN; *wa*, ring, circle, wheel 三輪車　*sanrinsha*, tricycle, three-wheeled vehicle
	軐	軡	幹	車輪　　*sharin*, wheel 首輪　　*kubiwa*, collar (for a dog)
631 15 strokes	輪	輪	輪	2

類	丷	米	米	RUI, a kind, a variety; *tagu(i)*, a kind, a type; an equal, a match
	米 ナ	米 天	米 天	種類　　*shurui*, kind, sort 親類　　*shinrui*, a relative 分類　　*bunrui*, classification
632 18 strokes	米 天	類	類	3

令	丿	人	亼	REI, proclamation, law, order 号令　　*gōrei*, (word of) command
	今	令		命令　　*meirei*, command, order 指令　　*shirei*, order, instructions
633 5 strokes				2

冷	丶	冫	⺀	REI; *tsume(tai)*, cold; *hi(eru)*, to grow cold, feel chilly; *hi(ya)*, cold water; *hi(yakasu)*, to banter; *hi(yasu)*, to cool (v.t.); *sa(meru)* (v.i.), to cool off; *sa(masu)* (v.t.), to let cool
	冫人	冷	冷	冷水　　*reisui*, cold water 冷気　　*reiki*, cold air 冷蔵　　*reizō*, cold storage,
634 7 strokes	冷			✓ 3 refrigeration

127

例	ノ	イ	仁	REI, example; *tato(eru)*, to liken to; *tato(eba)*, for example
	仴	佰	佰	例外　　*reigai*, exception 実例　　*jitsurei*, (concrete) example 例年　　*reinen*, ordinary year, every year
635 **8 strokes**	例	例		3

歴	一	厂	斤	REKI, to pass, to travel about
	斤	麻	麻	歴史　　*rekishi*, history 経歴　　*keireki*, background (of a person), career 履歴書 *rirekisho*, personal history
636 **14 strokes**	歴	歴	歴	2

連	一	厂	冖	REN, a ream (of paper), a group; ~*ren*, suffix for "group"; *tsu(reru)*, to take along; *tsura(naru)* (v.i.), *tsura(neru)* (v.t.), to range; ~*zure*, suffix for "companion"
	冒	車	車	
637 **10 strokes**	車	連	連	連絡　　*renraku*, connection, communication, contact 連盟　　*renmei*, league　3

老	一	十	土	RŌ, old age; *o(i)*, old age, the aged; *o(iru)*, to grow old; *fu(keru)*, to grow old
	少	耂	老	老人　　*rōjin*, old man 老木　　*rōboku*, aged tree
638 **6 strokes**				養老院 *yōrōin*, asylum for the aged　3

労	丶	゛	゛゛	RŌ, labor, service, trouble
	⺍	丷	学	苦労　　*kurō*, toil, care 勤労　　*kinrō*, labor 労働者 *rōdōsha*, laborer
639 **7 strokes**	労			3

録 640 16 strokes	金 鈩 鈩	釒 鈩 鍒	釸 鈩 録	ROKU, to copy, to write down 記録　*kiroku*, record 新記録　*shinkiroku*, new record 録音　*rokuon*, (sound) recording, transcription 〔2〕
圧 641 5 strokes	一 斤	厂 圧	厂	ATSU, pressure 気圧　*kiatsu*, atmospheric pressure 圧力　*atsuryoku*, pressure 電圧　*den'atsu*, voltage 〔2〕
移 642 11 strokes	一 禾 秒	二 禾 移	千 禾 移	I; *utsu(ru)*, to move (to a place, into a house), to change (v.i.), to sink into, to be infectious; *utsu(su)*, to remove (v.t.), to infect 移民　*imin*, immigration (emigration), immigrant 移り変わる　*utsurikawaru*, to change, to shift 〔2〕
因 643 6 strokes	丨 円	冂 因	冂 因	IN, cause; *yo(ru)*, to be due to, to be based on 原因　*gen'in*, cause 因果　*inga*, cause and effect, fate 因襲　*inshū*, long-established custom 〔3〕
永 644 5 strokes	丶 永	訁 永	刁	EI, long, eternal, perpetual; *naga(i)*, everlasting 永遠　*eien*, eternity 永眠　*eimin*, death 永住　*eijū*, permanent residence 〔2〕

営 645 12 strokes	丶 ⸜ ⸝ 営 営	⸜ 丷 営 営	⸝ 営	EI; *itona(mi)*, occupation; *itona(mu)*, to run (a hotel), to perform (a religious service) 経営　*keiei*, management, operation 営業　*eigyō*, business, trade, operation　②
衛 646 16 strokes	彳 彳 律	彳 仟 律	彳 律 衛	EI, to protect, to defend 衛生　*eisei*, hygiene 防衛　*bōei*, defense 守衛　*shuei*, guard, watchman　①
易 647 8 strokes	丨 日 易	冂 月 易	日 弓	EKI, divination; I; *yasa(shii)*, easy 容易　*yōi*, easy 貿易　*bōeki*, trade 易者　*ekisha*, fortuneteller　③
益 648 10 strokes	丶 䒑 羊	⸝ 兴 益	丷 兴 益	EKI, YAKU, benefit, profit 利益　*rieki*, gain, benefit 有益　*yūeki*, instructive, profitable 益虫　*ekichū*, useful insect　①
液 649 11 strokes	氵 汐 液	氵 浐 液	氵 汸 液	EKI, liquid, fluid, juice 液体　*ekitai*, liquid 血液　*ketsueki*, blood 消毒液　*shōdoku-eki*, antiseptic solution　②

| 演 650 14 strokes | シ 氵 氵 汽 沪 沪 清 沪 演 演 | EN; *en(jiru)*, to act, to perform a play, to create (a comic scene), to commit (a blunder) 演説　*enzetsu*, speech 演技　*engi*, acting 演奏　*ensō*, (musical) performance |

3

| 応 651 7 strokes | 、 亠 广 广 応 応 応 | Ō, *ō(jiru)*, to answer, to comply with, to apply for, to accept; *kota(eru)*, to answer, to respond 応援　*ōen*, aid, cheering 応用　*ōyō*, practical application 応接間　*ōsetsuma*, parlor |

1

| 往 652 8 strokes | ′ ′ 彳 彳 彳 彳 徉 往 | Ō, to go; ancient times 往来　*ōrai*, (street) traffic, going and coming, street 往復　*ōfuku*, going and returning, round trip 立往生　*tachi-ōjō*, standstill |

1

| 桜 653 10 strokes | 木 朮 朮 朼 桜 桜 桜 | Ō; *sakura*, cherry tree, cherry blossom, pink 桜花　*ōka*, cherry blossoms (lit.) 桜肉　*sakuraniku*, horsemeat 山桜　*yamazakura*, wild cherry |

1

| 恩 654 10 strokes | 丨 冂 日 円 因 因 因 恩 恩 | ON, favor, kindness 恩人　*onjin*, benefactor 謝恩　*shaon*, expression of gratitude 恩返し　*ongaeshi*, requital of another's favor |

1

可	一	一	一	KA, good, approval
				可決　　*kaketsu*, approval
	口	可		可能　　*kanō*, possibility
655				不可能 *fukanō*, impossibility
5 strokes				③

仮	ノ	イ	イ	KA, KE; *kari*, temporary, false
				仮定　　*katei*, supposition
	仮	仮	仮	仮装　　*kasō*, disguise
656				仮病　　*kebyō*, pretended illness
6 strokes				①

価	ノ	イ	イ	KA; *atai*, price, value
				定価　　*teika*, fixed price
	仁	価	価	価値　　*kachi*, value
	価	価		物価　　*bukka*, prices of
657				commodities
8 strokes				①

河	、	冫	氵	KA; *kawa*, river
				河口　　*kakō*, mouth of a river
	汀	沂	沪	銀河　　*ginga*, Milky Way
	河	河		運河　　*unga*, canal
658				
8 strokes				②

過	丶	冂	冎	KA; *su(giru)*, to elapse, to pass, to exceed; *su(gosu)*, to pass (a day), to go to excess; *ayama(chi)*, error, mishap
	冎	呙	咼	
	咼	過	過	通過　　*tsūka*, passage
659				経過　　*keika*, progress, lapse
12 strokes				過去　　*kako*, past, past tense ③

132

賀	コ	カ	加	GA, congratulations
	加	智	智	年賀　nenga, New Year's greetings
660 12 strokes	智	賀	賀	年賀状　nengajō, New Year's card 祝賀　shukuga, celebration, congratulation [1]

快	丶	八	忄	KAI; kokoroyo(i), pleasant, refreshing
	忄	忄	快	快晴　kaisei, fine weather 愉快　yukai, pleasant
661 7 strokes	快			快活　kaikatsu, cheerful [2]

解	广	角	角	KAI, explanation; to(ku), to untie, to solve; to(keru) (v.i.), to relent, become loose; hodo(ku), to untie
	郍	郍	解	理解　rikai, understanding 解散　kaisan, breaking up, dissolution
662 13 strokes	郍	解	解	分解　bunkai, analysis, decomposition [3]

格	一	十	才	KAKU, KŌ, status, case (in grammar)
	木	杦	枚	性格　seikaku, personality, character 人格　jinkaku, character
663 10 strokes	格			価格　kakaku, price 格子　kōshi, grid, lattice [3]

確	石	石	矿	KAKU; tashi(ka), sure, accurate, reliable; tashi(kameru), to ascertain, to confirm
	矿	矿	矿	正確　seikaku, correctness 確実　kakujitsu, certainty
664 15 strokes	矿	碎	確	確定　kakutei, decision [3]

133

額	`	宀	宀	GAKU, framed picture, amount (of money); *hitai*, forehead
	宀	安	客	金額 *kingaku*, amount of money 総額 *sōgaku*, sum total 多額 *tagaku*, large sum
665 18 strokes	額	額	額	②

刊	一	二	干	KAN, publication, edition
	刑	刊		刊行 *kankō*, publication 週刊 *shūkan*, weekly publication 新刊 *shinkan*, new publication
666 5 strokes				②

幹	一	十	古	KAN; *miki*, trunk of a tree
	卓	乾	乾	幹部 *kanbu*, the executive, leading members 根幹 *konkan*, basis, root 幹線 *kansen*, trunk line
667 13 strokes	幹	幹	幹	①

慣	`	ハ	忄	KAN; *na(reru)*, to get accustomed (to), to become inured (to)

	忄	忄	忄	習慣 *shūkan*, habit, custom
				慣用 *kan'yō*, common use,
				    practice
				見慣れる *minareru*, to get used
				    to seeing, to be
				    familiar (with)

668 14 strokes	忄	慣	慣	③

眼	l	冂	目	GAN; *manako*, eye
	目	目	目	肉眼 *nikugan*, naked eye 近眼 *kingan*, near-sightedness 双眼鏡 *sōgankyō*, binoculars
669 11 strokes	眼	眼	眼	①

基	一	十	廿	KI; *motoi*, foundation, basis; *moto(zuku)*, to be based on
	廿	甘	其	基本　*kihon*, foundation, basis, standard
670 11 strokes	其	其	基	基地　*kichi*, (air, etc.) base 基礎　*kiso*, foundation, basis ⬜1

寄	丶	八	宀	KI; *yo(ru)*, to approach, to drop in, to gather (v.i.); *yo(seru)*, to draw up (a chair), to push (a desk) aside
	宀	宀	安	寄港　*kikō*, call at a port
671 11 strokes	宝	客	寄	寄付　*kifu*, contribution 寄与　*kiyo*, contribution, service ⬛3

規	一	二	圭	KI, compass
	夫	知	邦	規律　*kiritsu*, order, discipline 規模　*kibo*, scale, scope 規準　*kijun*, standard
672 11 strokes	邦	規	規	⬛3

技	一	十	扌	GI, *waza*, art, skill
	扩	扩	抄	技師　*gishi*, engineer 競技　*kyōgi*, sporting events, contest
673 7 strokes	技			技術　*gijutsu*, art, technique ⬜2

義	丶	丷	丷	GI, justice, morality, loyalty, relationship; prefix for "in-law," "artificial"
	半	羊	羊	主義　*shugi*, principle, ~ism
674 13 strokes	姜	義	義	義務　*gimu*, duty 義兄　*gikei*, elder brother-in-law ⬜1

135

逆	丶	⺍	⺝	GYAKU, inverse, reverse; *gyaku(ni)*, inversely, reversely; *saka(rau)*, to oppose, to go against
	芒	芐	屰	逆転　　*gyakuten*, reversal, going backward
675 9 strokes	屰	逆	逆	逆境　　*gyakkyō*, adversity 反逆　　*hangyaku*, treason ⬚2

久	ノ	ク	久	KYŪ, KU; *hisa(shii)*, long (time), lasting; *hisa(shiku)*, for a long time
				永久　　*eikyū*, permanence, eternity 久しぶり　*hisashiburi*, after a long time
676 3 strokes				久遠　　*kuon*, eternity ⬚2

旧	丨	刂	𠂉	KYŪ, old
	旧	旧		旧式　　*kyūshiki*, old-style 旧跡　　*kyūseki*, place of historic interest
677 5 strokes				旧暦　　*kyūreki*, lunar calendar ⬚2

居	⺆	⺋	尸	KYO, dwelling place; *i(ru)*, to be, to be present, to dwell
	尸	尽	居	住居　　*jūkyo*, dwelling 居眠り　*inemuri*, napping, dozing (n.)
678 8 strokes	居	居		居間　　*ima*, living room ⬚3

許	丶	二	言	KYO; *yuru(shi)*, permission, pardon, approval; *yuru(su)*, to permit, to forgive, to approve
	言	言	訁	許可　　*kyoka*, permission, license, admission, approval
679 11 strokes	許	許	許	特許　　*tokkyo*, patent, concession 免許　　*menkyo*, license, certificate ⬚3

境 680 14 strokes	土 坟 埒 埒 埒 増	圵 堷 培 境 境	垆 培 境 境 境	KYŌ, KEI; *sakai*, border, boundary, border line 境遇　*kyōgū*, circumstances, surroundings 国境　*kokkyō*, frontier 境内　*keidai*, precincts　②
均 681 7 strokes	一 圵 均	十 圴	土 均	KIN, level, equality 平均　*heikin*, average, balance 均等　*kintō*, equality, identity 均一　*kinitsu*, even, regular　②
禁 682 13 strokes	一 木 埜 禁	十 林 禁 禁	才 埜 禁 禁	KIN; *kin~*, prefix for "forbidden" or "prohibited"; *kin(jiru)*, to forbid, to abstain from 禁止　*kinshi*, prohibition, ban 禁煙　*kin'en*, "No Smoking" 禁酒　*kinshu*, abstinence from alcoholic beverages　②
句 683 5 strokes	ノ 句	勹 句	勹	KU, clause, phrase, verse, line 文句　*monku*, words, objection 語句　*goku*, words and phrases 句読点　*kutōten*, punctuation marks　①
群 684 13 strokes	ヨ 君 群	尹 君′ 群	君 君″ 群	GUN; *mu(re)*, group, flock, herd; *mu(reru)*, *mura(garu)*, to throng (v.i.) 魚群　*gyogun*, school of fish 群島　*guntō*, group of islands 群衆　*gunshū*, crowd (of people)　②

経	㇗	ㇰ	幺	KEI, circles of longitude; KYŌ, the sutras, (law, reason, way, ordinary course of things); *he(ru)*, to pass, to pass through
	幺	糸	糸	
685 11 strokes	紆	経	経	経費　　*keihi*, expenditure 経由　　*keiyu*, by way of, through 神経　　*shinkei*, nerve　　3

潔	冫	冫	汁	KETSU; *isagiyo(i)*, manly, brave, pure
	津	沽	渕	清潔　　*seiketsu*, clean 潔白　　*keppaku*, innocent, pure, upright
686 15 strokes	潔	潔	潔	簡潔　　*kanketsu*, concise　　1

件	ノ	イ	イ	KEN, matter
	仁	仁	件	事件　　*jiken*, event, matter 用件　　*yōken*, business 条件　　*jōken*, condition, terms
687 6 strokes				3

券	丶	丷	丷	KEN, bond, ticket
	丷	半	关	定期券　*teikiken*, commutation ticket 旅券　　*ryoken*, passport 入場券　*nyūjō-ken*, admission ticket, platform ticket
688 8 strokes	券	券		2

険	丁	了	阝	KEN; *kewa(shii)*, steep, fierce
	阝	阸	阾	危険　　*kiken*, danger 保険　　*hoken*, insurance 冒険　　*bōken*, adventure
689 11 strokes	险	険	険	3

検 690 12 strokes	一 十 才 木 オ 朴 朴 枱 検	**KEN**, to examine 探検 *tanken*, exploration 検診 *kenshin*, medical examination 検定 *kentei*, official approval [1]
限 691 9 strokes	フ ヲ ⻖ ⻖フ ⻖ヲ ⻖ヨ 阝 限 限	**GEN**; *kagi(ri)*, limit, end, as far as possible; *kagi(ru)*, to limit, to restrict 制限 *seigen*, limitation 期限 *kigen*, term 無限 *mugen*, infinity [3]
現 692 11 strokes	一 丁 干 王 玕 珇 珇 現 現	**GEN**, present, now; *ara(wareru)*, to show oneself, to come into sight, to be found (out); *ara(wasu)*, to manifest, to expose, to express 実現 *jitsugen*, realization 表現 *hyōgen*, expression 現代 *gendai*, present age ✓ [3]
減 693 12 strokes	丶 氵 汀 汀 沪 沪 減 減 減	**GEN**; *he(ru)*, to decrease (v.i.), to wear out; *he(rasu)*, to decrease (v.t.) 加減 *kagen*, state of health, degree, adjustment, influence, addition and subtraction 減少 *genshō*, diminution, decrease 減退 *gentai*, decline, failing [2]
故 694 9 strokes	一 十 十 古 古 古 古 故 故	**KO**, old, former times; reason; *yue* reason, cause 事故 *jiko*, accident, hindrance 故郷 *kokyō*, one's native place 故障 *koshō*, mishap, trouble, accident, hindrance [1]

139

個	ノ	イ	们	KO, individual, suffix for enumeration
	们	们	佣	個人　*kojin*, individual 個性　*kosei*, individual character, personality
695 10 strokes	佣	個	個	数個　*sūko*, several ☑ 2

護	言	言	言	GO, to protect, to defend
	訐	訐	護	保護　*hogo*, protection 看護婦 *kangofu*, trained nurse 弁護士 *bengoshi*, lawyer
696 20 strokes	謹	護	護	1

効	、	二	亠	KŌ, efficacy, effect; *ki(ku)*, to be effective
	六	亣	交	効果　*kōka*, effect, efficacy, result, sound effects 効力　*kōryoku*, effect, efficacy
697 8 strokes	刻	効		有効　*yūkō*, valid, effective, efficacious 2

厚	一	厂	厂	KŌ; *atsu(i)*, thick, cordial
	戸	戸	戸	厚紙　*atsugami*, thick paper, cardboard 厚意　*kōi*, kindness
698 9 strokes	厚	厚	厚	厚生　*kōsei*, public welfare 2

耕	一	三	丰	KŌ; *tagaya(su)*, to till
	耒	耒	耒	耕地　*kōchi*, arable (cultivated) land 耕作　*kōsaku*, cultivation
699 10 strokes	耒	耕	耕	農耕　*nōkō*, farm labor 2

140

鉱 700 13 strokes	𠂉 牟 金 釒 釒 釒 釾 鉱 鉱	**KŌ**, ore 鉱山　*kōzan*, mine 鉱物　*kōbutsu*, mineral 鉄鉱　*tekkō*, iron ore　　2
構 701 14 strokes	木 杧 杧 杧 槯 槯 構 構 構	**KŌ**; *kama(e)*, structure, posture; *kama(eru)*, to put oneself in a posture, to build 構成　*kōsei*, composition 構造　*kōzō*, structure, construction 心構え *kokorogamae*, mental attitude, preparation　　3
興 702 16 strokes	𠂆 𦥑 臼 卵 卵 卵 卵 興 興	**KŌ, KYŌ**; interest; *oko(ru)*, to prosper; *oko(su)*, to restore 興味　*kyōmi*, interest, appeal 興奮　*kōfun*, excitement 復興　*fukkō*, revival, reconstruction　　1
講 703 17 strokes	言 言 計 講 講 講 講 講 講	**KŌ**, investigation, lecture; to think out, to study, to explain 講演　*kōen*, lecture 講堂　*kōdō*, auditorium 講習　*kōshū*, short training course　　2
混 704 11 strokes	丶 氵 氵 沪 沪 沪 泥 混 混	**KON**; *ko(mu)*, to be crowded; *ma(zeru)*, to mix, to mingle; *ma(jiru)*, to be mixed, to be mingled; *ma(zaru)* (=*majiru*) 混乱　*konran*, confusion 混雑　*konzatsu*, congestion, confusion 混合　*kongō*, mixture　　2

141

査	一	十	才	SA, to examine, to investigate
	木	朩	杏	検査　　*kensa*, inspection, examination 巡査　　*junsa*, policeman 審査　　*shinsa*, screening
705 9 strokes	杏	杳	査	2

再	一	厂	冂	SAI, SA, re- (prefix); *futata(bi)*, again
	币	再	再	再建　　*saiken*, reconstruction 再会　　*saikai*, meeting again 再三　　*saisan*, again and again
706 6 strokes				2

災	く	⺍	巛	SAI; *wazawa(i)*, disaster, misfortune
	灬	災	災	災害　　*saigai*, disaster, calamity 災難　　*sainan*, misfortune, calamity 火災　　*kasai*, fire, conflagration
707 7 strokes	災			1

妻	一	⺕	⺕	SAI, my wife; *tsuma*, wife
	⺕	圭	妻	夫妻　　*fusai*, husband and wife 妻子　　*saishi*, wife and children 稲妻　　*inazuma*, lightning
708 8 strokes	妻	妻		3

採	一	扌	扌	SAI; *to(ru)*, to gather (fruit, etc.), to employ (a person), to adopt (a measure)
	扩	扩	扩	採集　　*saishū*, collection 採用　　*saiyō*, employment, adoption
709 11 strokes	护	拼	採	採掘　　*saikutsu*, mining　　2

際 710 14 strokes	㇇ ㇌ ㇖ ㇖ ㇖ ㇌ ㇌ 㗇 際	SAI, occasion; *kiwa*, verge, occasion 実際　*jissai*, actual state, truth, reality 国際　*kokusai*, international 交際　*kōsai*, intercourse, acquaintance, association <div align="right">✓ 3</div>
在 711 6 strokes	一 ナ オ 在 在 在	ZAI, country, suburbs, to exist; *a(ru)*, to be, to exist 存在　*sonzai*, existence, being 滞在　*taizai*, sojourn 現在　*genzai*, present time, present tense <div align="right">3</div>
財 712 10 strokes	丨 冂 月 目 貝 貝 貝 財 財	ZAI, SAI, treasure 財産　*zaisan*, property, fortune 財政　*zaisei*, finance(s) 私財　*shizai*, private property <div align="right">3</div>
罪 713 13 strokes	丶 冖 罒 罒 严 罪 罪 罪 罪	ZAI; *tsumi*, crime, sin 犯罪　*hanzai*, crime 罪悪　*zaiaku*, sin, crime 謝罪　*shazai*, apology <div align="right">3</div>
雑 714 14 strokes	丿 九 卆 杂 杂' 朱 雜 雜 雜	ZATSU, rough; ZŌ, miscellaneous, rough 複雑　*fukuzatsu*, complexity, complication 雑誌　*zasshi*, magazine 雑巾　*zōkin*, floorcloth, mopping cloth <div align="right">✓ 3</div>

酸	丆	酉	酉⁄	SAN, acid; *su(ppai)*, sour
	酉ㄥ	酉ㄥ	酉ㄥ	酸素　*sanso*, oxygen 塩酸　*ensan*, hydrochloric acid 酸化　*sanka*, oxidization
715 14 strokes	酉ㄥ	酸	酸	[1]

賛	一	二	夫	SAN, to praise, to assist, to agree
	夫	夫夫	替	賛成　*sansei*, approval, support 賛助　*sanjo*, support, help 協賛　*kyōsan*, cooperation
716 15 strokes	替	賛	賛	[3]

支	一	十	支	SHI, branch; to branch off, to support; *sasa(eru)*, to support, to hold
	支			支配　*shihai*, rule, management 支払う　*shiharau*, to pay
717 4 strokes				支店　*shiten*, a branch (store, office) [3]

志	一	十	士	SHI; *kokorozashi*, will, intention, ambition, aim, kindness; *kokoroza(su)*, to intend, to aim at
	士	志	志	意志　*ishi*, will 志望　*shibō*, desire
718 7 strokes	志			同志　*dōshi*, comrade [1]

枝	一	十	才	SHI; *eda*, branch, twig
	木	木	杧	枝葉　*shiyō*, minor details, side issues 枯れ枝　*kare-eda*, dead branch
719 8 strokes	枝	枝		小枝　*koeda*, twig [2]

144

師	ノ	イ	ｒ
	ｒ	佇	帥
720 10 strokes	帥	師	師

SHI, teacher, expert; army

牧師　　*bokushi*, pastor
教師　　*kyōshi*, teacher
師団　　*shidan*, division (army)

3

資	丶	ｼ	ﾝ
	汇	次	次
721 13 strokes	浐	資	資

SHI, wealth, help, nature

資源　　*shigen*, resource
資格　　*shikaku*, capacity,
　　　　qualification
物資　　*busshi*, goods, materials

3

飼	ノ	𠆢	仐
	食	食	飼
722 13 strokes	飼	飼	飼

SHI; *ka(u)*, to raise/keep/feed
(animals)

飼料　　　*shiryō*, fodder, animal-feed
飼い主　*kainushi*, animal owner
飼育　　　*shi'iku*, breeding, rearing

1

示	一	二	亍
	亓	示	
723 5 strokes			

JI, SHI; *shime(su)*, to show, to point
out

示唆　　*shisa*, suggestion
掲示　　*keiji*, notice
指示　　*shiji*, instructions, indication

3

似	ノ	イ	仏
	仏	仏	似
724 7 strokes	似		

JI; *ni(ru)*, to resemble

類似　　*ruiji*, similarity
似顔　　*nigao*, portrait, likeness
不似合　*funiai*, unbecoming

3

識 725 19 strokes	亠 言 訥	言 訕 識	言 諳 識	SHIKI, to know, to write down, to distinguish 知識　　*chishiki*, knowledge 標識　　*hyōshiki*, mark 常識　　*jōshiki*, common sense <div align="right">3</div>
質 726 15 strokes	´ 斤 質	厂 斦 質	斤 斦 質	SHITSU, quality, substance; to inquire; simple and honest; SHICHI, pawn 質問　　*shitsumon*, question 素質　　*soshitsu*, makings, quality 質屋　　*shichiya*, pawnshop <div align="right">4</div>
舍 727 8 strokes	ノ 全 舍	人 全 舍	人 全	SHA, house, lodging 校舎　　*kōsha*, school building 牛舎　　*gyūsha*, cowshed 宿舎　　*shukusha*, lodging <div align="right">1</div>
謝 728 17 strokes	丶 言 訬	亠 訁 謝	言 訃	SHA, to apologize, to thank; to apologize 感謝　　*kansha*, thanks 謝絶　　*shazetu*, refusal 謝礼　　*sharei*, remuneration, thanks <div align="right">1</div>
授 729 11 strokes	一 扌 护	扌 扩 授	扌 扩 授	JU; *sazu(keru)*, to grant, to instruct; *sazu(karu)*, to be blessed with 授業　　*jugyō*, lesson(s), teaching 教授　　*kyōju*, teaching, professor 授賞　　*jushō*, awarding a prize <div align="right">☑ 1</div>

146

修 730 10 strokes	ノ イ 化 化 伊 攸 攸 攸 修	SHŪ, SHU; *osa(meru)*, to study, to finish, to practice; *osa(maru)*, to behave well 修理　*shūri*, repair 改修　*kaishū*, improvement, repair 修正　*shūsei*, amendment　　1
述 731 8 strokes	一 十 才 朮 朮 求 述 述	JUTSU; *no(beru)*, to speak, to express, to state 著述　*chojutsu*, writing (of books), one's writings 口述　*kōjutsu*, oral statement 述語　*jutsugo*, predicate (gram.)　2
術 732 11 strokes	ク 彳 千 升 升 休 術 術 術	JUTSU, art, artifice, means, magic 手術　*shujutsu*, surgical operation 技術　*gijutsu*, technique 美術　*bijutsu*, art　　✓ 3
準 733 13 strokes	シ シ 汀 汀 汀 汁 淮 淮 準	JUN, water level; rule; to imitate; prefix denoting "semi-," "associate" 標準　*hyōjun*, standard 基準　*kijun*, standard 準急　*junkyū*, semi-express　2
序 734 7 strokes	、 亠 广 庁 庁 庌 序	JO, preface 順序　*junjo*, order, method 秩序　*chitsujo*, public order, discipline 序文　*jobun*, preface　　1

招	一	寸	扌
	扣	扣	招
735 8 strokes	招	招	

SHŌ; *mane(ku)*, to invite, to beckon

招待　　*shōtai*, invitation
招待状　*shōtaijō*, invitation card
招き猫　*manekineko*, figure of a beckoning cat

3

承	㇇	了	了
	手	手	序
736 8 strokes	承	承	

SHŌ; *uketamawa(ru)*, to hear

承知　*shōchi*, consent, knowledge
承認　*shōnin*, approval
了承　*ryōshō*, acknowledgment

2

証	一	二	二
	言	言	訂
737 12 strokes	訂	証	証

SHŌ, evidence, testimony

証明　*shōmei*, proof, certification
証人　*shōnin*, witness (law), surety
保証　*hoshō*, guarantee, security

1

条	ノ	ク	夂
	冬	冬	条
738 7 strokes	条		

JŌ, clause in a law or treaty, logic, stripe

条件　　*jōken*, terms, conditions
条約　　*jōyaku*, treaty
無条件　*mujōken*, unconditional

1

状	丨	丬	丬
	丬	状	状
739 7 strokes	状		

JŌ, state, condition, letter

状態　*jōtai*, state (of things), condition
現状　*genjō*, existing state of affairs, present condition
礼状　*reijō*, letter of thanks

3

常	ヽ	丷	业	JŌ; *tsune*, usual, ordinary; *toko-*, everlasting
	小	业	尚	非常に *hijō-ni*, very (much) 正常 *seijō*, normal 日常 *nichijō*, everyday
740 11 strokes	尚	常	常	③

情	ヽ	丶	忄	JŌ, feeling, sympathy; *nasa(ke)*, feeling, sympathy, love, mercy
	忄	忄	忄	愛情 *aijō*, affection 情け深い *nasakebukai*, compassionate
741 11 strokes	忄	情	情	情勢 *jōsei*, state of things ③

織	糸	紅	紒	SHOKU, SHIKI; *ori*, textile; *o(ru)*, to weave
	紒	紵	綪	織物 *orimono*, textile fabric 織機 *shokki*, weaving machine 組織 *soshiki*, organization
742 18 strokes	織	織	織	①

職	一	厂	耳	SHOKU, employment, duties
	耳	耶	瞄	職業 *shokugyō*, occupation, business 内職 *naishoku*, side job
743 18 strokes	職	職	職	職場 *shokuba*, place of work ③

制	ノ	⺊	匕	SEI, law, rule; *sei(suru)*, to restrain, to control
	仁	与	制	制度 *seido*, system, institution 制服 *seifuku*, uniform 制限 *seigen*, restriction
744 8 strokes	制	制		☑ ③

149

性	﹑	ハ	忄
	忄	忄	忄
745 8 strokes	忄	性	

SEI, sex, nature; SHŌ, nature, temperament

性質　　*seishitsu*, nature, property
習性　　*shūsei*, habit
気性　　*kishō*, temper

③

政	一	丁	丁
	下	正	正
746 9 strokes	政	政	政

SEI, SHŌ; *matsurigoto*, government

政府　　*seifu*, government
政治　　*seiji*, administration, politics
政策　　*seisaku*, policy

③

勢	土	士	夫
	坴	刲	執
747 13 strokes	執	埶	勢

SEI; *ikio(i)*, force, vigor, power, influence

勢力　　*seiryoku*, power, influence
大勢　　*taisei*, general trend; *ōzei*, large number of people
軍勢　　*gunzei*, number of soldiers, troops

②

精	﹑	丷	半
	米	米	米
748 14 strokes	精	精	精

SEI, SHŌ, spirit, vitality, essence

精神　　*seishin*, spirit, mind, soul
精巧　　*seikō*, exquisite (workmanship)
精進　　*shōjin*, diligence

③

製	﹑	﹋	仁
	与	朱	制
749 14 strokes	制	製	製

SEI, to manufacture, suffix for "make" or "manufacture"

製品　　*seihin*, manufactured goods
銀製　　*ginsei*, made of silver
米国製　*Beikokusei*, of American make

①

150

税	ノ	二	千	ZEI, tax
	禾	禾	利	税金　*zeikin*, tax 納税　*nōzei*, tax payment 税関　*zeikan*, custom house
750 12 strokes	秆	秒	税	2

責	一	十	主	SEKI; *se(meru)*, to blame, to urge, to torture
	主	青	青	責任　*sekinin*, responsibility 責任者 *sekininsha*, person 　　　　　responsible
751 11 strokes	青	責	責	無責任 *musekinin*, irresponsibility 3

績	く	幺	糸	SEKI, to spin; meritorious deed
	糹	糺	絆	成績　*seiseki*, result, record 功績　*kōseki*, meritorious deeds 紡績　*bōseki*, spinning
752 17 strokes	絆	績	績	2

接	扌	扩	扩	SETSU; *ses(suru)*, to come in contact with, to receive, to adjoin; *tsu(gu)*, to join together, to splice, to set (a broken bone)
	扩	扩	拉	直接　*chokusetsu*, directly 接待　*settai*, reception
753 11 strokes	接	接	接	接続　*setsuzoku*, junction ✓ 2

設	、	二	二	SETSU; *mō(keru)*, to establish
	言	言	言	設備　*setsubi*, equipment 設計　*sekkei*, plan, design (for 　　　　construction) 建設　*kensetsu*, construction
754 11 strokes	訳	設	設	2

舌	一	二	千	ZETSU; *shita*, tongue 舌打ち *shita-uchi*, click of the tongue, smacking one's lips 舌鼓 *shita-tsuzumi*, smacking of the lips
	千	舌	舌	
755 **6 strokes**				1
絶	㇗	幺	糸	ZETSU; *ta(eru)*, to cease, to become extinct; *ta(tsu)*, to sever, to discontinue
	糸	紆	絈	絶対 *zettai*, absoluteness 絶頂 *zetchō*, peak, zenith, summit
756 **12 strokes**	絡	絡	絶	気絶 *kizetsu*, fainting　3
銭	ノ	人	今	SEN, former unit of money (a hundredth part of a yen); *zeni* money
	牟	金	金	金銭 *kinsen*, money こづかい銭 *kozukaisen*, pocket money
757 **14 strokes**	鈩	銭	銭	小銭 *kozeni*, small change　1
祖	丶	㇇	ネ	SO, ancestor, founder 祖国 *sokoku*, fatherland 祖母 *sobo*, grandmother 先祖 *senzo*, ancestor
	ネ	礻	初	
758 **9 strokes**	袑	袒	祖	3
素	一	十	圭	SO, SU, white, origin, source 素朴 *soboku*, simple 要素 *yōso*, element, important factor
	圭	耒	耒	
759 **10 strokes**	耒	素	素	素顔 *sugao*, unpainted face　1

152

総	く	幺	糸	**SŌ, whole, general**
	糸	糸	紣	総理大臣 *sōri-daijin*, prime minister
				総員 *sōin*, entire staff, all hands, full force
760 14 strokes	総	総	総	総選挙 *sōsenkyo*, general election [2]

造	ノ	牛	牛	**ZŌ**; *tsuku(ri)*, structure, build (n.); *tsuku(ru)*, to make, to create, to build; *~zuku(ri)*, made of ~ (suffix denoting type of structure)
	生	牛	告	
				木造 *mokuzō*, made of wood
				人造 *jinzō*, artificial
761 10 strokes	告	造	造	石造り *ishizukuri*, built of stone [2]

像	ノ	イ	广	**ZŌ, image, figure**
	仴	伃	伃	銅像 *dōzō*, bronze statue
				仏像 *butsuzō*, image of Buddha
				現像 *genzō*, development (of a film)
762 14 strokes	傊	像	像	[2]

増	一	十	土	**ZŌ**; *ma(su)*, to increase (v.i. & v.t.); *fu(eru)* (v.i.), to increase, to proliferate; *fu(yasu)* (v.t.), to increase, to add (to)
	圤	圤	圤	
				増加 *zōka*, increase
				増強 *zōkyō*, reinforcement
763 14 strokes	圤	増	増	増進 *zōshin*, promotion [3]

則	丨	冂	月	**SOKU, law; to act on**
	月	目	貝	法則 *hōsoku*, law
				規則 *kisoku*, rule
				原則 *gensoku*, principle
764 9 strokes	貝	則	則	[2]

153

測	丶	冫	氵	SOKU; *haka(ru)*, to fathom, to measure
	沪	沪	測	観測 *kansoku*, observation 測量 *sokuryō*, surveying 測定 *sokutei*, measurement
765 12 strokes	測	測	測	[2]
属	一	コ	尸	ZOKU, genus (biol.); *zoku(suru)*, to belong to
	尸	戸	居	金属 *kinzoku*, metal 所属 *shozoku*, one's position 付属病院 *fuzoku-byōin*, attached
766 12 strokes	属	属	属	hospital [1]
率	丶	亠	玄	SOTSU; *hiki(iru)*, to lead, to command; RITSU, rate
	玄	玄	泫	能率 *nōritsu*, efficiency 出席率 *shussekiritsu*, percentage of attendance
767 11 strokes	泫	淬	率	統率 *tōsotsu*, command, leadership [1]
損	一	才	扌	SON, loss, disadvantage; *son(suru)*, to suffer a loss; *soko(nau)*, *soko(neru)*, to hurt, to damage
	扩	捐	捐	損害 *songai*, loss, damage 損失 *sonshitsu*, loss 破損 *hason*, damage, breakdown
768 13 strokes	捐	損	損	[2]
退	⁊	⁊	ヨ	TAI; *shirizo(ku)*, to retreat, to withdraw, to retire (v.i.); *shirizo(keru)*, to drive back, to keep away, to refuse (v.t.)
	𦙞	𦙞	艮	退場 *taijō*, leaving, walk-out, exit 退治 *taiji*, stamping out, subjugation
769 9 strokes	退	退	退	後退 *kōtai*, retreat [3]

154

貸	ノ	イ	仁
	代	代	侁
770 12 strokes	侁	貸	貸

TAI; *ka(shi)*, loan; *ka(su)*, to lend, to loan, to hire out

貸家　　*kashiya*, house for rent
貸ボート *kashibōto*, boat for hire
貸借　　*taishaku*, borrowing and lending

☑ 4

態	厶	厶	亻
	台	台	育
771 14 strokes	育	能	態

TAI, appearance, state of affairs

態度　　*taido*, attitude
状態　　*jōtai*, state (of things) condition
容態　　*yōdai*, condition (of a patient)

1

団	丨	冂	冂
	用	団	団
772 6 strokes			

DAN; TON, round, group, party

団体　　*dantai*, party, organization
楽団　　*gakudan*, band (musical)
布団　　*futon*, Japanese quilt

2

断	丷	丷	半
	米	迷	迷
773 11 strokes	断	断	断

DAN; *kotowa(ru)*, to decline, to refuse, to give notice, to ask leave; *ta(tsu)*, to sever, to give up (drinking), to exterminate

断食　　*danjiki*, a fast
油断　　*yudan*, negligence, carelessness, unpreparedness
判断　　*handan*, judgment

3

築	ᄊ	ᄊ	ᄊ
	竺	竺	竺
774 16 strokes	筑	筑	築

CHIKU; *kizu(ku)*, to build

建築　　*kenchiku*, building
築造　　*chikuzō*, construction
新築　　*shinchiku*, new building

2

張	フ	コ	弓	CHŌ; *ha(ri)*, tension, expansion; *ha(ru)*, to stretch, to spread, to cover
	引	孖	殍	見張り　　*mihari*, lookout 引っ張る　*hipparu*, to pull 主張　　　*shuchō*, insistence,
775 11 strokes	張	張	張	opinion <div align="right">1</div>

提	一	十	扌	TEI; *sa(geru)*, to carry in one's hand
	押	担	押	提出　　*teishutsu*, presentation 　　　　(of a thesis), filing (of an 　　　　application) 提供　　*teikyō*, offer, tender (law)
776 12 strokes	捍	捍	提	提案　　*teian*, suggestion, proposition <div align="right">1</div>

程	ノ	ニ	千	TEI, degree, rule; *hodo*, extent, limit
	禾	和	和	程度　　*teido*, degree, standard, limit 日程　　*nittei*, day's program, 　　　　schedule
777 12 strokes	秆	程	程	行程　　*kōtei*, distance <div align="right">3</div>

適	丶	亠	亠	TEKI; *teki(suru)*, to be fit for
	广	斉	斉	適当　　*tekitō*, suitable, moderate 適任　　*tekinin*, fitness 快適　　*kaiteki*, agreeable
778 14 strokes	商	商	適	<div align="right">3</div>

敵	亠	方	斉	TEKI, *kataki*, enemy, opponent
	商	商	商	強敵　　*kyōteki*, formidable enemy 敵意　　*teki-i*, hostile feeling 敵国　　*tekikoku*, enemy country
779 15 strokes	敵	敵	敵	<div align="right">1</div>

156

統	⺃	幺	糸	**TŌ**; *su(beru)*, to control
	糸	糽	紵	統計　　*tōkei*, statistics 大統領　*daitōryō*, president (of a country) 伝統　　*dentō*, tradition
780 12 strokes	統	絞	統	▢1

銅	⼃	⺈	牟	**DŌ**, copper
	金	金	釒	青銅　　*seidō*, bronze 銅線　　*dōsen*, copper wire 銅山　　*dōzan*, copper mine
781 14 strokes	釦	釦	銅	▢2

導	丶	丷	丷	**DŌ**; *michibi(ki)*, guidance; *michibi(ku)*, to guide, to lead
	丷	首	道	指導　　　*shidō*, guidance 指導者　　*shidōsha*, leader 補導　　　*hodō*, guidance
782 15 strokes	道	導	導	▢2

徳	彳	行	彳	**TOKU**, virtue, power of commanding love and respect
	彳	徔	徔	道徳　　*dōtoku*, morality 徳望　　*tokubō*, moral influence 人徳　　*jintoku*, natural virtue
783 14 strokes	徔	徳	徳	▢1

独	丿	犭	犭	**DOKU**; *hito(ri)*, one person; Germany
	犭	狆	狆	独立　　*dokuritsu*, independence 独特　　*dokutoku*, peculiar, unique 独唱　　*dokushō*, vocal solo
784 9 strokes	独	独	独	▢1

任	ノ	イ	仁	NIN, duty; *maka(seru)*, to entrust, to leave (v.t.)
	仁	仟	任	責任 *sekinin*, responsibility 転任 *tennin*, change of post 任務 *ninmu*, duty
785 6 strokes				3

燃	丶	丷	丬	NEN; *mo(eru)*, to burn (v.i.); *mo(yasu)*, to burn (v.t.)
	火	灯	炒	燃料 *nenryō*, fuel 燃焼 *nenshō*, combustion 不燃性 *funensei*, incombustible
786 16 strokes	炒	燃	燃	2

能	ㄥ	ム	仁	NŌ, ability, expert, skill, the *Noh*
	㐅	宣	育	能力 *nōryoku*, ability, capacity, faculty 才能 *sainō*, talent 能率 *nōritsu*, efficiency
787 10 strokes	育	能	能	3

破	一	ア	石	HA; *yabu(re)*, a tear (rent); *yabu(ru)*, to tear, to break (a promise)
	石	矴	矿	破損 *hason*, breakdown 破産 *hasan*, bankruptcy 難破 *nanpa*, shipwreck
788 10 strokes	矿	破	破	3

犯	ノ	犭	犭	HAN; *oka(su)*, to commit, to violate, to rape
	犭	犯		犯罪 *hanzai*, crime 犯人 *hannin*, criminal 防犯 *bōhan*, crime prevention
789 5 strokes				3

判 790 7 strokes	丶 ⺍ 半 判	⸜ 半	⸌ 半	HAN, to decide; seal for stamping; BAN, size 判断 *handan*, judgment, divination 裁判 *saiban*, justice, trial, judgment 大判 *ō-ban*, large size (paper, book) 3
版 791 8 strokes	丿 片 版	丨 片 版	尸 𠂆	HAN, plate, printing, edition 版画 *hanga*, woodblock print 版権 *hanken*, copyright 出版 *shuppan*, publication 2
比 792 4 strokes	一 比	上	匕	HI, ratio, comparison; *kura(beru)*, to compare 比較 *hikaku*, comparison 比率 *hiritsu*, ratio 比例 *hirei*, proportion 2
肥 793 8 strokes	丿 月 肛	刀 肌 肥	月 肥	HI; *ko(eru)*, to grow fat; *koyashi*, manure, fertilizer; *ko(yasu)*, to fertilize, to fatten, to enrich (oneself) 肥料 *hiryō*, manure, fertilizer たい肥 *taihi*, compost 1
非 794 8 strokes	丿 彐 非	丿 非 非	非 非	HI, fault, wrong; non-, un- 非常に *hijō-ni*, very 非常口 *hijōguchi*, emergency door 非難 *hinan*, censure ✓ 3

159

備 795 12 strokes	ノ	イ	亻
	广	俨	伊
	俨	備	備

BI; *sona(e)*, preparation(s); *sona(eru)*, to furnish, to prepare; *sona(waru)*, to be possessed of, to be furnished with

準備	*junbi*, preparation(s)
守備	*shubi*, defense
予備	*yobi*, reserve	[3]

俵 796 10 strokes	ノ	イ	亻
	什	佳	伊
	佳	俵	俵

HYŌ; *tawara*, straw bag

土俵	*dohyō*, sandbag; sumō (wrestling) ring
一俵	*ippyō*, one straw bag
炭俵	*sumidawara*, charcoal sack	[1]

評 797 12 strokes	、	二	言
	言	言	言
	訂	訂	評

HYŌ, criticism; *hyō(suru)*, to criticize, to comment

評判	*hyōban*, reputation, popularity, rumor
評価	*hyōka*, appraisal, appreciation
批評	*hihyō*, criticism	[1]

貧 798 11 strokes	ノ	八	今
	分	分	貧
	貧	貧	貧

HIN, BIN, poverty; *mazu(shii)*, poor

貧弱	*hinjaku*, meager, poor
貧乏	*binbō*, poverty
貧困	*hinkon*, poverty, lack	[3]

| 布 799 5 strokes | ノ | ナ | 才 |
| | 右 | 布 | |

FU; *nuno*, cloth

毛布	*mōfu*, blanket
配布	*haifu*, distribution
綿布	*menpu*, cotton cloth	[2]

婦	く	女	女′	**FU, woman, wife**
	女″	女″	女″	婦人　*fujin*, woman 主婦　*shufu*, housewife 夫婦　*fūfu*, husband and wife
800 11 strokes	女″	婦	婦	✓ ③

富	`	⺍	宀	**FU, FŪ;** *tomi*, riches; *to(mu)*, to be rich, to abound (in)
	官	官	宜	豊富　*hōfu*, abundance 富貴　*fuki, fūki, fukki*, rich and noble
801 12 strokes	富	富	富	富裕　*fuyū*, riches, wealth ③

武	一	二	干	**BU, MU, military**
	干	走	正	武装　*busō*, arms, weapons 武器　*buki*, weapon 武力　*buryoku*, military power
802 8 strokes	武	武		②

復	ノ	ク	彳	**FUKU, re-, again, repeat**
	彳	彳	徊	回復　*kaifuku*, recovery 復興　*fukkō*, revival, reconstruction
803 12 strokes	復	復	復	復活　*fukkatsu*, revival, resurrection ②

複	⺀	衤	衤	**FUKU, to repeat; prefix for "double"**
	衤	衤	袖	複雑　*fukuzatsu*, complication, complexity
804 14 strokes	複	複	複	複製　*fukusei*, reproduction 重複　*chōfuku, jūfuku*, duplication, repetition ②

仏 805 4 strokes	ノ 仏	イ	化	BUTSU; *hotoke*, Buddha; FUTSU, France 大仏　*daibutsu*, colossal statue of Buddha 仏像　*butsuzō*, image of Buddha 仏教　*bukkyō*, Buddhism　　　②
編 806 15 strokes	糸 紗 絹	糸 紆 編	糸 絹 編	HEN, editing; *a(mu)*, to knit, to edit 編集　*henshū*, editing 編集者 *henshūsha*, editor 編成　*hensei*, formation　　　②
弁 807 5 strokes	㇉ 斉	㇛ 弁	㇔	BEN, speech 弁論　*benron*, debate 弁護人 *bengonin*, counsel 弁当　*bentō*, lunch　　　①
保 808 9 strokes	ノ 仴 伲	イ 仴 保	仃 但 保	HO; *tamo(tsu)*, to keep, to maintain 保護　*hogo*, protection 保存　*hozon*, preservation 保険　*hoken*, insurance　　　①
墓 809 13 strokes	一 苩 莫	艹 莒 莫	艹 草 墓	BO; *haka*, grave 墓地　*bochi*, graveyard 墓石　*boseki*, *haka-ishi*, gravestone 墓参り *hakamairi*, visit to a grave　　①

報	土	士	吉	HŌ, report; *muku(i)*, retribution; *muku(iru)*, to reward, to return (a favor)
	圭	幸	幸	報告　*hōkoku*, report 時報　*jihō*, announcement of time 電報　*denpō*, telegram
810 12 strokes	靪	靪	報	3

豊	冂	曲	曲	HŌ; *yuta(ka)*, abundance
	曲	曲	曹	豊年　*hōnen*, year of abundance 豊作　*hōsaku*, good harvest 豊富　*hōfu*, abundance, wealth
811 13 strokes	曹	曹	豊	2

防	⁊	阝	阝	BŌ; *fuse(gu)*, to defend, to keep off, to prevent
	阝'	阡	防	予防　*yobō*, prevention 消防　*shōbō*, fire fighting 防波堤　*bōhatei*, breakwater
812 7 strokes	防			2

貿	⼃	⼂	厶	BŌ, to purchase, to exchange
	幻	幻	留	貿易商　*bōekishō*, trader 貿易会社　*bōekigaisha*, trading firm 貿易風　*bōekifū*, trade wind
813 12 strokes	留	貿	貿	2

暴	曰	旦	昜	BŌ, BAKU, violent; to disclose; *aba(ku)*, to divulge; *aba(reru)*, to behave violently
	昱	異	異	暴力　*bōryoku*, violence, force 乱暴　*ranbō*, violence, unreasonableness 暴露　*bakuro*, disclosure
814 15 strokes	暴	暴	暴	2

	マ	予	矛	MU; *tsuto(maru)*, to be qualified for; *tsuto(meru)*, to discharge one's duties, to enact (a role)
務	矛	矛	矛	事務所 *jimusho*, office 勤務 *kinmu*, service, duty 義務 *gimu*, duty
815 11 strokes	矜	務	務	3

	一	艹	芌	MU; *yume*, dream, vision
夢	苗	莤	苗	悪夢 *akumu*, nightmare 夢中 *muchū*, unconsciousness; ecstasy, rapture 夢幻 *mugen*, dreams, visions
816 13 strokes	夢	夢	夢	3

	丶	⺍	丷	MEI; *mayo(u)*, to be puzzled, to lose one's way, to go astray, to be tempted by; *mayo(wasu)*, to lead astray, to puzzle, to tempt
迷	半	半	米	迷信 *meishin*, superstition 迷惑 *meiwaku*, trouble, annoyance
817 9 strokes	迷	迷	迷	3

	く	幺	糸	MEN; *wata*, cotton
綿	糸'	糹	紹	綿屋 *wataya*, cotton shop (dealer) 綿密 *menmitsu*, minute, careful 綿花 *menka*, raw cotton
818 14 strokes	綿	綿	綿	2

	亘	車	車	YU, to send
輸	軡	軡	輸	輸出 *yushutsu*, export 輸血 *yuketsu*, blood transfusion 輸送 *yusō*, transportation
819 16 strokes	輸	輸	輸	2

余	ノ	人	스
	스	仐	余
820 7 strokes	余		

YO, more (than), above; *ama(ri)*, the remainder, the balance; ~*ama(ri)*, more than, over; *ama(ru)*, to remain, to be beyond (one's power); *ama(su)*, to leave over

余分　　*yobun*, surplus
余暇　　*yoka*, spare time
余地　　*yochi*, room, scope　　3

預	フ	マ	ヌ
	予	予	予
821 13 strokes	預	預	預

YO; *azu(karu)*, to keep, to take charge of, to refrain from, to receive; *azu(keru)*, to deposit, to put into the charge of

預金　　*yokin*, money on deposit
預り物　*azukarimono*, item left in someone's charge
預り証　*azukarishō*, deposit receipt　　2

容	丶	丷	宀
	宀	穴	灾
822 10 strokes	灾	容	容

YŌ, figure; to admit

形容詞　*keiyōshi*, adjective
内容　　*naiyō*, content, substance
容積　　*yōseki*, capacity, cubic measure　　3

略	丨	冂	冂
	田	田	田'
823 11 strokes	畩	畩	略

RYAKU, abbreviation, omission, outline; *ryaku(su)*, to omit

計略　　*keiryaku*, stratagem, plan, plot
省略　　*shōryaku*, omission
略称　　*ryakushō*, abbreviation　　2

留	ノ	乇	厶
	幻	卯	卯
824 10 strokes	卯	留	留

RYŪ, RU; *to(meru)* (v.t.), *to(maru)* (v.i.), to fasten, to stop

停留所　*teiryūjo*, streetcar (bus) stop
留学　　*ryūgaku*, studying abroad
留守　　*rusu*, absence　　☑ 3

165

領	令	令	令	RYŌ, chief point; to control
	鈴	領	領	要領 *yōryō*, the point, knack 領土 *ryōdo*, territory 領事 *ryōji*, consul
825 14 strokes	領	領	領	2

異	丶	口	曰	I; *koto(naru)*, to be different, to be unusual
	甲	田	曻	異常 *ijō*, unusual 異論 *iron*, different opinion, objection
826 11 strokes	畢	異	異	異様 *iyō*, strange, odd, extraordinary 1

遺	口	中	虫	I, YUI, to leave behind, to bequeath
	贵	書	貴	遺族 *izoku*, bereaved family 遺跡 *iseki*, remains, relics 遺言 *yuigon*, will, testament
827 15 strokes	遺	遺	遺	1

域	一	士	圵	IKI, region, limits
	圵	垣	域	地域 *chi-iki*, region, area 区域 *kuiki*, domain, zone, limits 領域 *ryōiki*, territory, sphere
828 11 strokes	域	域		2

宇	丶	丷	宀	U, canopy of heaven, space, eaves
	宀	宀	宇	宇宙 *uchū*, universe, cosmos 宇宙服 *uchūfuku*, space suit 堂宇 *dō-u*, hall, temple, edifice
829 6 strokes				2

映	丨	冂	日	EI; *utsu(ru)*, to be reflected, match, come out (of photos); *utsu(su)*, to project, reflect; *ha(eru)*, to shine (v.i.)
	日	旷	旷	映画 *eiga*, film, movie 上映 *jōei*, screening
830 9 strokes	旷	映	映	反映 *han'ei*, reflection, influence ✓ 4

延	ノ	千	千	EN; *no(biru)*, to be postponed, to be extended; *no(basu)*, to postpone, to extend; *no(be)*, total
	正	正	延	延長 *enchō*, prolongation, extension
831 8 strokes	延	延		延着 *enchaku*, late arrival 延期 *enki*, postponement 2

沿	丶	冫	氵	EN; *so(u)*, to run along, lie along
	氵	沿	沿	沿岸 *engan*, coast, shore 沿道 *endō*, roadside
832 8 strokes	沿	沿		川沿い *kawazoi*, riverside 1

我	ノ	二	于	GA; *ware*, self, oneself, I
	手	我	我	我々 *ware-ware*, we 無我 *muga*, selflessness, ecstasy 我流 *garyū*, one's own way,
833 7 strokes	我			self-taught method 1

灰	一	厂	厂	KAI; *hai*, ash, ashes
	灰	灰	灰	石灰 *sekkai*, lime 灰色 *hai-iro*, grey 火山灰 *kazanbai*, volcanic ash
834 6 strokes				2

拡	一	扌	扌	KAKU, to extend, to unfold, to spread
	扌	扩	扩	拡大 *kakudai*, magnification 拡張 *kakuchō*, extension, expansion
835 8 strokes	拡	拡		拡声機 *kakuseiki*, loud-speaker [1]

革	一	十	廿	KAKU, leather; to reform
	廿	芇	芇	革命 *kakumei*, revolution 革新 *kakushin*, innovation, reform
836 9 strokes	苩	莒	革	改革 *kaikaku*, reform [2]

閣	丨	冂	冂	KAKU, tower, pavilion, the Cabinet
	門	門	閃	内閣 *naikaku*, the Cabinet 閣僚 *kakuryō*, Cabinet member 閣下 *kakka*, Your Excellency
837 14 strokes	閃	閃	閣	[1]

割	、	冂	宀	KATSU; *wa(ru)*, to split, divide, separate (v.t.); *wa(reru)*, to break, split (v.i.); *wa(ri)* proportion, rate; *sa(ku)*, to cut, spare
	宀	宀	宔	分割 *bunkatsu*, division, partition 割合 *wariai*, rate, ratio
838 12 strokes	害	害	割	割引 *waribiki*, discount, rebate [3]

株	一	十	才	*kabu*, shares, stocks, speculation in shares; stub
	木	朮	朾	切り株 *kirikabu*, stump 株式会社 *kabushiki-kaisha*, joint-stock corporation
839 10 strokes	枏	株	株	株券 *kabuken*, share certificate [1]

干 840 3 strokes	一	二	干	KAN, to dry, to drain, shield, thrust; *ho(su)*, to dry, to drain (v.t.); *hi(ru)*, to dry, to ebb (v.i.) 干し草 *hoshikusa*, dry grass, hay 干潮 *kanchō*, *hishio*, ebb tide 干渉 *kanshō*, interference, intervention 　2
巻 841 9 strokes	丶	丷	䒑	KAN; *ma(ki)*, volume, manuscript roll; *ma(ku)*, to roll, wind (v.t.) 巻頭 *kantō*, the beginning part of a book 巻物 *makimono*, a scroll 竜巻 *tatsumaki*, whirlwind, tornado 　2
	丬	半	关	
	芣	兹	巻	
看 842 9 strokes	一	二	三	KAN, to see, to observe, to examine 看護 *kango*, nursing, caring for 看守 *kanshu*, warder, jailer 看板 *kanban*, signboard, sign, placard 　1
	手	弄	看	
	看	看	看	
簡 843 18 strokes	⺮	⺮	竹	KAN, simple, brief; document 簡単 *kantan*, simple, easy 簡易 *kan'i*, easy, elementary 書簡 *shokan*, letter, correspondence 　2
	筥	筥	筥	
	簡	簡	簡	
危 844 6 strokes	ノ	⺈	𠂊	KI; *abu(nai)*, dangerous, critical (of condition), doubtful; *aya(ui)*, dangerous, doubtful 危険 *kiken*, danger 危篤 *kitoku*, critical condition (illness) 危機 *kiki*, crisis 　3
	𠂉	产	危	

169

机	一	十	才	KI; *tsukue*, desk
	木	朾	机	机上の *kijō no*, theoretical, impractical 事務机 *jimuzukue*, office desk 机一杯 *tsukue-ippai*, a deskful
845 6 strokes				[2]

揮	一	寸	扌	KI, to wield, to brandish
	扩	护	护	指揮　　　*shiki*, command; conducting (of music) 発揮　　　*hakki*, display, exhibition 揮発性　*kihatsusei*, volatility
846 12 strokes	揎	揎	揮	[1]

貴	口	中	虫	KI, noble, dear, precious; *tatto(bu)*, to esteem, to prize; *tatto(i)*, valuables, precious
	虫	昔	青	貴重　　　*kichō*, precious 貴金属　*kikinzoku*, precious metals 貴重品　*kichōhin*, valuables
847 12 strokes	書	貴	貴	[1]

疑	⺊	ヒ	匕	GI; *utaga(i)*, doubt, suspicion; *utaga(u)*, to doubt, to suspect
	髪	髪	斝	疑問　　　*gimon*, question, doubt 質疑　　　*shitsugi*, question 疑惑　　　*giwaku*, suspicion, doubt
848 14 strokes	髪	疑	疑	[3]

吸	丶	口	口	KYŪ; *su(u)*, to sip, to breathe in, to suck, to smoke (tobacco)
	叨	吸	吸	吸収　　　*kyūshū*, absorption 吸血鬼 *kyūketsuki*, vampire 呼吸　　　*kokyū*, breathing, respiration
849 6 strokes				[3]

供 850 8 strokes	ノ 仕 供	イ 仕 供	仁 供	KYŌ; *tomo*, attendant; *sona(eru)*, to offer (to a god) 供給　　*kyōkyū*, supply, provision 提供　　*teikyō*, offer 供出　　*kyōshutsu*, quota delivery　　3
胸 851 10 strokes	) 肝 胸	刀 肑 胸	月 肑 胸	KYŌ; *mune*, chest, heart, mind 度胸　　*dokyō*, courage 胸焼け　*muneyake*, heartburn 胸囲　　*kyōi*, chest measurement　　2
郷 852 11 strokes	く 幻 組	乡 彐 組	彡 組 郷	KYŌ, GŌ, country, village, native place 郷土　　*kyōdo*, one's native place; local 近郷　　*kingō*, neighboring districts 郷愁　　*kyōshū*, nostalgia, homesickness　　1
勤 853 12 strokes	一 莒 菫	十 苗 勤	艹 革 勤	KIN; *tsuto(me)*, duties, service; *tsuto(meru)*, to serve (in an office) 勤務　　*kinmu*, service, duty 勤勉　　*kinben*, diligence 出勤　　*shukkin*, attendance　　3
筋 854 12 strokes	ノ 筘 筘	ト 竹 筘	竹 筘 筋	KIN; *suji*, muscle, sinew; thread, plot, line; sources 筋肉　　*kinniku*, muscle 筋道　　*sujimichi*, reason, logic 筋書き　*sujigaki*, outline, plan　　1

171

系	一	㇀	幺
	幺	卒	系
855 7 strokes	系		

KEI, system, family line

系統　　*keitō*, system, family line
系図　　*keizu*, genealogical table
家系　　*kakei*, family line

1

敬	一	艹	艹
	苟	苟	苟
856 12 strokes	苟	苟	敬

KEI; *uyama(u)*, to respect

尊敬　　*sonkei*, respect
敬語　　*keigo*, honorific word
敬意　　*kei-i*, respects

2

警	一	艹	艹
	苟	苟	敬
857 19 strokes	警	警	警

KEI, to warn, to caution

警察　　*keisatsu*, police
警告　　*keikoku*, warning, caution
警報　　*keihō*, alarm, warning

3

劇	⺊	广	虍
	虏	虎	虏
858 15 strokes	虏	豦	劇

GEKI, drama, play; intense, severe

劇場　　*gekijō*, theater
演劇　　*engeki*, play, theatrical performance
劇薬　　*gekiyaku*, powerful medicine

2

激	氵	氵	泊
	泊	滂	澎
859 16 strokes	澎	激	激

GEKI; *geki(suru)*, to become excited/agitated; *hage(shii)*, violent, intense, passionate

感激　　*kangeki*, deep emotion
急激　　*kyūgeki*, sudden, abrupt
激烈　　*gekiretsu*, severe, intense, violent

1

穴	、	ハ	宀	KETSU; *ana*, cave, hole
	宀	穴		墓穴　*boketsu*, a grave 穴埋め　*ana-ume*, stopgap 穴居　*kekkyo*, cave-dwelling
860 5 strokes				☐1

絹	く	幺	幺	KEN; *kinu*, silk
	糸	糸	紀	絹糸　*kinu-ito*, silk thread 絹織物　*kinu-orimono*, silk fabrics 人絹　*jinken*, artificial silk, rayon
861 13 strokes	紹	絹	絹	☐1

権	木	朾	朾	KEN, GON, weight, authority, power
	栌	栌	栌	人権　*jinken*, human rights 版権　*hanken*, copyright 政権　*seiken*, political power
862 15 strokes	栌	栌	権	☐3

憲	、	ハ	宀	KEN, law, regulation
	宀	宇	宝	憲法　*kenpō*, constitution 憲兵　*kenpei*, military police, 　　　　shore patrol 憲章　*kenshō*, charter, constitution
863 16 strokes	害	憲	憲	☐1

源	氵	汀	沪	GEN; *minamoto*, origin, source
	沪	沪	沪	資源　*shigen*, resources 源氏　*Genji*, Minamoto Clan 水源　*suigen*, head of a 　　　　stream/river
864 13 strokes	源	源	源	☐1

173

	丶	丷	丷	GEN, GON, severe, strict, austere; *kibi(shii)*, strict, harsh; *ogoso(ka)*, solemn, severe
厳	丷	产	产	厳禁 *genkin*, strict prohibition 厳格 *genkaku*, stern, austere 荘厳 *sōgon*, sublime, solemn
865 17 strokes	产	岸	厳	☐1

	⁷	コ	己	KO, KI, myself, oneself, I
己				自己 *jiko*, one's self, self 利己主義 *rikoshugi*, egoism 知己 *chiki*, acquaintance, appreciative friend
866 3 strokes				☐1

	丶	口	口	KO, to call, to breathe; *yo(bu)*, to call, to invite, to name
呼	口ノ	口	口	点呼 *tenko*, roll call 呼び物 *yobimono*, drawcard, attraction
867 8 strokes	吁	呼		呼気 *koki*, exhalation ☐3

	丶	㇊	言	GO; *ayama(ri)*, fault, mistake, error; *ayama(ru)*, to err, to mistake
誤	言	訂	訳	誤解 *gokai*, misunderstanding 誤字 *goji*, wrong word 誤訳 *goyaku*, mistranslation
868 14 strokes	誤	誤	誤	☐3

	一	厂	厏	KŌ, empress, queen
后	斤	后	后	皇后 *kōgō*, Empress (of Japan) 皇太后 *kōtaikō*, Empress Dowager (of Japan), Queen Mother (of England)
869 6 strokes				☐1

孝	一	十	土	KŌ, filial duty
	耂	耂	考	孝行 *kōkō,* filial piety 孝心 *kōshin,* filial affection 孝養 *kōyō,* discharge of filial duties
870 7 strokes	孝			1

皇	'	イ	白	KŌ, Ō, monarch, emperor
	白	白	白	皇太子 *kōtaishi,* Crown Prince (of Japan) 皇室 *kōshitsu,* Imperial Family (of Japan)
871 9 strokes	皇	皇	皇	天皇 *tennō,* Emperor (of Japan)
				1

紅	∠	幺	幺	KŌ, KU; *kurenai,* crimson; *beni,* lipstick, rouge
	糸	糸	糸	口紅 *kuchibeni,* lipstick 紅茶 *kōcha,* black tea
872 9 strokes	紅	紅	紅	紅葉 *kōyō,* crimson foliage; *momiji,* maple
				2

降	ㄱ	阝	阝	KŌ; *fu(ru),* to fall (of rain/snow); *o(riru),* to come down, to get off (a vehicle, etc.); *o(rosu),* to lower
	阝	阝	阝	(三日)以降 *(mikka) ikō,* (falling) on and after (the 3rd)
873 10 strokes	降	降	降	乗り降り *noriori,* getting on and off 降雨 *kō-u,* rainfall ☑ 3

鋼	𠆢	仝	全	KŌ; *hagane,* steel
	金	金	釘	鋼鉄 *kōtetsu,* steel 鋼色 *hagane-iro,* steel-blue 製鋼 *seikō,* steelmaking
874 16 strokes	釘	鋼	鋼	1

刻	、	二	亠	KOKU, engrave; short period of time; kiza(mu), to cut fine, to carve, to engrave
	亥	亥	亥	
875 8 strokes	刻	刻		時刻 jikoku, time 深刻 shinkoku, grave, serious 彫刻 chōkoku, carving, engraving, sculpture [3]

穀	士	壴	声	KOKU, grain, cereals
	壴	索	索	穀物 kokumotsu, grain, cereals 雑穀 zakkoku, minor cereals 穀類 kokurui, cereals, grain
876 14 strokes	榖	穀	穀	[1]

骨	㇒	冂	冂	KOTSU; hone, bone, frame, "backbone"
	冎	冎	咼	骨折り hone-ori, pains, trouble, effort 骨折 kossetsu, a fracture 気骨 kikotsu, spirit, grit, mettle
877 10 strokes	骨	骨	骨	[2]

困	丨	冂	冂	KON; koma(ru), to be in trouble/in a fix
	用	困	困	困難 konnan, difficulty, adversity 困窮 konkyū, destitution 貧困 hinkon, poverty, indigence
878 7 strokes	困			✓ [3]

砂	一	厂	石	SA, SHA; suna, sand
	石	石	石	砂糖 satō, sugar 砂金 sakin, gold dust 砂利 jari, gravel
879 9 strokes	砂	砂	砂	[2]

176

座 880 10 strokes	丶	亠	广
	广	庁	庐
	庐	座	座

ZA, seat, gathering, constellation; *suwa(ru)*, to sit

座席　*zaseki*, seat
星座　*seiza*, constellation
銀座　*Ginza*, the Ginza (major street/district in Tokyo)

3

済 881 11 strokes	氵	氵	氵
	氵	汝	済
	済	済	済

SAI; *su(mu)*, to end, to be settled; *su(masu)*, to finish, to pay back (a debt), to manage with (little money, etc.)

経済　*keizai*, economics, thrift
不経済　*fukeizai*, bad economy
返済　*hensai*, repayment

3

裁 882 12 strokes	十	土	圭
	圭	圭	表
	裁	裁	裁

SAI; *saba(ku)*, to judge; *ta(tsu)*, to cut (cloth etc.)

裁判　*saiban*, trial
裁縫　*saihō*, needlework
独裁　*dokusai*, dictatorship

1

策 883 12 strokes	ノ	⺮	⺮
	⺮	竺	笁
	第	第	策

SAKU, policy, scheme, measure, plan

政策　*seisaku*, policy
策略　*sakuryaku*, stratagem
対策　*taisaku*, counterplan

1

| 冊 884 5 strokes | 丨 | 冂 | 冂 |
| | 冊 | 冊 | |

SATSU, SAKU; counter for books and magazines

一冊　*issatsu*, one volume
冊子　*sasshi*, booklet, pamphlet, brochure
別冊　*bessatsu*, separate volume

2

蚕	一	二	チ	SAN; *kaiko*, silkworm
	天	天	吞	養蚕　*yōsan*, sericulture 蚕室　*sanshitsu*, silkworm rearing room
885 10 strokes	吞	蚕	蚕	養蚕地 *yōsanchi*, silkworm raising district [1]

至	一	エ	ム	SHI; *ita(ru)*, to reach, to go so far (as to), to come, to lead to, to be brought to
	云	卒	至	至急　*shikyū*, urgency 冬至　*tōji*, winter solstice
886 6 strokes				夏至　*geshi*, summer solstice [1]

私	一	二	千	SHI; *watakushi*, *watashi*, I, personal (affairs), privacy
	千	禾	私	私用　*shiyō*, private use (business) 私物　*shibutsu*, private property
887 7 strokes	私			私有　*shiyū*, private ownership ✓ [4]

姿	、	ン	ソ	SHI; *sugata*, shape, figure; appearance, condition
	ツ	次	次	姿勢　*shisei*, posture, pose, stance 容姿　*yōshi*, one's form, appearance
888 9 strokes	姿	姿	姿	後ろ姿 *ushirosugata*, view from the back [1]

視	、	ラ	ネ	SHI, to look at carefully
	ネ	礻	初	視界　*shikai*, field of vision 視力　*shiryoku*, eyesight, vision
889 11 strokes	祖	視	視	無視　*mushi*, disregard [1]

詞	、	ニ	言	SHI, speech, words
	言	訂	訶	歌詞　　*kashi*, words (of a song) 名詞　　*meishi*, noun 形容詞 *keiyōshi*, adjective
890 12 strokes	詞			2

誌	、	ニ	言	SHI, document, magazine, record
	言	言	計	雑誌　　*zasshi*, magazine 週刊誌 *shūkanshi*, weekly 　　　　magazine 地誌　　*chishi*, a topography
891 14 strokes	計	誌	誌	2

磁	一	ア	石	JI, magnet; porcelain
	石	石ソ	砿	磁石　*jishaku*, magnet, compass 磁気　*jiki*, magnetism 磁器　*jiki*, porcelain ware
892 14 strokes	磁	磁	磁	1

射	'	イ	勺	SHA; *i(ru)*, to shoot (an arrow); to strike (one's eyes)
	勺	身	身	射撃　　*shageki*, firing, shooting 発射　　*hassha*, discharge, fire 日射病 *nisshabyō*, sunstroke, 　　　　heatstroke
893 10 strokes	射	射		1

捨	一	扌	扌	SHA; *su(teru)*, to throw away, to abandon
	扲	拾	拎	捨て子 *sutego*, abandoned child 喜捨　　*kisha*, charity, alms 取捨　　*shusha*, adoption or 　　　　rejection; choice
894 11 strokes	拎	捨	捨	2

179

尺 895 4 strokes	ㄱ 尺	ㄱ	ㄹ	SHAKU, old unit of length (approx 30 cm); length 尺度 *shakudo*, linear measure, scale, gauge 尺貫法 *shakkanhō*, Japanese system of weights and measures 尺八 *shakuhachi*, shakuhachi flute [1]
若 896 8 strokes	一 サ 若	十 芋 若	艹 芋	JAKU; *waka(i)*, young; immature; *mo(shikuwa)*, or 若者 *wakamono*, young people 若々しい *wakawakashii*, youthful, young-looking 若干 *jakkan*, some, a few, a little ☑ [3]
樹 897 16 strokes	木 杧 桔	杧 桔 椬	枓 桔 樹	JU, tree, plant; *ki*, tree 樹木 *jumoku*, trees and shrubs 樹脂 *jushi*, resin 樹立 *juritsu*, establishment, founding [1]
収 898 4 strokes	ㅣ 収	ㅐ	収	SHŪ; *osa(meru)*, to obtain, to pay (taxes), to accept, to store, to seize; *osa(maru)*, to be restored, contented 収穫 *shūkaku*, harvest 収容 *shūyō*, admission, accommodation 収入 *shūnyū*, income [3]
宗 899 8 strokes	` 宀 宗	丷 宀 宗	宀 宁	SHŪ, SŌ, foundation, source, origin 宗教 *shūkyō*, religion 宗派 *shūha*, sect 宗匠 *sōshō*, master (in an art), teacher [1]

180

就	丶	古	亠	SHŪ, JU, to sit, to engage in, to be completed; *tsu(ku)*, to engage in, to set about (a job)
	京	京	京	就学　　*shūgaku*, entering school 就職　　*shūshoku*, finding 　　　　　employment
900 12 strokes	京	就	就	成就　　*jōju*, accomplishment, 　　　　　realization　　　　　1

衆	宀	血	血	SHŪ, many
	血	卒	卆	衆議院　*Shūgi-in*, House of 　　　　　Representatives 観衆　　*kanshū*, spectators
901 12 strokes	尞	衆	衆	民衆　　*minshū*, the masses　1

従	ノ	彳	彳	JŪ; *shitaga(u)*, to obey, to comply with, to observe (rules), to yield to, to follow
	彳	彳	彳	服従　　*fukujū*, obedience 従事　　*jūji*, engaging in (business)
902 10 strokes	従	従	従	従業員　*jūgyōin*, employee　1

縦	く	幺	幺	JŪ; *tate*, length, height; warp
	糸	糸	紛	操縦　　*sōjū*, handling, operation 縦書き　*tategaki*, vertical script 縦横　　*tateyoko*, *jūō*, length and 　　　　　breadth
903 16 strokes	絆	縦	縦	1

縮	く	幺	幺	SHUKU; *chiji(meru)*, to shrink (v.t.); *chiji(mu)*, *chiji(maru)*, to shrink (v.i.); *chiji(reru)*, to be frizzy, wavy
	糸	糸'	紵	縮小　　*shukushō*, reduction, 　　　　　curtailment, retrenchment
904 17 strokes	紵	縮	縮	縮れ毛　*chijirege*, curly hair 軍縮　　*gunshuku*, arms reduction　1

181

熟	亠	亯	亭	JUKU; *juku(suru)*, *u(reru)*, to ripen, to mature
	享	孰	孰	成熟　*seijuku*, ripeness, maturation 未熟　*mijuku*, immature 熟練　*jukuren*, skill, dexterity, mastery
905 15 strokes	孰	熟	熟	[1]
純	く	幺	幺	JUN, purity, innocence
	糸	糸	糹	単純　*tanjun*, simple 純粋　*junsui*, pure, genuine 純和風　*jun-wafū*, purely Japanese style
906 10 strokes	紅	純	純	[2]
処	ノ	ク	久	SHO; *sho(suru)*, to manage, to deal with, to sentence, to conduct oneself
	処	処		処理　*shori*, management, transaction 処置　*shochi*, measure, treatment (medical)
907 5 strokes				処分　*shobun*, disposal, punishment　[3]
署	冖	罒	罒	SHO, station (police, fire, etc.); (public) office; write, sign
	罒	里	罗	警察署　*keisatsusho*, police station 署長　*shochō*, head of a government office
908 13 strokes	署	署	署	署名　*shomei*, signature　[2]
諸	言	言	計	SHO, many
	計	訐	訐	諸国　*shokoku*, various countries 諸君　*shokun*, gentlemen, you 諸島　*shotō*, group of islands
909 15 strokes	諸	諸	諸	[2]

除

910
10 strokes

JO, JI, division (math.); *nozo(ku)*, to take off, to remove, to exclude, to omit

除幕式 *jomakushiki*, unveiling ceremony
除名 *jomei*, dismissal from membership
駆除 *kujo*, extermination

3

将

911
10 strokes

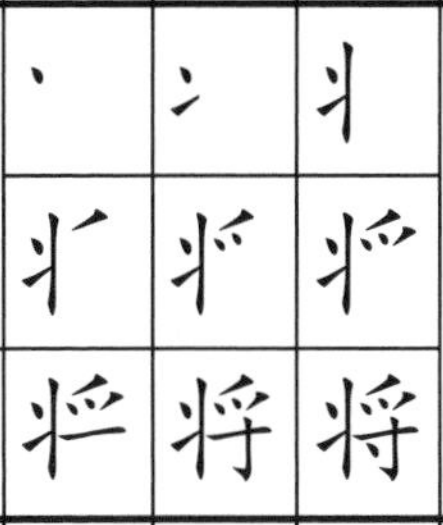

SHŌ, to lead; about to

大将 *taishō*, a general, leader
将棋 *shōgi*, Japanese chess
将来 *shōrai*, the future

2

傷

912
13 strokes

SHŌ; *kizu*, wound, injury, cut; *kizu(tsukeru)*, to injure; *kizu(tsuku)*, to get injured; *ita(mu)*, to be painful

傷害 *shōgai*, wound, injury, accident
死傷者 *shishōsha*, casualties
傷跡 *kizuato*, scar

1

障

913
14 strokes

SHŌ, to hinder; to separate; *sawa(ru)*, to hinder, to interfere with, to harm

障害 *shōgai*, obstacle, impediment
故障 *koshō*, obstacle, impediment, breakdown
障子 *shōji*, paper sliding door

1

城

914
9 strokes

JŌ; *shiro*, castle

城跡 *shiroato*, castle ruins/site
城下町 *jōkamachi*, castle town
姫路城 *Himeji-jō*, Himeji Castle

2

蒸	一	艹	艹	JŌ; *mu(su)*, to steam, be steamy; *mu(rasu)*, to steam (v.t.); *mu(reru)*, to be steamed, steamy, stuffy, musty (v.i.)
	芗	茅	茅	
915 13 strokes	茲	蒸	蒸	蒸気　　　*jōki*, steam, vapour 蒸し暑い　*mushiatsui*, hot and muggy 蒸発　　　*jōhatsu*, evaporation, 　　　　　　strange disappearance ②

針	ノ	𠂉	𠂉	SHIN; *hari*, needle, pin, pointer
	牟	余	金	針金　　*harigane*, wire 方針　　*hōshin*, policy, line 秒針　　*byōshin*, second-hand (of a 　　　　　watch)
916 10 strokes	金	金	針	②

仁	ノ	イ	仁	JIN, perfect virtue, benevolence, humanity
	仁			仁徳　　*jintoku*, benevolence 仁義　　*jingi*, humanity and justice, 　　　　　humanity, duty, gamblers' 　　　　　moral code
917 4 strokes				仁愛　　*jin'ai*, benevolence ①

垂	一	二	三	SUI; *ta(reru)*, to hang down, dangle (v.i.); *ta(rasu)*, to drip, dribble, spill (v.t.)
	𠂆	乒	岳	垂直の　　*suichoku*, vertical, 　　　　　　perpendicular 雨垂れ　　*amadare*, raindrops, 　　　　　　eavesdrops
918 8 strokes	垂	垂		垂れ飾り *tarekazari*, pendant ①

推	一	扌	扌	SUI; *o(su)*, to infer, to guess, to recommend, to boost (a candidate)
	扣	扩	扩	推理　　*suiri*, reasoning 推定　　*suitei*, inference, 　　　　　presumption
919 11 strokes	扗	推	推	推薦　　*suisen*, recommendation ①

寸	一	寸	寸	**SUN**, old unit of length (approx. 3 cm) 寸法　*sunpō*, measurements; plan 寸分　*sunbun*, a little 寸前　*sunzen*, just before
920 3 strokes				1
盛	ノ 成 盛	厂 成 盛	厉 盛 盛	**SEI, JŌ**, abundant, plentiful; *mo(ru)*, to pile up; *saka(n)*, prosperous; *saka(ri)*, prime, heyday 盛大　*seidai*, splendid, prosperous 大盛り　*ōmori*, large serve, helping 繁盛　*hanjō*, prosperity, success
921 11 strokes				1
聖	一 耳	丁 耳	匸 耶	**SEI**, sage, saint 聖人　*seijin*, sage, saint 聖書　*seisho*, the Bible 神聖　*shinsei*, sacred, holy
922 13 strokes	耶	聖	聖	1
誠	一 訁	言 訂	言 訪	**SEI**; *makoto*, sincerity, truth 誠実　*seijitsu*, sincerity, faithfulness 誠意　*sei-i*, sincerity, good faith 至誠　*shisei*, sincerity, one's true heart
923 13 strokes	試	誠	誠	1
宣	丶 宀	ソ 宀	宀 官	**SEN**, to promulgate, to state 宣言　*sengen*, declaration 宣伝　*senden*, propaganda 宣教師　*senkyōshi*, missionary
924 9 strokes	官	官	宣	1

185

専	一	厂	万	SEN, sole, exclusive; *moppa(ra)*, wholly, exclusively
	万	甹	申	専門 *senmon*, specialty 専用 *sen'yō*, exclusive use 専売 *senbai*, monopoly
925 9 strokes	亩	専	専	☑ 2

泉	'	⺊	白	SEN; *izumi*, spring, fountain, source
	白	白	臬	温泉 *onsen*, hot spring 泉水 *sensui*, garden pond, fountain
926 9 strokes	臬	泉	泉	源泉 *gensen*, source, origin 2

洗	'	⺀	氵	SEN; *ara(u)*, to wash, cleanse
	氵	汇	汁	洗濯 *sentaku*, washing, laundry 洗剤 *senzai*, washing powder 洗練 *senren*, polishing, refinement
927 9 strokes	洪	泆	洗	☑ 3

染	'	⺀	氵	SEN; *so(meru)*, to dye; *shi(miru)*, to pierce, to penetrate, to soak into; to smart; *shi(mi)*, a stain
	氵	氿	洂	染料 *senryō*, dyestuffs, dyes 染み抜き *shiminuki*, stain remover
928 9 strokes	染	染	染	汚染 *osen*, pollution 1

善	'	⺀	꼭	ZEN, good, goodness, virtue; *yo(i)*, virtuous, goodnatured
	꼭	羊	羊	親善 *shinzen*, amity, friendship 最善 *saizen*, the best
929 12 strokes	羊	善	善	慈善 *jizen*, charity 1

奏

930
9 strokes

SŌ; *kana(deru)*, to play/perform on (an instrument)

演奏	*ensō*, (musical) performance, recital
伴奏	*bansō*, (musical) accompainment
合奏	*gassō*, concert, ensemble

1

窓

931
11 strokes

SŌ; *mado*, window

窓口	*madoguchi*, service window
同窓会	*dōsōkai*, alumni association
窓際	*madogiwa*, by the window

3

創

932
12 strokes

SŌ, *tsukuru*, origin, beginning

創立	*sōritsu*, establishment
創作	*sōsaku*, literary creation, original work
独創的	*dokusōteki*, original, creative

1

装

933
12 strokes

SŌ, SHŌ; *yoso-o(u)*, to dress, wear; to pretend

装置	*sōchi*, equipment, device
衣装	*ishō*, clothes, costume
変装	*hensō*, disguise

2

層

934
14 strokes

SŌ, layer, stratum

下層階級	*kasōkaikyū*, the lower classes
断層	*dansō*, (geological) fault
高層ビル	*kōsō-biru*, high-rise building

2

操	一	寸	扌	SŌ, to grasp, to manage, principle; *misao*, chastity, virtue; *ayatsu(ru)*, to operate (machine), manipulate
	扌	护	押	操作　　　*sōsa*, manipulation, operation
935 16 strokes	揀	捤	操	操り人形　*ayatsuri-ningyō*, puppet 貞操　　　*teisō*, chastity　　　　[1]

蔵	一	十	艹	ZŌ; *kura*, warehouse; *zō(suru)*, to own, to have
	广	芦	苣	冷蔵庫 *reizōko*, refrigerator 貯蔵　　*chozō*, storage
936 15 strokes	莅	蔵	蔵	蔵書　　*zōsho*, one's library 　　　　　　　　　　　　　　[2]

臓	丿	刀	月	ZŌ, entrails
	肝	肝	肝	肝臓　*kanzō*, the liver 内臓　*naizō*, internal organs 心臓　*shinzō*, the heart
937 19 strokes	肝	臓	臓	[2]

存	一	ナ	才	SON, ZON, to exist; *zon(jiru)*, to know, to think
	疒	存	存	保存　*hozon*, preservation 生存　*seizon*, existence, life, survival
938 6 strokes				存在　*sonzai*, existence, being 　　　　　　　　　　　　　[3]

尊	⺌	兯	丷	SON; *tatto(i)*, noble, valuable; *tatto(bu)*, to respect, to value
	芮	酋	酉	尊敬　*sonkei*, respect 尊重　*sonchō*, respect, deference
939 12 strokes	酋	尊	尊	本尊　*honzon*, principal image, idol 　　　　　　　　　　　　　[2]

宅	丶	宀	宀	TAKU, home; to dwell
	宀	宅	宅	住宅　*jūtaku*, a dwelling, housing 自宅　*jitaku*, one's own home 宅地　*takuchi*, residential land
940 6 strokes				3

担	一	扌	扌	TAN; *katsu(gu)*, to carry on the shoulder; *nina(u)*, to carry; take upon oneself
	扌	扣	担	担架　*tanka*, a stretcher 担当　*tantō*, being in charge (of)
941 8 strokes	担	担		負担　*futan*, burden　　2

探	扌	扌	扩	TAN; *sagu(ru)*, to search, look for, explore; *saga(su)*, to search
	扩	扨	挧	探求　*tankyū*, search, enquiry, research 探検　*tanken*, exploration, expedition
942 11 strokes	挧	探	探	探知　*tanchi*, detection　　3

誕	言	訂	訂	TAN, be born, to give birth
	訂	証	証	誕生日　*tanjōbi*, birthday 降誕　*kōtan*, holy birth 生誕　*seitan*, birth, nativity
943 15 strokes	誕	誕	誕	1

段	丶	厂	广	DAN, platform, step, grade
	阝	阝	阝	階段　*kaidan*, steps, stairs 段階　*dankai*, stage, phase, grade 手段　*shudan*, a means, way
944 9 strokes	阝	段	段	3

暖	丨	日	日丨	DAN; *atata(kai)*, warm; *atata(meru)*, to warm (v.t.); *atata(maru)*, to warm up (v.i.)
	日丷	日丷	日丷	
945 13 strokes	日丷	暖	暖	暖房　　*danbō*, heating 暖流　　*danryū*, warm current 温暖　　*ondan*, warm, mild, temperate　　　　　[1]

値	亻	亻	什	CHI; *ne*, price; *atai*, price, value, merit
	什	佶	佶	値段　　*nedan*, price 価値　　*kachi*, value, worth, merit 数値　　*sūchi*, numerical value
946 10 strokes	侑	値	値	[3]

宙	丶	丷	宀	CHŪ, heaven, sky, space, air
	宀	宀	宙	宇宙　　*uchū*, the universe, space 宙返り　*chūgaeri*, somersault 航宙　　*kōchū*, space flight
947 8 strokes	宙	宙		[1]

忠	丶	冖	口	CHŪ, loyalty, faithfulness
	中	中	忠	忠告　　*chūkoku*, (friendly) advice 忠義　　*chūgi*, loyalty 忠実　　*chūjitsu*, faithful
948 8 strokes	忠	忠		[1]

著	一	十	艹	CHO; *ichijiru(shii)*, remarkable, notable, conspicuous; *ara(wasu)*, to write (a book)
	艹	艹	芏	著書　　*chosho*, book, work 著者　　*chosha*, writer, author 著名　　*chomei*, famous
949 11 strokes	芓	著	著	[2]

| 庁 950 5 strokes | 、 | 亠 | 广 |
| | 广 | 庁 | |

CHŌ, hall, government office

官庁　　kanchō, government office
環境庁　Kankyōchō, Environment
　　　　Agency
庁令　　chōrei, official ordinance

2

頂 951 11 strokes	丁	厂	广
	厂	疒	頂
	頂	頂	頂

CHŌ; itada(ku), to receive (humble),
be capped; itadaki, top, summit

頂点　　chōten, zenith, peak
頂き物　itadakimono, a gift one has
　　　　received
絶頂　　zetchō, summit (of
　　　　mountain); zenith

3

潮 952 15 strokes	氵	氵	泮
	洺	渣	淖
	潮	潮	潮

CHŌ; shio, tide, seawater

潮流　chōryū, tide, current; trend
満潮　manchō, high tide
潮風　shiokaze, sea breeze

1

賃 953 13 strokes	ノ	イ	仁
	仁	任	任
	侼	眚	賃

CHIN, wages, rent

賃金　　chingin, wages
家賃　　yachin, house rent
電車賃　denshachin, carfare

1

痛 954 12 strokes	、	广	疒
	疒	疒	疔
	疖	痛	痛

TSŪ; ita(mu), to feel pain, ache;
ita(i), painful

頭痛　zutsū, headache
苦痛　kutsū, pain, anguish
痛烈　tsūretsu, severe, bitter,
　　　scathing

✓ 3

展	⁷	コ	尸	**TEN, to open, to exhibit** 展望車 *tenbōsha*, observation car 発展 *hatten*, expansion, development, prosperity 展示会 *tenjikai*, exhibition
	尸	屏	屈	
955 10 strokes	展	展	展	☐1
討	、	二	三	**TŌ; *u(tsu)*, to subjugate, to attack** 検討 *kentō*, examination, investigation 討論 *tōron*, debate 討議 *tōgi*, discussion
	言	言	討	
956 10 strokes	討			☐1
党	⼁	⺉	⺍	**TŌ, party, faction** 政党 *seitō*, political party 党派 *tōha*, party, faction, clique 悪党 *akutō*, bad guy 甘党 *amatō*, sweet tooth
	⺍	屵	씃	
957 10 strokes	尚	労	党	☐2
糖	丶	丷	半	**TŌ, sugar** 砂糖 *satō*, sugar 糖分 *tōbun*, sugar content 糖尿病 *tōnyōbyō*, diabetes
	米	籵	籵	
958 16 strokes	粏	糘	糖	☐1
届	⁷	コ	尸	*todo(ku)*, to reach; *todo(keru)*, to forward, to send, to report 欠席届け *kessekitodoke*, notice of one's absence 届け先 *todokesaki*, receiver's address 行き届く *yukitodoku*, to be attentive (to details), to be careful
	尺	吊	吊	
959 8 strokes	届	届		☐2

難	一	サ	古	NAN, disaster, difficulty; *kata(i)*, difficult, impossible; *muzuka(shii)*, difficult
	莒	菓	菓	難破 *nanpa*, shipwreck 非難 *hinan*, (adverse) criticism, censure
960 18 strokes	斳	斳	難	困難 *konnan*, difficulty, trouble, suffering ☑ ③

乳	ノ	⺆	⺈	NYŪ; *chi-*, *chichi*, milk, breasts
	⺥	孚	孚	牛乳 *gyūnyū*, milk 乳製品 *nyūseihin*, dairy products 乳首 *chikubi*, *chichikubi*, nipple
961 8 strokes	孚	乳		②

認	亠	言	言	NIN; *mito(meru)*, to see, to recognize; to approve of, to judge, to regard (as)
	訂	訒	認	承認 *shōnin*, approval, consent, recognition
962 14 strokes	認	認	認	公認 *kōnin*, official recognition 認識 *ninshiki*, cognition ③

納	⼂	幺	幺	NŌ, NA, TŌ; *osa(meru)*, to put away, to pay, to supply, to dedicate, to obtain, to accept, to put back
	幺	糸	糹	納入 *nōnyū*, payment, delivery 納屋 *naya*, barn
963 10 strokes	納	納	納	出納 *suitō*, receipts and disbursements ①

脳	ノ	月	月	NŌ, brain(s)
	月	肦	肦	頭脳 *zunō*, brain(s) 主脳 *shunō*, focus 脳障害 *nōshōgai*, brain injury
964 11 strokes	肦	脳	脳	②

派	丶	冫	氵	HA, group, party, school
	汀	沪	沪	左派　　　　*saha*, left wing, radical 派遣　　　　*haken*, dispatch
965 9 strokes	沂	浙	派	[1]

拝	一	扌	扌	HAI; *oga(mu)*, to worship, to pray to
	扩	扩	扩	拝見　　　　*haiken*, inspection, looking 　　　　　　over (polite speech) 拝啓　　　　*haikei*, Dear Sir, Dear 　　　　　　Madam, etc. (salutation in a 　　　　　　letter)
966 8 strokes	拝	拝		参拝　　　　*sanpai*, worship　　　　[2]

背	丶	丬	北	HAI; *se*, the back, stature, behind; *sei*, stature, height; *somu(ku)*, to disobey, rebel; *somu(keru)*, to turn one's back
	北	北	北	背景　　　　*haikei*, background, setting; 　　　　　　affiliations 背中　　　　*senaka*, the back
967 9 strokes	背	背	背	背が高い　*se/sei ga takai*, 　　　　　　be tall　　　　　　[✓][3]

肺	丿	几	月	HAI, lung(s)
	月	月'	肝	肺臓　　　　*haizō*, the lungs 肺病　　　　*haibyō*, lung disease 肺炎　　　　*haien*, pneumonia
968 9 strokes	肝	肺	肺	[1]

俳	丿	亻	亻	HAI, amusement; actor
	亻	俳	俳	俳句　　　　*haiku*, 17-syllable Japanese 　　　　　　verse 俳味　　　　*haimi*, refined taste
969 10 strokes	俳	俳	俳	俳優　　　　*haiyū*, actor　　　　　[1]

班	一	丁	王	HAN, squad, group
				救護班　*kyūgohan*, relief squad
	王	刲	珌	作業班　*sagyōhan*, work squad
970				班長　　*hanchō*, squad leader
10 strokes	珋	珋	班	1

晩	日	日′	日″	BAN, evening, night
				今晩　　*konban*, this evening, tonight
	日″	昡	晄	晩御飯 *bangohan*, evening meal, dinner
971				晩年　　*bannen*, late in life, evening years
12 strokes	晄	晩	晩	✓ 3

否	一	丆	不	HI; *ina*, no
				否定　　*hitei*, denial
	不	丕	否	拒否　　*kyohi*, refusal, rejection
972				安否　　*anpi*, safety, well-being
7 strokes	否			3

批	一	寸	才	HI, to criticize, to comment on; to strike
				批難　　*hinan*, (adverse) criticism
	扌	批	批	批評　　*hihyō*, commentary
973				批判　　*hihan*, comment, criticism
7 strokes	批			1

秘	丿	二	千	HI, secret, mysterious; *hi(meru)*, to conceal
				秘密　　*himitsu*, a secret
	禾	禾	利	神秘　　*shinpi*, mystery
974				秘書　　*hisho*, secretary
10 strokes	秘	秘	秘	1

腹	月	肵	肸	FUKU; *hara*, abdomen, belly; heart, mind
	肪	胪	胪	満腹　　*manpuku*, full stomach 腹立ち　*haradachi*, anger 腹切り　*harakiri*, suicide by 　　　　disembowelment
975 13 strokes	胪	胪	腹	[3]

奮	大	大	否	FUN; *furu(u)*, to rouse oneself
	否	卒	奔	興奮　　*kōfun*, excitement 奮闘　　*funtō*, hard fighting, 　　　　strenuous efforts 発奮　　*happun*, being inspired,
976 16 strokes	奞	奞	奮	rousing oneself [1]

並	、	丷	丷	HEI; *nami*, common, ordinary; *nara(beru)*, to place in order; *nara(bu)*, to form a line/be in line; *nara(bi ni)*, and
	并	并	並	並列　　*heiretsu*, a row 月並み　*tsukinami (no)*, 　　　　commonplace
977 8 strokes	並	並		並木　　*namiki*, row of trees [2]

陛	⁊	⻖	阝	HEI, stairs of a palace
	阝-	阹	阹	陛下　　*heika*, His (Her) Majesty, 　　　　Your Majesty 天皇陛下 *tennō-heika*, His Majesty 　　　　the Emperor (of Japan)
978 10 strokes	陕	陛	陛	皇后陛下 *kōgō-heika*, Her Majesty 　　　　the Empress (of Japan) [1]

閉	丨	冂	冃	HEI; *to(jiru)*, to shut/close (v.t.); *shi(meru)*, to shut/close (v.t.); *shi(maru)*, to shut/close (v.i.)
	冃	門	門	閉店　　*heiten*, closing a shop 閉口　　*heikō (suru)*, be 　　　　dumbfounded
979 11 strokes	門	閉	閉	閉鎖　　*heisa*, closing, lockout [3]

片	ノ	ノ゛	片	HEN; *kata*, piece, scrap; incomplete; one side
	片			断片　　*danpen*, fragment, scrap 破片　　*hahen*, broken piece, splinter (of glass, etc.) 片手　　*katate*, one hand
980 4 strokes				[2]

補	ﾌ	ネ	ネ	HO; *ogina(u)*, to supply, to compensate (for), to supplement
	衤	祈	袻	候補　　*kōho*, candidacy, candidate 補助　　*hojo*, assistance, supplement, subsidy 補給　　*hokyū*, supply
981 12 strokes	袻	補	補	[2]

暮	一	艹	艹	BO; *ku(re)*, nightfall, year-end; end; *ku(reru)*, to grow dark, end; *ku(rasu)*, to make a living
	苧	苩	莒	歳暮　　　　　　*seibo*, end of year, end-of-year present 夕暮れ　　　　　*yūgure*, evening 一人暮らし　*hitorigurashi*, single life, celibacy
982 14 strokes	莫	莫	暮	[3]

宝	、	丷	宀	HŌ; *takara*, treasure, riches
	宀	宁	宇	宝石　　*hōseki*, precious stone, gem 国宝　　*kokuhō*, a national treasure 宝箱　　*takarabako*, treasure chest
983 8 strokes	宝	宝		[2]

訪	、	二	言	HŌ; *otozu(reru)*, *tazu(neru)*, to visit, call on
	言	言	言	訪問　　*hōmon*, visit 来訪　　*raihō*, visit 訪米　　*hōbei*, visiting America
984 11 strokes	訂	訪	訪	[3]

亡	`	亠	亡	BŌ, MŌ, to perish, to flee; *na(ki)*, the late (of deceased persons); *na(kunaru)*, to pass away, die; *na(kusu)*, to lose (a loved one)
985 **3 strokes**				亡命　　*bōmei*, exile 死亡　　*shibō*, death 亡き森氏　*naki Mori-shi*, the late 　　　　　　　Mr Mori　⬚3
忘	`	亠	亡	BŌ; *wasu(reru)*, to forget, leave behind
	亡	忘	忘	忘年会　*bōnenkai*, year-end party 忘れ物　*wasuremono*, a forgotten 　　　　　　　item
986 **7 strokes**	忘			物忘れ　*monowasure*, forgetfulness 　　　　　　　✓⬚3
棒	一	十	木	BŌ, stick, club
	村	杆	棒	鉄棒　　　*tetsubō, kanabō*, iron bar, 　　　　　　　crowbar 棒グラフ　*bōgurafu*, bar graph 編み棒　　*amibō*, knitting needle
987 **12 strokes**	栱	棒	棒	⬚2
枚	一	十	才	MAI, counter for thin or flat objects
	木	朮	朾	枚数　　*maisū*, number of pages 数枚　　*sūmai*, a few (sheets of 　　　　　　paper, shirts, etc.) 枚挙　　*maikyo*, enumerate, count
988 **8 strokes**	朾	枚		✓⬚2
幕	一	艹	昔	MAKU, curtain; act (of a play), BAKU
	茸	苩	莫	幕切れ　*makugire*, fall of the curtain 幕内　　*makunouchi*, high-ranking 　　　　　　sumo wrestlers
989 **13 strokes**	莫	幕	幕	幕府　　*bakufu*, Shogunate 　　　　　　　⬚1

密 990 11 strokes	、	宀	宀	
	少	宓	宓	MITSU, dense, fine (of texture); secret
				綿密　*menmitsu*, detailed, meticulous
	宓	密	密	密度　*mitsudo*, density 秘密　*himitsu*, a secret [1]

盟 991 13 strokes	冂	日	明	MEI, to swear, to pledge
	明	明	眀	連盟　*renmei*, league 同盟　*dōmei*, alliance 加盟　*kamei*, joining (an alliance), participation
	朙	盟	盟	[1]

模 992 14 strokes	一	十	木	MO, BO, mould; to model after
	杧	栉	槙	模範　*mohan*, model, paragon 縮尺模型　*shukushakumokei*, scale model
	槙	模	模	規模　*kibo*, scale, scope [1]

訳 993 11 strokes	、	言	言	YAKU, translation; *wake*, reason, meaning, circumstances; *yaku(suru)*, to translate
	言	言	訂	翻訳　*hon'yaku*, translation 通訳　*tsūyaku*, interpretation, interpreter
	訂	訳	訳	言い訳　*iiwake*, excuse, apology [1]

郵 994 11 strokes	一	二	三	YŪ, posthouse, mail
	舌	岳	垂	郵便　*yūbin*, mail, post 郵便局　*yūbinkyoku*, post office
	垂	郵	郵	郵送　*yūsō*, transport, transportation [2]

優	亻	亻	佰	YŪ, excellent; abundant; actor; *yasa(shii)*, gentle, graceful, kindly; *sugu(reru)*, to excel, be superior
	価	偄	偄	優越　*yūetsu*, superiority, supremacy
995 **17 strokes**	優	優	優	優先　*yūsen*, priority 俳優　*haiyū*, actor　③

幼	ㄥ	ㄠ	ㄠ	YŌ; *osana(i)*, young, childish, immature
	幻	幼		幼児　*yōji*, baby, infant 幼虫　*yōchū*, larva
996 **5 strokes**				幼稚園　*yōchien*, kindergarten　②

欲	丿	八	夕	YOKU, avarice, desire; *hos(suru)* to desire, to wish; *ho(shii)*, want, desire
	父	谷	谷	欲ばり　*yokubari*, greedy person, miser
997 **11 strokes**	谷	欲	欲	欲望　*yokubō*, desire 食欲　*shokuyoku*, appetite　③

翌	ㄱ	ㄋ	刃	YOKU, the next, the following (day, etc.)
	羽	羽	翌	翌日　*yokujitsu*, the next day 翌年　*yokunen*, the next year
998 **11 strokes**	翌	翌	翌	翌々年　*yokuyokunen*, two years later　②

乱	ノ	二	千	RAN; *mida(reru)*, to fall into disorder/disarray, be corrupt; *mida(su)*, to throw into disorder/disarray, to disturb, to agitate
	千	舌	舌	混乱　*konran*, confusion 乱雑　*ranzatsu*, disorderly, confused
999 **7 strokes**	乱			反乱　*hanran*, rebellion, revolt　②

卵	ˊ	ˊ	ˊ	RAN; *tamago*, egg, spawn; budding, emergent
	夘	夘	夘	卵黄 *ran'ō*, egg yolk 卵白 *ranpaku*, albumen, egg white
1,000 **7 strokes**	卵			生卵 *namatamago*, raw egg <div align="right">2</div>

覧	丨	乛	臣	RAN, to see, to look at
	臣	臣一	臣一	遊覧 *yūran*, sightseeing, excursion 展覧会 *tenrankai*, exhibition
1,001 **17 strokes**	覧	覧	覧	一覧 *ichiran*, a look, check, summary <div align="right">1</div>

裏	一	亠	言	RI; *ura*, reverse side, back, opposite, inner, lining
	审	軍	軍	裏面 *rimen*, back, inside, "behind the scenes" 裏付け *urazuke*, backing, support
1,002 **13 strokes**	裏	裏	裏	裏打ち *urauchi*, backing, lining <div align="right">2</div>

律	ˊ	ˊ	彳	RITSU, law, degree
	彳	彳	彳	法律 *hōritsu*, law 規律 *kiritsu*, order, discipline, regulations
1,003 **9 strokes**	律	律	律	旋律 *senritsu*, melody <div align="right">2</div>

臨	丨	厂	臣	RIN; *nozo(mu)*, to face, to meet, to be present at
	臣	臣	臣	臨終 *rinjū*, the hour of death 臨時 *rinji*, special, extra, temporary
1,004 **18 strokes**	臨	臨	臨	臨席 *rinseki*, attendance <div align="right">1</div>

201

朗	`	㇇	㇆	RŌ; *hoga(raka)*, clear, bright, cheerful, melodious
	自	良	𦨞	朗読 *rōdoku*, reading aloud, recitation 朗報 *rōhō*, glad tidings 明朗 *meirō*, bright, clear, open-hearted
1,005 10 strokes	朗	朗	朗	[1]
論	言	言	言	RON, argument, opinion, essay
	診	論	論	結論 *ketsuron*, conclusion 討論 *tōron*, debate, discussion 理論 *riron*, theory
1,006 15 strokes	論	論	論	[3]

The 2,136
GENERAL-USE CHARACTERS

1 STROKE

| 一 | 1
page 1 | 乙 | OTSU, second in a series, grade B; chic, witty; strange [1] |

2 STROKES

丁	367 page 74	入	28 page 6
七	7 page 2	八	8 page 2
九	9 page 2	刀	198 page 40
了	RYŌ, to come to an end, to understand [2]	力	38 page 8
二	2 page 1	十	10 page 3
人	39 page 8	又	*mata*, and, again, also [1]

3 STROKES

丈	JŌ, old unit of length (3.316 yd.), length; *take*, height, stature [1]	凡	BON, generally, all; roughly, ordinary [1]
与	YO; *ata(eru)*, to give, to award, to supply, to cause (damage), to assign (a task) [3]	刃	JIN; *ha*, edge (of a knife, sword, etc.), blade [1]
万	227 page 46	千	12 page 3
三	3 page 1	及	KYŪ; *oyo(bi)*, and; *oyo(bu)*, to reach, to equal, to extend [1]
下	24 page 5	口	34 page 7
上	23 page 5	土	19 page 4
丸	101 page 21	士	521 page 105
久	676 page 136	夕	54 page 11
乞	*ko(u)*, to ask, request	大	25 page 6
亡	985 page 198	女	41 page 9

子	40 page 9	己	866 page 174
寸	920 page 185	巾	KIN; towel; width
小	27 page 6	干	840 page 169
山	58 page 12	弓	107 page 22
川	59 page 12	才	139 page 28
工	125 page 26		

4 STROKES

不	600 page 121	予	425 page 86
中	26 page 6	互	GO; taga(i), each other, one another, mutual [3]
丹	TAN, cinnabar, red; elixir of life [1]	井	SEI, SHŌ; i (lit.), well (n.) [1]
乏	BŌ; tobo(shii), scanty, short (of food, money) [1]	五	5 page 2

介	KAI, to come between, to aid; *kai(shite)*, through the good offices of [2]	刈	*ka(ru)*, to mow, to reap, to prune, to shear, to cut (hair) [1]
仁	917 page 184	切	173 page 35
仏	805 page 162	分	218 page 44
今	138 page 28	匂	*nio(u)*, fragrant; scent
元	117 page 24	勾	KŌ; be bent
六	6 page 2	化	258 page 52
公	126 page 26	匹	HITSU, an equal; HIKI, suffix for counting small animals, rolls of cloth [2]
円	50 page 11	区	282 page 57
内	207 page 42	升	SHŌ, old unit of capacity (3.81 pt.); *masu*, a unit of measure [1]
冗	JŌ, waste, uselessness, surplus [1]	午	122 page 25
凶	KYŌ, evil, calamity [1]	厄	YAKU, misfortune, disaster [1]

友	234 page 47	幻	GEN; *maboroshi*, vision, phantom 1
双	SŌ, both, pair; to rival; *futa-*, a pair 2	弔	CHŌ; *tomura(i)*, funeral, condolence; *tomura(u)*, to condole, to mourn 1
反	393 page 79	引	81 page 17
収	898 page 180	心	164 page 33
夫	601 page 121	戸	120 page 25
太	181 page 37 1	手	35 page 8
天	67 page 14	支	717 page 144
孔	KŌ, hole; extremely; to pass 1	文	77 page 16
少	160 page 33	斗	TO, old unit of capacity, *it-to* (one-*to*) 19.04 qt 1
尺	895 page 180	斤	KIN, old unit of weight (1.323 lb.) 1
屯	TON, barracks 1	方	223 page 45

日	13 page 3	火	15 page 4
月	14 page 3	▲ 爪	*tsume*, *tsuma*, claw; nail; talon
木	17 page 4	▲ 父	216 page 44
欠	496 page 100	片	980 page 197
止	143 page 29	▲ 牙	GA, GE; *kiba*, tusk, fang
比	792 page 159	牛	108 page 22
毛	230 page 47	犬	73 page 15
氏	522 page 105	王	47 page 10
水	16 page 4		

5 STROKES

| 丙 | HEI, third class, the third in a series, grade | 且 | *ka(tsu)*, besides, moreover, at the same time |

1

丘	KYŪ; *oka*, hill [1]	兄	114 page 23
世	344 page 69	冊	884 page 177
▲ 丼	*donburi*, *don*, bowl; bowl of food	写	313 page 63
主	315 page 64	冬	199 page 40
以	443 page 89	処	907 page 182
仙	SEN, hermit, wizard [1]	凸	TOTSU, convex [1]
令	633 page 127	凹	Ō, concave [1]
他	354 page 71	出	29 page 6
仕	301 page 61	刊	666 page 134
付	602 page 121	功	502 page 101
代	358 page 72	加	453 page 91

包	611 page 123	台	183 page 37
北	224 page 45	右	22 page 5
半	214 page 43	可	655 page 132
占	SEN; *urana(i)*, divination; *urana(u)*, to divine; *shi(meru)*, to occupy, to hold (a seat) 2	古	121 page 25
去	276 page 56	囚	SHŪ, to capture; captivity, slavery, prisoner 1
叱	SHITSU; *shika(ru)*, scold	四	4 page 1
号	297 page 60	圧	641 page 129
句	683 page 137	外	96 page 20
召	SHŌ; *me(su)*, honorific for "to wear," "to summon" 2	央	254 page 51
史	523 page 105	失	529 page 106
司	524 page 105	奴	DO, manservant, fellow, guy 1

尼	NI; *ama*, nun [1]	弁	807 page 162
▲ 尻	*shiri*, buttocks, rear end; hips	必	597 page 120
巧	KŌ; *taku(mi)*, skill [1]	払	FUTSU; *hara(u)*, to pay, to clear away, to lop off (branches), to dispose [3]
巨	KYO, many, much, huge, gigantic [2]	打	355 page 72
左	21 page 5	斥	SEKI, to drive away, to keep away, to refuse [1]
布	799 page 160	▲ 旦	TAN, DAN; dawn; morning
市	144 page 29	旧	677 page 136
平	411 page 83	札	513 page 103
幼	996 page 200	末	615 page 124
庁	950 page 191	未	617 page 124
広	127 page 26	本	76 page 16

正	79 page 16	甘	KAN; *ama(i)*, sweet, indulgent, flattering, over-optimistic, easy to deal with [2]
母	222 page 45	生	44 page 9
民	619 page 124	用	235 page 48
永	644 page 129	由	421 page 85
氷	401 page 81	甲	KŌ, grade A, the former; back (of the hand); shell (of a tortoise); KAN [1]
▲ 氾	HAN; spread out; wide	申	338 page 68
汁	JŪ; *shiru*, soup, juice, gravy [1]	田	60 page 13
犯	789 page 158	白	53 page 11
玄	GEN, dark, black, abstruse; heaven; quiet [1]	皮	396 page 80
玉	48 page 10	皿	300 page 61
▲ 瓦	GA; *kawara*, tile	目	30 page 7

矛	MU; *hoko*, halberd [1]	穴	860 page 173
矢	145 page 30	立	37 page 8
石	72 page 15	込	*ko(mu)*, to be crowded; *ko(meru)*, to load (a gun), to include; to concentrate (on) [3]
示	723 page 145	辺	608 page 122
礼	436 page 88		

6 STROKES

両	434 page 87	伎	KI, GI; skill
争	558 page 112	企	KI; *kuwada(te)*, attempt, plan, intrigue; *kuwada(teru)*, to attempt, to plan [1]
交	128 page 26	任	785 page 158
件	687 page 138	仰	GYŌ, KŌ; *ao(gu)*, to look up at (to), to ask for; *ō(se)*, another's word or instructions [1]
伐	BATSU, to attack, to fell; to boast	伏	FUKU; *fu(seru)*, to turn over (v.t.), to cover, to conceal, to lay (an ambush) [1]

仲	571 page 115	再	706 page 142
伝	580 page 117	列	437 page 88
休	80 page 17	刑	KEI, punishment, penalty [1]
会	93 page 19	劣	RETSU, *oto(ru)*, be inferior to, be worse than
仮	656 page 132	匠	SHŌ, workman, artisan; idea *takumi*, artisan, master
全	347 page 70	危	844 page169
兆	573 page 115	印	448 page 90
充	JŪ, to fill; *a(teru)*, to allot, to appropriate [1]	后	869 page 174
光	129 page 26	吏	RI an official [1]
先	43 page 9	叫	KYŌ; *sake(bu)*, to exclaim, to shout, to cry for [2]
共	484 page 97	吐	TO; *ha(ku)*, to vomit, to spew, to emit, to confess, to express [1]

吉	KICHI, good luck, good omen; KITSU [1]	在	711 page 143
向	294 page 59	地	184 page 37
吸	849 page 170	多	180 page 37
各	462 page 93	妃	HI, empress, married princess [1]
合	134 page 27	妄	MŌ, BŌ, arbitrary, reckless [1]
名	55 page 12	如	JO, NYO, as if, looking like; to equal, to reach [1]
同	204 page 41	好	503 page 101
因	643 page 129	存	938 page 188
団	772 page 155	字	78 page 16
回	92 page 19	宅	940 page 189
壮	SŌ, powerful, influential, brave [1]	宇	829 page 166

守	316 page 64	忙	BŌ; *isoga(shii)*, busy [3]
安	242 page 49	成	545 page 110
寺	149 page 30	扱	*atsuka(u)*, to deal with, to receive, to manage, to deal in, to work (manipulate) [1]
尽	JIN; *tsu(kusu)*, to render service to; to exhaust, to use up; *tsu(kiru)*, to be used up [1]	旨	SHI; *mune*, purport, effect, principle, command [1]
巡	JUN; *megu(ru)*, to go one's rounds, to patrol, to travel about [1]	旬	JUN, period of ten days; SHUN, in season [1]
州	320 page 65	曲	279 page 56
帆	HAN; *ho*, sail, canvas [1]	早	56 page 12
年	20 page 5	机	845 page 170
弐	NI, two (used in legal documents) [1]	朴	BOKU, simple, plain [1]
式	311 page 63	朽	KYŪ; *ku(chiru)*, to rot, to perish, to remain in obscurity [1]
当	200 page 41	朱	SHU, cinnabar, vermilion [1]

次	308 page 62	百	11 page 3
死	302 page 61	竹	71 page 15
毎	225 page 46	米	220 page 45
気	68 page 14	糸	75 page 16
池	185 page 38	缶	KAN, a can ②
汎	HAN; pan-	羊	426 page 86
江	KŌ, *e*, inlet, bay	羽	82 page 17
汗	KAN, *ase*, sweat	老	638 page 128
汚	O, *kitana(i)*, dirt, *kega(reru)*, to get dirty, *yogo(su)* to stain	考	130 page 27
灯	583 page 117	耳	32 page 7
灰	834 page 167	肉	209 page 42

肌	*hada*, skin ②	芝	*shiba*, turf, grass ①
有	423 page 85	芋	*imo*, taro, Irish potato, sweet potato, etc. ①
自	150 page 31	虫	74 page 15
至	886 page 178	血	288 page 58
臼	KYŪ; *usu*, mortar	行	131 page 27
舌	755 page 152	衣	444 page 89
舟	SHŪ; *fune*, boat, ship ②	西	169 page 34
色	162 page 33	迅	JIN, swift, quick, fast ①

7 STROKES

串	*kushi*, spit, skewer	亜	A, sub~, near~ (used as prefix); Asia ①
乱	999 page 200	似	724 page 145

但	*tada(shi)*, but, provided (that) [1]	余	820 page 165
佐	SA, to help [1]	何	86 page 18
伺	SHI; *ukaga(u)*, to visit, to ask, to hear [2]	克	KOKU, to be able to do, to conquer [1]
伴	HAN, BAN; *tomo(nau)*, to accompany, to take with [1]	児	526 page 106
伯	HAKU, a count, a chief, elder brother [1]	兵	606 page 122
位	445 page 90	冶	YA; melting
伸	SHIN; *no(beru)*, to extend; to spread; *no(biru)*, to extend, to grow; to collapse (v.i.); *no(basu)*, to lengthen, to stretch [2]	冷	634 page 127
住	325 page 66	初	535 page 108
体	182 page 37	別	607 page 122
低	575 page 116	判	790 page 159
作	141 page 29	利	626 page 126

助	330 page 67	呉	GO, ancient province of China [1]
努	582 page 117	否	972 page 195
励	REI; hage(mu), to strive, to make an effort [1]	含	GAN; fuku(mu), to contain, to include, to keep in one's mouth, to harbor, to cherish [2]
労	639 page 128	告	507 page 102
医	244 page 49	君	285 page 58
却	KYAKU, to reject, to withdraw [1]	吹	SUI; fu(ku); to blow, to breathe out, to play (a wind instrument), to talk big [3]
卵	1,000 page 201	囲	446 page 90
即	SOKU, at once; namely, nothing but; accession [1]	困	878 page 176
▲ 呂	RO; backbone	図	167 page 34
呈	TEI; tei(suru), to offer (congratulations), to present (a tragic sight) [1]	壱	ICHI, one (used in legal documents) [1]
吟	GIN; gin(jiru), to recite (a poem) [1]	坂	394 page 79

坊	BŌ, sonny, boy, priest, priest's lodge [2]	完	464 page 93
坑	KŌ, hole, mine pit, cave [1]	寿	JU; *kotobuki*, congratulations; longevity [1]
均	681 page 137	対	356 page 72
声	170 page 35	尿	NYŌ, urine [1]
売	211 page 43	尾	BI, suffix for counting fish; *o*, tail, ridge, trail (of a shooting star) [1]
妨	BŌ; *samata(geru)*, to obstruct, to disturb, to prevent [1]	局	280 page 57
妥	DA, peaceful, calm [1]	岐	KI, fork of a road [1]
妊	NIN, to conceive, to become pregnant [1]	希	470 page 95
▲妖	YŌ, *aya(shii)*, attractive; bewitching	序	734 page 147
妙	MYŌ, strange, mysterious; clever, admirable [1]	床	SHŌ; *toko*, bed, alcove; *yuka*, floor [3]
孝	870 page 175	廷	TEI, public office [1]

221

▲ 弄	RŌ, *rō(suru)*, *moteaso(bu)*, play with; trifle with	我	833 page 167
弟	194 page 39	戻	REI; *modo(ru)*, to return, go back; *modo(su)*, to give back, restore [3]
形	115 page 24	把	HA, bundle, sheaf, to grasp [1]
役	419 page 84	批	973 page 195
忘	986 page 198	抄	SHŌ, to excerpt; extract, excerpt [1]
志	718 page 144	扶	FU, to help [1]
忌	KI; *i(mu)*, to abhor, to detest, to avoid, to taboo; *i(mawashii)*, odious, offensive [1]	抑	YOKU, to restrain, to hold down, to stop; *osa(eru)*, to hold down, to restrain [1]
忍	NIN; *shino(bu)*, to endure (pain); *shino(baseru)*, to conceal [1]	抗	KŌ, to resist, to confront [1]
応	651 page 131	技	673 page 135
快	661 page 133	折	551 page 111
戒	KAI; *imashi(meru)*, to admonish, to warn; *imashi(me)*, admonition, warning, lesson [1]	投	378 page 76

抜	BATSU; *nu(ku)*, to pull out, to outstrip, to omit, to remove, to capture [3]	求	478 page 96
択	TAKU, to choose, to select, to sort out [1]	汰	TA; luxury; select
攻	KŌ; *se(meru)*, to attack, to assault; *se(me)*, attack [1]	沃	YOKU; fertility
改	458 page 92	沢	TAKU; *sawa*, marsh, swamp [1]
更	KŌ, to renew, reform; *sara(ni)*, again, still more; *fu(keru)*, to grow late [3]	▲ 沙	SA; sand
材	511 page 103	沖	CHŪ; *oki*, offing, open sea [1]
杉	*sugi*, cryptomeria, a Japanese cedar [1]	没	BOTSU, rejection (of a manuscript); *bos(suru)*, to sink, to set (sun), to die [1]
村	62 page 13	汽	104 page 21
▲ 束	561 page 113	沈	CHIN; *shizu(mu)*, to sink, to feel depressed [2]
▲ 条	738 page 148	決	289 page 58
来	237 page 48	災	707 page 142

状	739 page 148	肝	KAN, vital point; *kimo*, the liver; pluck, mind [1]
狂	KYŌ, ~addict; *kuru(i)*, disorder, warp; *kuru(u)*, to go mad, to get out of order [1]	臣	543 page 109
町	61 page 13	良	628 page 126
男	42 page 9	▲ 芯	SHIN; wick; core
社	153 page 31	芸	495 page 100
秀	SHŪ, excellent; to surpass, to excel; *hii(deru)*, to surpass, to excel [1]	芳	HŌ; *kanba(shii)*, fragrant [1]
私	887 page 178	花	70 page 15
究	271 page 55	見	31 page 7
▲ 系	855 page 172	角	97 page 20
肖	SHŌ, to resemble, to pattern after, to copy after [1]	言	118 page 24
肘	*hiji*, elbow; arm	谷	135 page 28

豆	379 page 76	返	412 page 83
貝	49 page 10	近	113 page 23
▲ 那		51 page 11	NA, what
赤	51 page 11	那	NA, what
走	179 page 36	邦	HŌ, country, land, Japan [1]
足	36 page 8	里	238 page 48
身	339 page 68	▲ 阪	HAN; *saka*, slope; incline
車	63 page 13	防	812 page 163
辛	SHIN, bitter, hard, severe; *kara(i)*, pungent, spicy, hot, salty [2]	麦	213 page 43
迎	GEI; *muka(eru)*, to meet, to welcome, to invite; *muka(e)*, meeting, greeter [3]		

8 STROKES

並	977 page 196	乳	961 page 193

事	309 page 62	供	850 page 171
享	KYŌ, to receive, to enjoy [1]	使	303 page 61
京	110 page 23	免	MEN, exempt; *manuka(reru)*, to avoid, to be exempt [1]
侮	BU; *anado(ru)*, to look down upon, to hold in contempt [1]	具	284 page 57
価	657 page 132	典	579 page 116
舎	727 page 146	券	688 page 138
併	HEI; *awa(seru)*, to amalgamate, to combine [1]	▲ 刹	SATSU, SETSU; temple
依	I, E, to depend on [2]	到	TŌ, to reach, to go or come to [3]
侍	JI, samurai; *ji(suru)*, to attend on [1]	刷	514 page 103
例	635 page 128	刺	SHI, name card; thorn, splinter; *sa(su)*, to sting, to pierce, to stab [2]
佳	KA, good, beautiful [1]	制	744 page 149

226

刻	875 page 176	味	415 page 84
劾	GAI, to investigate thoroughly [1]	命	416 page 84
効	697 page 140	周	532 page 107
卒	564 page 113	呼	867 page 174
卓	TAKU, to excel, to surpass; table, desk [1]	和	440 page 89
協	485 page 98	固	501 page 101
参	517 page 104	国	136 page 28
叔	SHUKU, younger brother of one's parent [1]	坪	tsubo, old unit of area (3.952 sq. yd.) [1]
受	319 page 64	垂	918 page 184
取	317 page 64	夜	232 page 47
▲ 呪	JU; noro(u), spell; curse; incantation	▲ 奈	NA; what

227

奔	HON, to run, to rush [1]	学	45 page 10
奉	HŌ; *hō(jiru)*, to serve, to obey; *tatematsu(ru)*, to dedicate, to offer [1]	宙	947 page 190
奇	KI, unusual, rare, surpassing, strange, mysterious [1]	▲ 宛	EN; *a(teru)*, address
姓	SEI, surname, family name; SHŌ [2]	宗	899 page 180
▲ 妬	TO; *neta(mu)*, jealous; envy	官	465 page 94
妹	226 page 46	定	371 page 75
妻	708 page 142	宜	GI, all right, good, just, proper, natural [1]
姉	146 page 30	実	312 page 63
始	304 page 61	宝	983 page 197
委	245 page 50	尚	SHŌ; *nao*, furthermore, yet [1]
季	471 page 95	届	959 page 192

228

屈	KUTSU; *kus(suru)*, to yield to, to be daunted, to bend [1]	延	831 page 167
居	678 page 136	弦	GEN, *tsuru*, string (for musical instruments), bowstring, chord [1]
岳	GAKU; *take* (lit.), peak, mountain [1]	▲弥	*ya*; all the more; increasingly
岬	*misaki*, cape, promontory [1]	径	492 page 99
岸	267 page 54	征	SEI, to subjugate [1]
▲岡	*oka*, hill, knoll	彼	HI; *kare*, he; *ka(no)*, that [3]
岩	102 page 21	往	652 page 131
幸	295 page 60	念	590 page 119
府	603 page 121	忠	948 page 190
底	576 page 116	怖	FU, to fear, to be afraid; *kowa(i)*, frightening, afraid [3]
店	195 page 40	怪	KAI, mystery, apparition; *aya(shii)*, suspicious; *aya(shimu)*, to doubt, to suspect [1]

性	745 page 150	披	HI, open [1]
房	BŌ, chamber, house; *fusa*, cluster, tuft, fringe [1]	拡	835 page 168
所	328 page 66	抽	CHŪ, to draw out, to pull [1]
拒	KYO; *koba(mu)*, to refuse, to decline, to resist, to deny [1]	抵	TEI, to touch, to go against [1]
承	736 page 148	担	941 page 189
拐	KAI, to falsify, to kidnap [1]	拙	SETSU, *tsutana(i)*, clumsy, unskillful, inexpert [1]
▲ 拉	RATSU, *ras(suru)*, drag along; kidnap	拘	KŌ, to catch, to affect, to adhere to [1]
抹	MATSU, to erase, to rub [1]	招	735 page 148
拠	KYO, KO to depend on, to be based on, to hold; foundation, ground, authority [1]	抱	HŌ; *da(ku)*, to hug; *ida(ku)*, to hold (a belief); *kaka(eru)*, to employ, hold [3]
拍	HAKU, HYŌ to clap; musical time, beat [1]	拝	966 page 194
拓	TAKU, clearing, reclamation; production of copies by rubbing [1]	押	Ō; *o(su)*, to push, to press; *o(shi)*, influence, audacity; *osa(eru)*, to repress [3]

230

放	414 page 83	枢	SŪ, pivot, vital point, center [1]
旺	Ō; flourishing, successful, vigorous	枕	*makura*, pillow
昆	KON, elder brother, posterity; sometimes used for its sound value [1]	林	64 page 13
易	647 page 130	枝	719 page 144
昔	346 page 70	松	536 page 108
昇	SHŌ, to rise, to go up; *nobo(ru)*, to ascend, to rise [2]	果	454 page 91
明	228 page 46	板	395 page 80
析	SEKI, to divide, to tear, to break [1]	東	201 page 41
枚	988 page 198	欧	Ō Europe [2]
枠	*waku*, frame, spindle, limit [1]	歩	221 page 45
杯	HAI, suffix for counting cupfuls, glassfuls, etc.; *sakazuki*, sake cup [3]	武	802 page 161

殴	Ō, to beat, to strike; *nagu(ru)*, to strike, to beat [1]	波	387 page 78
毒	588 page 118	河	658 page 132
況	KYŌ, state of things; still more [2]	注	365 page 74
泳	252 page 51	泣	479 page 96
沼	SHŌ; *numa*, swamp, marsh, bog [1]	泥	DEI; doro, mud [2]
泌	HITSU, HI to ooze out [1]	油	422 page 85
泡	HŌ; *awa*, foam, bubbles [1]	法	612 page 123
沸	FUTSU; *wa(ku)*, to boil, to seethe, to ferment (v.i.) [2]	炉	RO, fireplace, hearth, smelting furnace [1]
沿	832 page 167	炎	EN to burn; *hono-o*, flame, blaze [1]
泊	HAKU; *to(maru)*, to stay overnight, to stop over; *to(meru)*, to lodge (v.t.) [2]	炊	SUI; *ta(ku)*, to cook, to boil [1]
治	527 page 106	版	791 page 159

牧	614 page 123	突	TOTSU, sudden; *tsu(ku)*, to pierce, to thrust, to strike, to attack ③
物	410 page 83	空	66 page 14
▲ 狙	SO; *nera(u)*, aim at; stalk ①	者	314 page 63
▲ 玩	GAN, play, take pleasure in	肪	BŌ, fat, grease, tallow ①
画	91 page 19	肢	SHI, limbs ①
的	578 page 116 ①	肯	KŌ, to consent, to agree; daringly, boldly ②
盲	MŌ; *mekura*, blindness, blind person; ignorance ②	▲ 股	KO; *mata*, thigh; crotch; yarn; strand
直	192 page 39	育	247 page 50
知	186 page 38	肥	793 page 159
祉	SHI, blessing, happiness	服	408 page 82
祈	KI; *ino(ru)*, to pray, to invoke, to wish; *ino(ri)*, prayer, wish	肩	KEN; *kata*, shoulder ②

茎	KEI; *kuki*, stalk, stem [1]	述	731 page 147
茂	MO; *shige(ru)*, to grow thick, to grow rank [1]	迫	HAKU; *sema(ru)*, to press, to urge, to draw near [1]
芽	457 page 92	邸	TEI, mansion, residence [1]
苗	BYŌ; *nae*, seedling, sapling [1]	邪	JA, wrong, injustice, evil [1]
▲ 苛	KA; *iji(meru)*; *saina(mu)*, torment, scold	▲ 采	SAI; form, appearance
若	896 page 180	金	18 page 4
英	449 page 90	長	189 page 38
苦	283 page 57	門	231 page 47
▲ 虎	KO; *tora*, tiger	▲ 阜	FU; hill; mound
表	402 page 81	阻	SO, steep; to separate, to obstruct; *haba(mu)*, to obstruct, to hinder [1]
迭	TETSU, to change places with; by turns [1]	附	FU, to stick to, to adhere to [1]

雨	69 page 14	非	794 page 159
青	52 page 11	斉	SEI, equal, similar 1

9 STROKES

衷	CHŪ, heart, sincerity 1	侵	SHIN; *oka(su)*, to invade, to violate 1
乗	336 page 68	便	610 page 123
亭	TEI, restaurant, pavilion 1	俗	ZOKU, customs, manners; vulgar 1
▲ 侶	RYO; companion; follower	信	544 page 109
侯	KŌ, feudal lord; marquis 1	保	808 page 162
促	SOKU; *unaga(su)*, to urge 1	冠	KAN; *kanmuri*, crown 1
俊	SHUN, to be excellent, to surpass, to be high 1	則	764 page 153
係	286 page 58	削	SAKU; *kezu(ru)*, to shave (wood), to sharpen, to delete, to curtail 1

前	177 page 36	咽	IN; choked; smothered
勃	BOTSU, suddenness; rise	咲	*sa(ku)*, to bloom, to blossom 2
勅	CHOKU, Imperial edict 1	哀	AI; *awa(re)*, pathos, misery, pity; *awa(remu)*, to feel pity for 1
勇	622 page 125	品	405 page 82
卑	HI; *iya(shii)*, base, vulgar, low-lived; *iya(shimeru)*, to despise 1	垣	*kaki*, fence, hedge 1
南	208 page 42	型	493 page 99
単	569 page 114	城	914 page 183
卸	*oro(su)*, to sell wholesale; *oroshi*, wholesale 1	変	609 page 122
厘	RIN, old unit of money (0.001 yen); old unit of length (about 0.0119 in.) 1	契	KEI; *chigi(ru)*, to pledge, to promise 1
厚	698 page 140	奏	930 page 187
叙	JO, preface; *jo(suru)*, to describe, to confer (a rank) upon 1	姻	IN, to get married 1

236

姿	888 page 178	巻	841 page 169
威	I, majestic, solemn; to threaten [1]	帝	TEI, emperor, sovereign, Mikado [1]
孤	KO, orphan; solitary, alone [1]	帥	SUI, to command an army [1]
室	152 page 31	幽	YŪ, faint, profound, quiet [1]
宣	924 page 185	度	377 page 76
客	270 page 55	建	498 page 100
封	FŪ, seal; *fū(jiru)*, to prevent, to enclose, to blockade, to seal; HŌ fief [2]	弧	KO, arc [1]
専	925 page 186	待	357 page 72
屋	256 page 52	律	1,003 page 201
峠	*tōge*, mountain pass, ridge, peak, crisis [1]	後	123 page 25
峡	KYŌ, gorge, ravine [1]	怠	TAI; *okota(ru)*, to neglect, *nama(keru)*, to be lazy [1]

怨 ▲	EN, ON; *ura(mu)*, *ura(mi)*, *ura(meshii)*, grudge, resentment		挑	CHŌ; *ido(mu)*, to challenge, to strive [1]
怒	DO; *ika(ru)* (lit.), to get angry; *oko(ru)*, to get angry [3]		挟	KYŌ; *hasa(mu)*, to put (hold) between; *hasa(maru)*, to be sandwiched between [2]
急	272 page 55		拾	321 page 65
思	147 page 30		持	310 page 63
恨	KON; *ura(mi)*, spite, grudge; *ura(mu)*, to bear a grudge; *ura(meshii)*, hateful [1]		指	305 page 62
悔	KAI; *ku(iru)*, to regret; *kuya(mi)*, condolence; *kuya(mu)*, to mourn, to repent [1]		政	746 page 150
恒	KŌ, always, eternal [1]		故	694 page 139
拶 ▲	SATSU; be imminent		施	SHI, SE; *hodoko(su)*, to give in charity; to perform, to administer [1]
拷	GŌ, to beat, to strike [1]		昧 ▲	MAI; dark; foolish
括	KATSU, to fasten, to bind, to tie up [1]		映	830 page 167
拭	SHOKU; *fu(ku)*, *nugu(u)*, wipe; mop; swab		昨	512 page 103

星	171 page 35	査	705 page 142
春	158 page 32	柱	366 page 74
昭	331 page 67	架	KA; ka(suru), to build, to span (a river with a bridge, etc.) [1]
昼	188 page 38	柔	JŪ, NYŪ; yawa(rakai), soft, tender, mild, mellow [2]
是	ZE, right, just [1]	枯	KO; ka(reru), to wither, to mature (v.i.); ka(rasu), to blight [2]
▲栃	tochi, horse chestnut	栄	450 page 91
▲柵	SAKU; stockade, fence	染	928 page 186
▲柿	kaki, persimmon	段	944 page 189
柄	HEI; e, handle; gara, pattern, design, build, character, nature [1]	泉	926 page 186
某	BŌ, a certain person, Mr. So-and-so; one, a, a certain ~ (used as prefix) [1]	津	tsu, harbor, ferry [1]
柳	RYŪ, yanagi, willow tree [1]	洪	KŌ, flood, vast [1]

洞	DŌ; *hora*, cave, excavation [1]	牲	SEI, sacrifice, victim [1]
派	965 page 194	狭	KYŌ; *sema(i)*, narrow, small; *seba(meru)* (v.t.), to narrow, to reduce [1]
浄	JŌ, pure, innocent [1]	狩	SHU; *ka(ri)*, hunting, gathering, (maple- etc.) viewing; *ka(ru)*, to hunt [1]
浅	554 page 111	独	784 page 157
洋	427 page 86	珍	CHIN; *mezura(shii)*, rare, novel, unusual [2]
洗	927 page 186	甚	JIN; *hanaha(da)*, extremely, immensely; *hanaha(dashii)*, extreme, enormous [1]
活	99 page 20	界	260 page 53
海	94 page 19	畑	391 page 79
為	I, to do, to make, to think; benefit, reason, cause, purpose [1]	▲ 畏	I; *oso(reru)*, fear; *kashiko(maru)*, to obey, humble oneself; *kashiko(i)*, majestic
点	196 page 40	疫	EKI, epidemic [1]
炭	361 page 73	発	392 page 79

皆	KAI; *mina, minna*, all, everything, everyone [3]	研	290 page 59
皇	871 page 175	砂	879 page 176
盆	BON, tray; the Bon Festival (Buddhist celebration held in Japan in mid-July) [1]	祖	758 page 152
盾	JUN; *tate*, shield [1]	祝	533 page 107
▲ 冒	BŌ; *oka(su)*, to brave, to defy, to attack, to damage, to profane [1]	神	340 page 69
省	546 page 110	秒	403 page 81
眉	BI, MI; *mayu*, eyebrow	科	87 page 18
県	291 page 59	秋	156 page 32
看	842 page 169	窃	SETSU, to steal, to rob
相	348 page 70	糾	KYŪ, to investigate, to examine, to twist, to twine around [1]
砕	SAI; *kuda(ku)* (v.t.), to smash, to simplify; *kuda(keru)* (v.i.), to be broken, softened [1]	紀	472 page 95 [1]

241

約	621 page 125	臭	SHŪ, smell, stink; *kusa(i)*, ill-smelling, suspicious; *~kusa(i)*, smelling of ~; *nio(u)*, to stink ☐1	
紅	872 page 175	▲ 茨	*ibara*, briar, thorn	
級	273 page 55	荘	SŌ, majestic, solemn; villa ☐1	
美	398 page 80	草	57 page 12	
耐	TAI; *ta(eru)*, to endure, to bear, to stand (v.t.) ☐1	茶	187 page 38	
胞	HŌ, placenta ☐1	荒	KŌ; *ara(i)*, violent, wild; *a(reru)*, to be rough, dilapidated; *a(rasu)*, to lay waste ☐2	
胎	TAI, to conceive; womb, fetus ☐1	虐	GYAKU, to treat harshly, to spoil; *shiita(geru)*, to oppress, to persecute ☐1	
胆	TAN, liver; spirit, courage ☐1	▲ 虹	KŌ; *niji*, rainbow	
肺	968 page 194	要	623 page 125	
胃	447 page 90	訂	TEI, to correct, to establish ☐1	
背	967 page 194	▲ 訃	FU; report of someone's death	

計	116 page 24	追	370 page 75
貞	TEI right, just, chaste [1]	郊	KŌ, suburbs, the country [2]
負	406 page 82	郎	RŌ, man, male — used as suffix in men's given names [1]
赴	FU, to go; *omomu(ku)*, to proceed (towards) [1]	重	326 page 66
軌	KI, space between two wheels, print of a wheel [1]	限	691 page 139
軍	490 page 99	面	417 page 84
迷	817 page 164	革	836 page 168
逃	TŌ; *ni(geru)*, to flee; *noga(reru)*, to escape, avoid; *ni(gasu)*, to set free [3]	音	33 page 7
送	349 page 70	風	217 page 44
退	769 page 154	飛	595 page 120
逆	675 page 136	食	163 page 33

首	155 page 32	香	KŌ, incense; *ka* (lit.), perfume, fragrance; *kao(ri)*, fragrance; *kao(ru)* to be fragrant 2

10 STROKES

倣	HŌ; *nara(u)*, to model after, to imitate 1	倉	559 page 112
▲ 俺	*ore*, I, myself	倒	TŌ; *tao(reru)*, to fall, to break down, to go to ruin; *tao(su)*, to fell, to overthrow 3
俵	796 page 160	値	946 page 190
倫	RIN, principles, duty, rules 1	個	695 page 140
倹	KEN, frugal, modest, humble 1	借	530 page 107
俸	HŌ, salary 1	修	730 page 147
候	504 page 101	▲ 党	957 page 192
倍	389 page 78	兼	KEN, and, in addition, concurrently; *ka(neru)*, to combine, be unable to (suffix) 1
俳	969 page 194	冥	MEI, MYŌ, dark

▲ 凄	SEI; *sugo(i)*, *susa(majii)*, uncanny, weird, threatening, horrible	▲ 唄	*uta*, song
准	JUN, rule; to imitate, to approve [1]	唆	SA; *sosonoka(su)*, to tempt, to instigate [1]
凍	TŌ; *kō(ru)*, to freeze (v.i.); *kogo(eru)*, to be benumbed with cold [2]	唇	SHIN; *kuchibiru*, lips [1]
剖	BŌ, to divide, to distinguish [1]	員	248 page 50
剤	ZAI, medicine, drug [1]	▲ 哺	HO; nurse; suckle
▲ 剥	HAKU; *ha(gasu)*, *ha(gu)*, *ha(gareru)*, *ha(geru)*, come off; peel; fade	哲	TETSU, wise, sagacious
剛	GŌ, inflexible, stubborn, stiff, hard [1]	唐	TŌ, Tang, (an ancient Chinese dynasty); *kara*, China (old name used in Japan) [1]
剣	KEN, *tsurugi*, sword [1]	埋	MAI; *u(meru)*, to bury, to fill up; *u(maru)*, to be buried, to be filled up [2]
勉	413 page 83	夏	88 page 18
匿	TOKU, to give refuge to, to conceal, to hide, to keep secret [1]	姫	*hime*, princess, young lady of birth; also used as prefix for "small" or "dainty" [1]
原	119 page 24	娠	SHIN, to conceive, to become pregnant [1]

娘	*musume*, girl, daughter [3]	将	911 page 183
娯	GO, to enjoy, to take pleasure in [1]	展	955 page 192
孫	565 page 114	峰	HŌ; *mine*, peak, back (of a sword) [1]
宰	SAI, to administer, to manage, to take charge of; chief, head [1]	島	380 page 77
宴	EN, feast, banquet [1]	差	508 page 102
害	460 page 93	席	549 page 110
宵	SHŌ; *yoi*, evening [1]	師	720 page 145
容	822 page 165	帯	566 page 114
宮	274 page 55	帰	106 page 22
家	89 page 18	庫	292 page 59
射	893 page 179	庭	372 page 75

座	880 page 177	恩	654 page 131
弱	154 page 31	恋	REN; *koi*, love; *koi(shii)*, dear, beloved [2]
除	910 page 183	恐	KYŌ; *oso(re)*, fear, anxiety; *oso(reru)*, to fear; *oso(roshii)*, fearful, fierce, awful　[3]
徐	JO, slowly, gently [1]	悩	NŌ; *naya(mi)*, affliction, trouble, pain; *naya(mu)*, to be troubled with　[2]
徒	581 page 117	悦	ETSU, to be glad, to rejoice [1]
従	902 page 181	悟	GO; *sato(ru)*, to be spiritually awakened, to perceive, to comprehend　[1]
▲ 恣	SHI; selfish; self-indulgent; arbitrary	扇	SEN; *ōgi*, folding fan [1]
恭	KYŌ, respectful, reverent; *uyauya(shii)*, reverent　[1]	▲ 拳	KEN; *kobushi*, fist
恥	CHI; *haji*, shame, disgrace; *ha(jiru)*, to be ashamed of; *ha(zukashii)*, embarrassing　[3]	挙	482 page 97
恵	KEI, E; *megu(mi)*, grace, blessing; *megu(mu)*, to give in charity　[1]	▲ 捉	SOKU; *tora(eru)*; catch; capture
息	351 page 71	▲ 挨	AI; *hira(ku)*, push open

247

▲ 捗	CHOKU, make progress	書	159 page 32
▲ 挫	ZA, crush, break	栓	SEN, bolt, plug, faucet [1]
挿	SŌ; *sa(su)*, to insert, to put into [1]	栽	SAI, to plant [1]
捜	SŌ; *saga(su)*, to hunt for, to search for [2]	▲ 桁	*keta*, beam, girder; unit, column
捕	HO; *tora(eru)*, *to(ru)*, to catch, to seize; *tsuk(maeru)*, to catch, to arrest [3]	桟	SAN, crosspiece, jetty [1]
振	SHIN; *fu(reru)*, to shake, swing, lean to; *fu(ru)*, to wave, shake, wield, discard; *fu(ruu)*, to brandish, master, prosper [1]	核	KAKU, nucleus, kernel, core, stone (of a fruit) [1]
敏	BIN, clever, quick [1]	桑	SŌ; *kuwa*, mulberry [1]
料	629 page 126	桃	TŌ; *momo*, peach [1]
旅	433 page 87	桜	653 page 131
既	KI; *sude(ni)*, already, previously [1]	株	839 page 168
時	151 page 31	梅	592 page 119

案	442 page 89	涙	RUI; *namida*, tear (from the eye) [2]
格	663 page 133	浪	RŌ, billow; to wander about [1]
校	46 page 10	浦	*ura*, inlet, beach [1]
根	298 page 60	浸	SHIN; *hita(su)*, to soak, to wet; *hita(ru)*, to be immersed, to indulge [1]
殉	JUN; *jun(jiru)*, to follow even to death, to sacrifice oneself [1]	消	332 page 67
殊	SHU, especially; to be different; *koto(ni)*, especially [1]	浮	FU; *u(ku)*, to float, to be merry, to be left over; *u(kabu)*, to float, to come to mind [3]
残	520 page 105	流	432 page 87
殺	515 page 104	烈	RETSU, valiant, violent, brave, strong [1]
泰	TAI, peaceful, great, extravagant, extremely [1]	特	586 page 118
浜	HIN; *hama*, beach, shore [1]	班	970 page 195
浴	625 page 126	珠	SHU, pearl [1]

畔	HAN, vicinity; footpath between rice fields, edge [1]	砲	HŌ, gun, cannon [1]
畝	*une*, furrow, groove	破	788 page 158
畜	CHIKU, to raise cattle, to cultivate [2]	祥	SHŌ, good fortune, omen [1]
留	824 page 165	秩	CHITSU, order, rank [1]
症	SHŌ, nature of a disease [1]	租	SO, tribute [1]
疲	HI; *tsuka(re)*, fatigue; *tsuka(reru)*, to get tired, to become fatigued [3]	称	SHŌ, to praise; *shō(suru)*, to call, to name, to pretend [1]
疾	SHITSU, sickness; to fall ill; quick, swift [1]	秘	974 page 195
病	404 page 81	竜	RYŪ; *tatsu*, dragon [1]
益	648 page 130	笑	537 page 108
眠	MIN; *nemu(ri)*, sleep; *nemu(ru)*, to sleep; *nemu(i)*, sleepy [3]	粋	SUI, *iki*, essence, elegance; delicate, smart, stylish [1]
真	341 page 69	粉	605 page 122

索	SAKU, cable, rope; to seek for, to search for [1]	朕	CHIN, We, Our (formerly used by the Emperor of Japan in Imperial rescripts) [1]
紡	BŌ; *tsumu(gu)*, to spin (thread) [1]	朗	1,005 page 202
紋	MON, family insignia, crest, figures (in cloth) [1]	脅	KYŌ; *obiya(kasu)*, *odo(su)*, *odo(kasu)*, to threaten, to menace, to intimidate [1]
紛	FUN; *magi(reru)*, to be obscure, to be diverted, to be confused [1]	▲ 脊	SEKI; *se*, *sei*, stature; height
納	963 page 193	脈	618 page 124
純	906 page 182	▲ 脇	*waki*, the other way; side; supporting role
紙	148 page 30	脂	SHI; *abura*, fat, grease, tallow [2]
素	759 page 152	能	787 page 158
翁	Ō, old man, honorific title for an old man [1]	胴	DŌ, trunk (of the body), body armor [1]
耗	MŌ, KŌ, to decrease, to spend [1]	胸	851 page 171
耕	699 page 140	致	CHI, to do, to bring about; taste, appearance; *ita(su)*, to do (humbly) [1]

251

般	HAN, generally; to carry, to turn; to enjoy [2]	訓	489 page 98
航	505 page 102	記	105 page 22
荷	259 page 52	貢	KŌ, tribute, contribution; *mitsu(gu)*, to give financial support [1]
華	KA, flower, showiness, China; *hana(yaka)*, showy, splendid [1]	財	712 page 143
蚊	*ka*, mosquito [1]	起	268 page 54
蚕	885 page 178	軒	KEN, suffix for counting houses; *noki*, eaves [2]
衰	SUI; *otoro(eru)*, to become weak, to decline [1]	辱	JOKU, to put to shame, to disgrace; *hazukashi(meru)*, to humiliate, to violate [1]
▲ 袖	SHŪ; *sode*, sleeve; extension	逝	SEI; *i(ku)*, *yu(ku)*, to pass away, to die [1]
被	HI; *kōmu(ru)*, to suffer (damage, etc.), to receive (a favor, etc.) [2]	逓	TEI, alternately, by turns; to convey [1]
託	TAKU, to entrust to a person, to make a pretext of [1]	逐	CHIKU, to chase, to pursue [1]
討	956 page 192	途	TO, way, road [3]

透	TŌ, penetrate; *su(ku)*, to be transparent, leave gaps; *su(kasu)*, to make transparent, thin out [1]	針	916 page 184
速	352 page 71	陛	978 page 196
造	761 page 153	陥	KAN; *ochii(ru)*, to fall into, to yield, to cave in, to fall (to surrender to a siege) [1]
連	637 page 128	院	249 page 50
通	193 page 39	陣	JIN, camp, position (military), battle array [1]
郡	491 page 99	降	873 page 175
酒	318 page 64	隻	SEKI, suffix for counting ships [2]
▲酎	CHŪ; liquor	飢	KI; *u(e)*, hunger, starvation; *u(eru)*, to be hungry, to starve [1]
酌	SHAKU; *ku(mu)*, to ladle, to drink together, to consider [1]	馬	210 page 43
配	388 page 78	骨	877 page 176
▲釜	*kama*, iron pot, kettle	高	132 page 27

鬼	KI; *oni*, ogre, fiend, demon [1]		

11 STROKES

▲ 亀	KI; *kame*, tortoise, turtle	剰	JŌ, surplus; moreover [1]
乾	KAN to dry, to be thirsty; *kawa(ku)* (v.i.), *kawa(kasu)* (v.t.), to dry [2]	副	604 page 121
偵	TEI, spy [1]	務	815 page 164
停	577 page 116	勘	KAN, perception, intuition [1]
偶	GŪ, even number; by chance, accidentally [3]	動	384 page 77
側	562 page 113	喝	KATSU, scold, get hoarse [1]
偽	GI; *itsuwa(ru)*, to tell a lie, to pretend, to deceive [1]	唾	DA; *tsuba*, saliva; sputum
偏	HEN, left-hand radical; one-sided, biased; *kata(yoru)*, to be biased [1]	▲ 啓	KEI, to enlighten, to open [1]
健	499 page 100	唱	538 page 108

問	418 page 84	婆	BA, old woman, old mother 1
唯	YUI, merely, only, alone 1	婚	KON, marriage 2
商	333 page 67	婦	800 page 161
▲ 埼	SAI, cape; promontory	密	990 page 199
域	828 page 166	宿	327 page 66
培	BAI; *tsuchika(u)*, to cultivate, to foster 1	寂	JAKU, SEKI; *sabi(shii)*, lonesome, lonely, solitary; *sabi(reru)*, to mature, to mellow 1
▲ 堆	TAI; piled high	寄	671 page 135
堀	*hori*, ditch, moat 1	尉	I, military rank 1
堂	584 page 117	崎	*saki*, cape, promontory 1
執	SHITSU, SHŪ; *to(ru)*, to do (business, etc.), to manage, to take, to grasp 1	▲ 崖	GAI; *gake*, cliff, precipice
基	670 page 135	崇	SŪ, lofty, noble; to respect, to worship 1

255

崩	HŌ; *kuzu(reru)*, to collapse; *kuzu(su)*, to destroy, reduce, write in simplified form [1]	得	587 page 118
帳	368 page 74	患	KAN, sickness, anxiety, trouble [2]
常	740 page 149	悪	241 page 49
康	506 page 102	▲ 懼	GU; *oso(reru)*, fear, be overawed
庸	YŌ, moderate, ordinary, mediocre [1]	悠	YŪ, distance, leisure [1]
庶	SHO, various, all, many [1]	悼	TŌ; *ita(mu)*, to mourn over, to lament, to feel pity for [1]
張	775 page 156	惜	SEKI; *o(shii)*, regrettable; precious; wasteful; *o(shimu)*, to begrudge, to regret [1]
強	111 page 23	惨	SAN, cruel, horrible, appalling; *miji(me)*, wretched, cruel [1]
彩	SAI, coloration; to color; *irodo(ru)*, to paint, to color [1]	情	741 page 149
彫	CHŌ; *ho(ru)*, to carve, to engrave [1]	▲ 戚	SEKI; relative
術	732 page 147	措	SO, to put aside, to except, to dispose of; to place [1]

揭	KEI; *kaka(geru)*, to put up, to hoist, to carry [1]	探	942 page 189
据	*su(eru)*, to lay (a foundation), to install (a person); *su(waru)*, to become set/fixed [1]	推	919 page 184
描	BYŌ; *ega(ku)*, to picture, to describe, to draw; *ka(ku)*, to paint, to draw [1]	接	753 page 151
捻	NEN, twirl; twist; play with	掛	*ka(keru)*, to hang (v.t.), to sit on (a chair, etc.), to cover with [3]
控	KŌ; *hika(eru)*, to write down; to refrain from, to be moderate in, to wait [1]	敗	591 page 119
掘	KUTSU; *ho(ru)*, to dig, to dig up [2]	救	480 page 97
捨	894 page 179	教	112 page 23
掃	SŌ; *ha(ku)*, to sweep [2]	斎	SAI, religious purification; a room [1]
授	729 page 146	斜	SHA; *nana(me)*, slanting, oblique [1]
採	709 page 142	斬	ZAN; *ki(ru)*, beheading; murder
排	HAI, to reject; to display, to push open [1]	断	773 page 155

257

族	353 page 71	渉	SHŌ, to wade, to cross over, to walk about; to be related to [1]
旋	SEN, to rotate, to return [1]	淑	SHUKU, graceful, gentle [1]
曹	SŌ, an official, friend [1]	渇	KATSU, thirst; to be thirsty, to dry up; *kawa(ku)*, to feel thirsty [1]
▲ 曽	SŌ, ZO; once; before; formerly	渓	KEI, valley [1]
械	459 page 92	済	881 page 177
▲ 梨	RI; *nashi*, Japanese pear	涼	RYŌ, (lit.) coolness; *suzu(shii)*, cool [2]
▲ 梗	KŌ, KYŌ; close up	液	649 page 130
巣	560 page 113	渋	JŪ; *shibu*, astringent juice; *shibu(i)*, astringent, refined, sober; *shibu(ru)*, to demur [1]
欲	997 page 200	添	TEN; *so(eru)*, to annex (to), to add (to), to garnish (cooking); *so(u)*, to accompany [1]
殻	KAKU; *kara*, husk, shell [1]	淡	TAN; *awa(i)*, light (color, taste, etc.), transitory (love, joy, etc.) [1]
涯	GAI, shore [1]	▲ 淫	IN; licentiousness; *mida(ra)*, indecent, lewd

混	704 page 141	瓶	BIN, bottle, vase [2]
清	547 page 110	産	518 page 104
深	342 page 69	略	823 page 165
▲ 爽	SŌ; *sawa(yaka)*, refreshing; clear	異	826 page 166
猫	BYŌ; *neko*, cat [3]	▲ 痕	KON; *ato*, mark; footprint
猟	RYŌ, hunting, shooting [1]	盗	TŌ; *nusu(mu)*, to steal, to rob [3]
猛	MŌ, strong, valiant, brave, fierce, wild [1]	盛	921 page 185
率	767 page 154	眺	CHŌ; *naga(meru)*, to gaze at, to watch [1]
球	275 page 56	眼	669 page 134
理	239 page 48	票	598 page 120
現	692 page 139	祭	299 page 60

移	642 page 129	紺	KON, dark blue <div align="right">1</div>
窒	CHITSU, to block up, to obstruct; nitrogen <div align="right">1</div>	紳	SHIN, ceremonial sash; man of high birth <div align="right">1</div>
窓	931 page 187	累	RUI, trouble, involve- ment; to pile up, to trouble; to be acquainted with 1
章	334 page 67	組	178 page 36
笛	373 page 75	終	322 page 65
符	FU, tally, mark, sign, good omen, charm, talisman <div align="right">2</div>	細	140 page 29
第	359 page 72	経	685 page 138
粒	RYŪ; *tsubu*, grain, drop <div align="right">2</div>	▲ 羞	SHŪ; be ashamed
粗	SO, rough, loose, coarse, humble; *ara(i)*, coarse, rugged <div align="right">1</div>	翌	998 page 200
粘	NEN; *neba(ru)*, to be sticky; to persevere <div align="right">1</div>	習	323 page 65
紹	SHŌ, to introduce a person; to succeed to <div align="right">2</div>	粛	SHUKU, to be respectful, to be modest, to admon- ish, to be severe <div align="right">1</div>

望	613 page 123	菊	KIKU, chrysanthemum [1]
脚	KYAKU, leg, lower part, position, suffix for counting furniture with legs [1]	菜	509 page 102
脳	964 page 193	著	949 page 190
脱	DATSU, to omit, to escape; nu(gu), to take off shoes, coat, etc. [1]	虚	KYO, KO, empty, vain [1]
舶	HAKU, ocean-going ship [1]	蛍	KEI; hotaru, firefly [1]
▲ 舷	GEN; gunwale	蛇	JA, DA; hebi, snake [1]
船	175 page 36	袋	TAI; fukuro, bag, sack, pouch [2]
▲ 葛	KATSU; kuzu, arrowroot, kudzu	規	672 page 135
▲ 萎	I; na(eru),weaken, wither, droop; shibo(mu), shio(reru), shina(biru), wither, fade	視	889 page 178
菌	KIN, germ, fungus [1]	訟	SHŌ, to sue, to go to law [1]
菓	KA, fruit, nut, berry [2]	許	679 page 136

設	754 page 151	軟	NAN, soft, weak, feeble; *yawa(rakai)* soft, tender, mild, yellow [2]
訪	984 page 197	転	375 page 76
訳	993 page 199	逮	TAI, to catch, to arrest, to overtake, to pursue [1]
豚	TON; *buta*, pig [1]	週	157 page 32
▲ 貪	DON; *musabo(ru)*, coveting	逸	ITSU, to excel, to be lost, to be rash, to run off, to enjoy oneself [1]
貫	KAN, old unit of weight (8.27 lb.); *tsuranu(ku)*, to pierce, to carry out, to attain [1]	進	343 page 69
販	HAN, to sell, to deal in [2]	郭	KAKU, enclosure, red-light district [1]
責	751 page 151	郷	852 page 171
貨	455 page 92	部	407 page 82
貧	798 page 160	郵	994 page 199
赦	SHA, to forgive, to pardon [1]	都	376 page 76

酔	SUI; *yo(u)*, to get drunk, to become sick (sea, car, air), to be in ecstasy [1]	陸	627 page 126
釈	SHAKU, to interpret, to explain [1]	陰	IN, gloom, negative, the female principle (yin); *kage*, shadow, shade, back [1]
野	233 page 47	雪	174 page 35
釣	CHŌ; *tsu(ru)*, to fish, to entice; *tsu(ri)*, fishing, change (of money) [1]	▲ 頃	*koro*, time, about
閉	979 page 196	頂	951 page 191
陵	RYŌ; *misasagi*, Imperial mausoleum [1]	魚	109 page 22
隆	RYŪ high, prosperous, flourishing [1]	鳥	190 page 39
険	689 page 138	▲ 鹿	KA; *shika*, deer
陳	CHIN, to state, to display; to be old [1]	麻	MA; *asa*, hemp, flax [1]
陪	BAI, to attend upon; attendant [1]	黄	133 page 27
陶	TŌ pottery, porcelain [1]	黒	137 page 28

263

12 STROKES

傘	SAN; *kasa*, umbrella	喩	YU; *tato(eru)*, compare; illustrate
備	795 page 160	喚	KAN, to call, to cry, to summon
偉	I; *era(i)*, great, admirable	喪	SŌ, to lose, to ruin; *mo*, mourning
傍	BŌ, side, neighborhood	喉	KŌ; *nodo*, throat
創	932 page 187	喫	KITSU, to eat, to drink
割	838 page 168	営	645 page 130
募	BO; *tsuno(ru)*, to collect, to raise (troops, etc.); to grow intense	喜	473 page 95
勤	853 page 171	善	929 page 186
勝	335 page 68	圏	KEN, sphere, range [1]
博	593 page 119	堕	DA, to fall, to get into, to let fall, to lose [1]

堅	KEN; *kata(i)*, hard, tough, tight, firm, solid, strict, sound ☐1	婿	SEI; *muko*, son-in-law, bridegroom ☐1
塚	*tsuka*, mound, hillock ☐1	媒	BAI, intermediation, matchmaking, intermediary, go-between ☐1
塀	HEI, wall, fence ☐1	富	801 page 161
塔	TŌ, tower, pagoda, steeple ☐2	寒	263 page 53
堤	TEI; *tsutsumi*, bank (of a river, etc.) ☐1	尋	JIN; *tazu(neru)*, to ask, to look for ☐1
塁	RUI, base (in baseball), fort ☐1	尊	939 page 188
堪	KAN; *ta(eru)*, to endure, to bear, to withstand, to resist ☐1	就	900 page 181
場	161 page 33	属	766 page 154
報	810 page 163	▲ 嵐	RAN; *arashi*, storm, tempest
奥	Ō, interior; *oku*, interior, depths, heart ☐2	帽	BŌ, headgear, headdress ☐2
▲ 媛	EN; *hime*, beautiful woman, princess	幅	FUKU, scroll, suffix for counting scrolls; *haba*, width, difference in price ☐2

幾	KI; *iku~*, how many?, how much?, some (used as prefix) [3]	愉	YU, to rejoice, to enjoy oneself [1]
廊	RŌ, corridor, passage [1]	惰	DA, to be idle, to neglect [1]
廃	HAI, to abolish, abandon; *suta(ru)*, *suta(reru)*, to fall into disuse [1]	扉	HI; *tobira*, door, page [1]
弾	DAN; *hi(ku)*, to play a musical instrument; *hazu(mu)*, to spring back; *tama*, bullet [1]	掌	SHŌ, palm of the hand; to control, to preside over [1]
循	JUN, to obey, to observe, to follow; to revolve [1]	搭	TŌ, to load (a vehicle), to ride [1]
街	461 page 93	揮	846 page 170
復	803 page 161	援	EN, to help, to rescue, to pull [1]
御	GYO, GO; *on*, honorific prefix; *gyo(suru)*, to drive (a horse) [3]	握	AKU; *nigi(ru)*, to grasp, to clasp, to hold, to seize [1]
惑	WAKU; *mado(u)*, to be puzzled, to go astray, to be captivated by [1]	換	KAN; *ka(eru)*, to exchange, to change (v.t.); *ka(waru)*, to change (v.i.) [2]
悲	397 page 80	揺	YŌ; *yu(reru)*, to shake (v.i.), to swing, to flicker [1]
慌	KŌ, busy, flustered; *awa(teru)*, to be in a hurry, confused; *awa(tadashii)*, bustling, hurried [1]	揚	YŌ; *a(geru)*, to raise, to send up, to hoist; to fry [1]

提	776 page 156	普	FU, wide, universal, general 2
散	519 page 104	晩	971 page 195
敢	KAN, daring, boldly 1	最	510 page 103
敬	856 page 172	▲ 椅	I; chair
▲ 斑	HAN; *madara*, *mura*, spot; speck; unevenness; inequality	▲ 椎	TSUI; mallet; *shii*, oak
晶	SHŌ, bright; crystal 1	棋	KI, chessman, Japanese chess 1
暑	329 page 66	棺	KAN, casket, coffin 1
暁	GYŌ; *akatsuki*, dawn, daybreak 1	棟	TŌ; *mune*, ridge (of a roof) 1
替	TAI; *ka(eru)*, to exchange, to replace; *ka(waru)*, to be replaced, to take turns 2	棚	*tana*, shelf 1
景	494 page 99	森	65 page 14
晴	172 page 35	棒	987 page 198

植	337 page 68	港	296 page 60
検	690 page 139	湿	SHITSU; *shime(ru)*, to become damp, to moisten; *shime(su)*, to dampen [2]
極	488 page 98	測	765 page 154
款	KAN, sincerity, goodwill; article in a legal document [1]	湯	381 page 77
欺	GI; *azamu(ku)*, to deceive, to cheat [1]	温	257 page 52
殖	SHOKU; *fu(eru)* (v.i.), *fu(yasu)* (v.t.), to increase, multiply, grow [1]	渡	TO; *wata(ru)*, to go over; *wata(su)*, to hand over, span [3]
▲ 湧	YŪ, *wa(ku)*, boil; ferment; seethe	満	616 page 124
滋	JI, nourishing; to flourish, to be luxuriant [1]	減	693 page 139
湾	WAN, bay, gulf [2]	然	557 page 112
湖	293 page 59	焦	SHŌ; *ko(geru)* (v.i.), *ko(gasu)* (v.t.), to scorch, to burn; *ko(gareru)*, to yearn; *ase(ru)*, be impatient [1]
渦	KA; *uzu*, whirlpool, eddy [1]	煮	SHA; *ni(ru)*, to cook (v.t.); *ni(eru)* (v.i.), to be boiled, to be cooked [1]

268

焼	539 page 108	登	382 page 77
無	620 page 125	着	364 page 73
猶	YŪ, to hesitate; moreover, even, still; as if [1]	短	362 page 73
琴	KIN; *koto*, Japanese harp [1]	硫	RYŪ, sulfur [1]
番	215 page 44	硝	SHŌ, nitrate, gunpowder [1]
畳	JŌ, suffix for counting mats; *tatami*, mat; *tata(mu)*, to fold (up) [2]	硬	KŌ; *kata(i)*, hard, tough, stiff, firm [2]
疎	SO, estranged, sparse; *uto(i)*, estranged, ignorant of; *uto(mu)*, to neglect, to shun [1]	程	777 page 156
▲痩	SŌ; *ya(seru)*, become thin	税	750 page 151
痢	RI, diarrhea [1]	童	385 page 78
痘	TŌ, smallpox [1]	筒	TŌ; *tsutsu*, pipe, tube [2]
痛	954 page 191	策	883 page 177

269

答	202 page 41	絶	756 page 152
筋	854 page 171	結	497 page 100
等	383 page 77	期	269 page 54
筆	400 page 81	腕	WAN; *ude*, arm, talent, ability [2]
粧	SHŌ, to paint and powder, to embellish [1]	朝	191 page 39
絡	RAKU; *kara(meru)*, to twine around, to surround; *kara(mu)*, to get entangled, to pick a fight [2]	葬	SŌ; *hōmu(ru)*, to bury, to consign to oblivion, to shelve
絞	KŌ; *shibo(ru)*, to wring, to squeeze, to extort, to scold; *shi(meru)*, to strangle [1]	葉	428 page 86 [1]
紫	SHI; *murasaki*, purple, violet [1]	落	431 page 87
統	780 page 157	蛮	BAN, barbarian
絵	95 page 20	衆	901 page 181 [1]
給	481 page 97	裂	RETSU; *sa(ku)*, to tear, to rend (v.t.); *sa(keru)*, to tear, to rend (v.i.) [1]

裁	882 page 177	訴	SO; *utta(e)*, lawsuit, appeal, complaint; *utta(eru)*, to sue, to resort to, to appeal [1]
装	933 page 187	▲ 証	737 page 148
裕	YŪ, abundant, broad-minded, at ease [1]	象	540 page 109
補	981 page 197	費	596 page 120
覚	463 page 93	貼	CHŌ; counter for medicine packets; *ha(ru)*, to stick; to paste; to apply
詔	SHŌ; *mikotonori*, Imperial edict [1]	貿	813 page 163
詞	890 page 179	賀	660 page 133
詠	EI, poem, ode, recitation of poetry; *yo(mu)*, to compose a poem [1]	貯	572 page 115
詐	SA, to tell a lie, to pretend, to deceive [1]	貸	770 page 155
診	SHIN, to examine, to diagnose; *mi(ru)*, to examine (a patient) [1]	買	212 page 43
評	797 page 160	貴	847 page 170

越	ETSU; *ko(eru)*, to go over, to exceed; *ko(su)*, to cross, to exceed, to move (to) [3]	道	205 page 42
超	CHŌ, to exceed, super-; *ko(eru)* (v.i.), *ko(su)* (v.t.), to exceed, to transcend [2]	運	251 page 51
距	KYO, to separate, to be distant, to reach [1]	遊	424 page 85
軸	JIKU, axis, axle, scroll picture, holder, stalk [1]	酢	SAKU; *su*, vinegar [1]
軽	287 page 58	量	630 page 127
遇	GŪ, to treat, to deal with, to meet with, to come across [1]	鈍	DON; *nibu(i)*, dull, slow, blunt, dim; *nibu(ru)*, to become blunt, to weaken [2]
遂	SUI, at last; *to(geru)*, to accomplish, to attain [1]	閑	KAN, quiet, tranquil, leisure, time to spare [1]
遍	HEN, wide, universal [1]	間	100 page 21
達	568 page 114	開	261 page 53
遅	CHI, late, slow; *oku(reru)*, to be late; *oso(i)*, late [3]	随	ZUI, to follow, to accompany; freely; as one pleases [1]
過	659 page 132	隅	GŪ; *sumi*, corner [2]

隊	567 page 114	雲	83 page 17
階	262 page 53	項	KŌ, clause, paragraph, item [1]
陽	429 page 86	▲ 須	SU; by all means; necessarily
雄	YŪ, strong, valiant, brave, surpassing; *osu*, *o-*, male animal [1]	順	534 page 107
集	324 page 65	飯	594 page 119
雇	KO; *yato(u)*, to hire, to employ [2]	飲	250 page 51
雰	FUN, atmosphere [1]	歯	306 page 62

13 STROKES

▲ 僅	KIN; *wazu(ka)*, a little bit	債	SAI, debt, loan [1]
傑	KETSU, to excel, to surpass; man of great caliber [1]	働	585 page 118
▲ 傲	GŌ; be proud	催	SAI; *moyo-o(shi)*, meeting, auspices; *moyo-o(su)*, to hold (a meeting), to feel [1]

傾	KEI; *katamu(ki)*, inclination; *katamu(ku)* (v.i.), *katamu(keru)* (v.t.), to incline [2]	塊	KAI, clod, lump [1]
僧	SŌ, Buddhist priest, bonze [1]	▲ 填	TEN; fit in; go into
傷	912 page 183	墓	809 page 162
勢	747 page 150	塗	TO; *nu(ru)*, to paint, to plaster, to coat, to lacquer, to smear [2]
勧	KAN; *susu(meru)*, to advise, to persuade, to encourage [1]	塩	451 page 91
嗣	SHI, to succeed to, to inherit; heir, succession [1]	夢	816 page 164
▲ 嗅	KYŪ; *ka(gu)*, smell, scent	奨	SHŌ, to encourage, to promote [1]
嘆	TAN; *nage(ku)*, to bewail, to deplore, to sigh	▲ 嫉	SHITSU; jealous, envy
園	84 page 17	嫁	KA; *yome*, daughter-in-law, young wife, bride; *totsu(gu)*, to marry
塑	SO, earthen figure [1]	嫌	KEN; *kira(u)*, to dislike; *iya*, unpleasant, repugnant [1]
▲ 塞	SAI, SOKU; *fusa(gu)*, *fusa(garu)*, close, shut, obstruct	寛	KAN, generous, easy [1]

274

寝	SHIN; *ne(ru)*, to go to bed, to sleep, to lie down [3]	感	264 page 53
幕	989 page 198	慈	JI; *itsuku(shimu)*, to love, to cherish, to pity [1]
幹	667 page 134	▲ 慄	RITSU; fear; shudder
廉	REN, noble, lofty, pure; cheap [1]	慨	GAI, to deplore, to lament [1]
▲ 彙	I; same kind	慎	SHIN; *tsutsushi(mu)*, to be discreet, to refrain from [1]
微	BI, slight, little, faint, dim [1]	戦	555 page 112
想	350 page 71	搬	HAN, to carry, to transport, to remove [1]
愁	SHŪ, grief, sorrow, distress; *ure(eru)*, to lament, to grieve; *ure(i)*, grief, sorrow [1]	搾	SAKU, to squeeze, to compress; *shibo(ru)*, to press, to extract, to reprimand [1]
愚	GU; *oro(ka)*, foolish, stupid, silly [1]	摂	SETSU, to take, to cultivate, to act in place of [1]
意	246 page 50	携	KEI; *tazusa(eru)*, to carry in one's hand, to take with one [1]
愛	441 page 89	損	768 page 154

275

数	168 page 34	毀	KI; break, destroy
新	165 page 34	▲ 殿	DEN, TEN; ~dono, Mr., Mrs., etc. (used in formal letters); tono, lord, my lord [2]
暇	KA; hima, time, leisure, dismissal [1]	漠	BAKU, a desert, vague [1]
暖	945 page 190	▲ 溺	DEKI; obo(reru), drown; indulge
暗	243 page 49	滝	taki, waterfall, cataract, cascade [1]
▲ 楷	KAI; square character style; correctness	源	864 page 173
楼	RŌ, (lit.), stately mansion with two or more stories, watchtower [1]	溝	KŌ; mizo, ditch [1]
棄	KI, to throw away, to abandon, to reject [1]	溶	YŌ; to(keru), to melt, to dissolve (v.i.); to(kasu), to melt (v.t.) [2]
業	278 page 56	準	733 page 147
楽	98 page 20	滅	METSU; horo(biru), to go to ruin, to die out; horo(bosu), to ruin, to destroy [1]
歳	SAI, ~ years old (used as suffix); SEI, year, age, time [3]	滞	TAI; todokō(ru), to stagnate, to fall into arrears, to be left undone [1]

漢	265 page 54	督	TOKU, to control, to supervise, to urge [1]
滑	KATSU, KOTSU, smooth, even; to slide; *sube(ru)* to slide [1]	睡	SUI, to sleep, to doze [1]
▲ 煎	SEN; *i(ru)*, broil, parch, roast	碁	GO, the Japanese game of *go* [1]
煩	HAN; *wazura(u)*, to be worried, ill; *wazura(wasu)*, to trouble; *wazura(washii)*, troublesome [1]	禁	682 page 137
煙	EN; *kemuri*, smoke; *kemu(ru)*, to smoulder; *kemu(i)*, smoky [3]	禍	KA, misfortune, disaster, evil [1]
照	541 page 109	禅	ZEN, Dhyāna, the Zen sect of Buddhism, religious meditation [1]
献	KEN, KON, to dedicate, to offer, to present [1]	福	409 page 82
猿	EN; *saru*, monkey [1]	稚	CHI infant, young, childish, raw [1]
痴	CHI foolish, stupid [1]	▲ 窟	KUTSU; cavern
盟	991 page 199	節	552 page 111
▲ 睦	BOKU, *mutsu(majii)*, intimate; friendly, harmonious; *mutsu(mu)*, get along together	絹	861 page 173

続	563 page 113	▲ 腫	SHU; *ha(reru)*, *ha(rasu)*, tumor; swelling
継	KEI; *tsu(gi)* a patch; *tsu(gu)*, to inherit, to succeed to, to come into (property, etc.) [1]	腸	574 page 115
署	908 page 182	腰	YŌ; *koshi*, waist, loins [2]
罪	713 page 143	腹	975 page 196
置	570 page 115	艇	TEI, boat [1]
▲ 羨	SEN; *uraya(mu)*, *uraya(mashii)*, envious, be jealous	▲ 蓋	GAI; *futa*, cover, lid, flap
群	684 page 137	蓄	CHIKU, to store, to save; *takuwa(eru)*, to save, to store up [1]
義	674 page 135	蒸	915 page 184
聖	922 page 185	虞	*osore*, anxiety, apprehension [1]
▲ 腎	JIN; kidney	虜	RYO, captive, prisoner of war [1]
▲ 腺	SEN; gland	▲ 蜂	HŌ, *hachi*, bee; wasp

裏	1,002 page 201	誠	923 page 185
褐	KATSU, woolen kimono, dark brown [1]	詳	SHŌ; kuwa(shii), detailed, minute, well-informed [1]
▲裾	suso, cuff, hem; foot of a mountain	話	240 page 49
裸	RA; hadaka, nakedness, nude [1]	詰	KITSU; tsu(meru), to cram; tsu(maru), to be blocked; tsu(maranai), trifling; tsu(mari), in short [2]
触	SHOKU; fu(reru), to touch, to mention; to conflict with; to proclaim [2]	詩	307 page 62
解	662 page 133	試	525 page 106
▲詣	KEI; mō(deru), visit a temple	豊	811 page 163
該	GAI, that, the very, the ~ in question (used as prefix) [1]	▲賂	RO; bribe
誉	YO; homa(re), honor, credit, glory, reputation [1]	賄	WAI, wealth, bribe; to cater for; makana(u), to provide (meals, etc.), expenses [1]
▲詮	SEN; discussion; selection	賊	ZOKU, thief, robber, burglar [1]
誇	KO; hoko(ri), pride; hoko(ru), to be proud of, to boast of [1]	賃	953 page 191

資	721 page 145	遠	85 page 18
践	SEN, to step on, to go, to carry out [1]	酬	SHŪ, to reward, to recompense, to return, to repay [1]
跡	SEKI; *ato*, mark, trace, trail, wake, ruins [2]	酪	RAKU, dairy products [1]
路	439 page 88	鈴	REI; RIN, *suzu*, small bell [1]
跳	CHŌ, to jump, to leap, to flee; *ha(neru)*, *to(bu)*, to jump, to leap [1]	鉢	HACHI, bowl, pot [1]
較	KAKU, to compare [1]	鉛	EN; *namari*, lead (metal) [1]
載	SAI; *no(seru)*, to load, place on, put in print; *no(ru)*, to be put in print [1]	鉱	700 page 141
辞	528 page 106	鉄	374 page 75
農	386 page 78	隙	GEKI; *suki*, crevice, fissure
違	I; *chiga(u)*, to differ from, to be wrong; *chiga(eru)*, to change, to break [3]	隔	▲ KAKU; *heda(teru)*, to separate, to screen, to estrange; *heda(taru)*, to be distant from [1]
遣	KEN, to send, to dispatch, to bestow; *-zukai*, use of [1]	雅	GA, elegant, graceful [1]

零	REI, zero, to fall, to rain; fragment [2]	頑	GAN, stubborn, foolish [1]
雷	RAI; *kaminari*, thunder, thunderbolt [1]	預	821 page 165
電	197 page 40	飾	SHOKU; *kaza(ru)*, to ornament, to embellish, to exhibit, to affect [1]
靴	KA; *kutsu*, shoes [3]	飽	HŌ; *a(ki)*, weariness, tiresomeness; *a(kiru)*, to grow tired of, to become weary of [1]
頒	HAN, to distribute, to divide [1]	飼	722 page 145
▲ 頓	TON; suddenly, immediately, in a hurry	鼓	KO; *tsuzumi*, hand drum [1]

14 STROKES

像	762 page 153	境	680 page 137
僕	BOKU, manservant, I [1]	墨	BOKU; *sumi*, India ink, ink stick [1]
僚	RYŌ, an official; friend, colleague [1]	増	763 page 153
塾	JUKU, cram school, private school [1]	奪	DATSU; *uba(u)*, to take by force, to rob, to captivate [1]

嫡	CHAKU, heir, legitimate child [1]	憎	ZŌ; *niku(mu)*, to hate, to detest; *niku(i)*, *niku(rashii)*, hateful, provoking; *niku(shimi)*, hatred [2]
察	516 page 104	慣	668 page 134
寧	NEI, quiet, peaceful, easy; kind; rather [1]	摘	TEKI, to dislose, to reveal, to point out; *tsu(mu)*, to pick, to pluck [1]
寡	KA, few, little, small, scanty; alone; widow [1]	旗	474 page 95
層	934 page 187	暦	REKI; *koyomi*, calendar, almanac [1]
彰	SHŌ, manifest, clear, to elucidate [1]	暮	982 page 197
徳	783 page 157	様	430 page 87
徴	CHŌ, symptom, sign; effect, proof; to summon [1]	構	701 page 141
態	771 page 155	概	GAI, roughly, generally, as a rule [1]
慕	BO; *shita(u)*, to yearn for, to adore, to follow [1]	模	992 page 199
慢	MAN, to be idle, to neglect; to despise, to be naughty, to be selfish [1]	歌	90 page 19

282

歴	636 page 128	獄	GOKU, prison, jail 1
滴	TEKI; *shizuku*, a drop (of liquid); *shitata(ru)*, to trickle, to drip 2	▲ 瑠	RU; lapis lazuli
漬	*tsu(keru)* (v.t.), to pickle, to preserve, to soak; *tsu(karu)* (v.i.), to be soaked/steeped in 1	疑	848 page 170
漂	HYŌ, to wander about; to bleach; *tadayo(u)*, to drift, to float 1	▲ 瘍	YŌ; boil; carbuncle
漆	SHITSU; *urushi*, lacquer 1	碑	HI, monument, tombstone 1
漸	ZEN, gradually; to advance gradually; at last 1	磁	892 page 179
漏	RŌ; *mo(ru)*, to leak; *mo(reru)*, to leak, to get out (secret, etc.), to be omitted 1	穀	876 page 176
漫	MAN in spite of oneself, involuntarily, self-willfulness; vast, wide, lax 1	稲	TŌ; *ine*, rice plant 1
漁	483 page 97	種	531 page 107
演	650 page 131	端	TAN, right, correct, just; *hashi*, *hata*, *ha-*, end, tip, edge, border 1
▲ 熊	*kuma*, bear	▲ 箋	SEN; paper; label; letter

箇	KA (used as auxiliary in counting) [1]	綿	818 page 164
算	142 page 29	総	760 page 153
管	466 page 94	罰	BATSU, BACHI, penalty, punishment; *bas(suru)*, to punish, to penalize [1]
精	748 page 150	聞	219 page 44
▲綻	TAN, DAN; *hokoro(biru)*, ripped; unravel	腐	FU; *kusa(ru)*, to go bad, to rot; to be dejected, to lose heart [1]
維	I to keep; to fasten; fundamental principles [1]	膜	MAKU, membrane [1]
緒	SHO, beginning, lineage; clue; *o*, cord, string (of a musical instrument) [3]	▲蔑	BETSU, despise, ridicule, *sagesu(mu)*, ignore, neglect
綱	KŌ, basic principles; *tsuna*, rope, cable; last hope (of life, etc.) [1]	▲蜜	MITSU; honey; nectar
網	MŌ; *ami*, net, netting [1]	製	749 page 150
緑	435 page 88	複	804 page 161
練	438 page 88	誌	891 page 179

誓	SEI; *chika(i)*, oath, vow; *chika(u)*, to swear, to take a vow [1]	▲ 遜		SON; humble; modest
認	962 page 193	▲ 遡		SO; *sakanobo(ru)*, go upstream; retrace the past
誘	YŪ; *saso(i)*, invitation, temptation; *saso(u)*, to invite, to induce, to allure [1]	遭		SŌ, to encounter, to come across; *a(u)*, to encounter, to be confronted by [1]
誤	868 page 174	遮		SHA; *saegi(ru)*, to interrupt, to obstruct [1]
説	553 page 111	適		778 page 156
語	124 page 25	酵		KŌ, yeast, ferment, sake lees [1]
読	206 page 42	酷		KOKU, severity, cruelty, harshness [1]
豪	GŌ, to excel, to stand pre-eminent; strong, vigorous; Australia [1]	酸		715 page 144
▲ 貌	BŌ; form; appearance	銭		757 page 152
踊	YŌ; *odo(ri)*, dance; *odo(ru)*, to dance, to jump [2]	銘		MEI, signature, inscription, appellation, motto [1]
▲ 辣	RATSU; bitter	銅		781 page 157

285

銃	JŪ, gun, rifle [1]	静	548 page 110
銀	281 page 57	領	825 page 166
閥	BATSU, clique, faction, clan [1]	▲ 餅	HEI; *mochi*, rice cake
閣	837 page 168	▲ 餌	JI; *e, esa*, food, bait; prey
関	467 page 94	駄	DA, packhorse; sometimes used for its sound value [1]
際	710 page 143	駅	253 page 51
障	913 page 183	駆	KU, to drive a vehicle, to chase; *ka(keru)*, to run, to gallop [1]
隠	IN; *kaku(reru)*, to hide (v.i.), to disappear; *kaku(su)*, to hide (v.t.), to conceal [1]	髪	HATSU; *kami*, hair, hairdo [3]
雌	SHI; *mesu, me-*, female (animal, bird; *me-* is also used in the case of plants) [1]	魂	KON; *tamashii*, soul, spirit, ghost [1]
雑	714 page 143	鳴	229 page 46
需	JU, demand, request [1]	鼻	399 page 80

286

15 STROKES

億	452 page 91	墳	FUN, mound, tumulus, hillock, tomb 1
舗	HO, store; to pave 1	賓	HIN, guest 1
儀	GI, rule, ceremony, affair, matter 1	寮	RYŌ, boarding house, dormitory 1
劇	858 page 172	審	SHIN, detailed, full, clear, evident, obvious 1
勲	KUN, meritorious deed, distinguished service 1	導	782 page 157
嘱	SHOKU, to entrust, to request 1	履	RI, footwear; to walk; to do, to experience; *ha(ku)*, to put on, to wear (footwear) 1
▲ 嘲	CHŌ; *azake(ru)*, ridicule	幣	HEI, pendant paper strips in a Shinto shrine; riches, offering, money 1
器	475 page 96	弊	HEI, evil, abuse, vice, our (used as prefix denoting modesty) 1
噴	FUN; *fu(ku)*, to emit, to spout, to belch out 1	影	EI; *kage*, shadow, reflection, image, phantom, light 1
墜	TSUI, to fall, to drop 1	徹	TETSU, to pierce, to penetrate 1

287

衝	SHŌ, important position, focus; to attack, to strike against; to brave [1]	撃	GEKI; *u(tsu)*, to fire (a gun, etc.), to attack, to strike, to fight [1]
慮	RYO, to consider, to deliberate, to plan, to be anxious [1]	撲	BOKU, to strike, to beat [1]
慶	KEI, congratulation, happiness; to rejoice [1]	撤	TETSU; *tes(suru)*, to remove, to get rid of, to withdraw (an army, etc.) [1]
憂	YŪ; *ure(i)*, grief, anxiety, affliction; *ure(eru)*, to fear, to lament, to be worried [1]	撮	SATSU, to pinch, to pick, to gather, to take a photograph; *to(ru)*, to photograph, to film [1]
慰	I; *nagusa(me)*, comfort; *nagusa(mi)*, pastime; *nagusa(meru)*, to comfort, to console [1]	敷	FU; *shi(ku)*, to spread, to pave, to sit on (a cushion), to lay (a railway) [1]
▲ 憬	KEI; yearn for, admire	敵	779 page 156
▲ 憧	SHŌ; *akoga(reru)*, yearn after, long for	暫	ZAN, for a little while, for some time [1]
憤	FUN; *ikidō(ru)*, to be indignant, to resent [1]	暴	814 page 163
戯	GI, fun, play, flirtation; *tawamu(reru)*, to joke, to play, to flirt with [1]	槽	SŌ, tank, vat [1]
▲ 摯	SHI; gift; seriousness	標	599 page 120
摩	MA, to rub, to grind, to wear away; *ma(suru)* (lit.), to nearly touch, to scrape [1]	横	255 page 52

権	862 page 173		▲ 璃	RI; lapis lazuli
歓	KAN, to rejoice [1]		▲ 畿	KI; capital, suburbs of capital
潔	686 page 138		監	KAN, to watch over, to keep control over, to supervise; prison, jail [1]
澄	CHŌ; su(mu), to become clear or serene (moon, stream, sky, mind, etc.) [1]		盤	BAN, board (for chess, etc.), shallow basin, phonograph record, plate [1]
潜	SEN, dive, submerge, lurk; hiso(mu), to lie concealed, mogu(ru), to dive in, to crawl in [1]		確	664 page 133
潟	kata, lagoon [1]		▲ 稽	KEI; think, consider, quarrel
潤	JUN; uruo(i), moisture; profit; charm; uruo(su) (v.t.), to moisten; to profit [1]		稿	KŌ, draft, rough copy, manuscript [1]
▲ 潰	KAI; tsubu(su), tsubu(reru), crush, smash		穂	SUI; ho, ear (of wheat, etc.), head [1]
潮	952 page 191		稼	KA; kase(gu), to work, to earn [1]
熟	905 page 182		窯	YŌ; kama, kiln for baking tiles, ceramics, etc. [1]
熱	589 page 118		窮	KYŪ; kiwa(meru), to carry to extremes; kiwa(maru), to end, to reach the extreme [1]

箸	*hashi*, chopsticks	罷	HI, to pause, to intermit, to dismiss, to release, to get tired [1]
範	HAN, example, model [1]	膚	FU; *hada*, skin (of the body) [2]
箱	390 page 79	膝	*hiza*, knee; lap
緊	KIN, to shrink, to become tight, to contract; severe, strict, hard, solid [1]	舞	BU; *mai*, dancing, dance; *ma(u)*, to dance [3]
縄	JŌ; *nawa*, rope [1]	蔵	936 page 188
線	176 page 36	蔽	HEI; cover; shade; conceal
締	TEI; *shi(maru)*, to be shut, to be tight; *shi(meru)*, to tie, to tighten, to shut (v.t.) [1]	褒	HŌ; *ho(meru)*, to praise [1]
緩	KAN, slow, easy, slack, lenient; *yuru(i)*, loose, lenient [1]	謁	ETSU, (Imperial) audience; audience with persons of high rank [1]
編	806 page 162	諾	DAKU, consent, assent [1]
縁	EN, relation, ties, blood relation; fate; veranda, porch; *fuchi*, edge, verge [1]	誕	943 page 189
罵	BA; *nonoshi(ru)*, abuse; insult	誰	*dare*, who; someone

290

談	363 page 73		質	726 page 146
課	456 page 92		趣	SHU; *omomuki*, taste, elegance, grace, air, appearance, purport, effect [1]
請	SEI, SHIN; *ko(u)*, to beg, to ask, to request; *u(keru)*, to receive, to undertake [1]	▲	踪	SŌ; remains; clue; footprint
論	1,006 page 202		踏	TŌ; *fu(mu)*, to step on, to tread on; *fu(maeru)*, to step on, to be based on [1]
調	369 page 74		輩	HAI, fellows, companions [1]
諸	909 page 182		輝	KI; *kagaya(ku)*, to shine, to be radiant [1]
賠	BAI, to make up for, to compensate for [1]		輪	631 page 127
賦	FU (lit.), ode, poetical prose; tribute, levy, allotment [1]		遵	JUN, to obey, to observe, to abide by [1]
賜	SHI; *tamawa(ru)*, to deign to give, to grant, to award [1]		遷	SEN, to move from one location to another, to transfer [1]
賛	716 page 144		選	556 page 112
賞	542 page 109		遺	827 page 166

鋭	EI; *surudo(i)*, sharp, pointed, biting, acute, keen, smart [2]	養	624 page 125
鋳	CHŪ; *i(ru)*, to cast (metal), to found [1]	餓	GA, to be hungry, to starve [1]
閲	ETSU (lit.), inspection, examination; to examine, to inspect, to peruse, to elapse [1]	▲ 駒	*koma*, pony, horse
震	SHIN; *furu(u)*, *furu(eru)*, to shake (v.i.), to tremble; *furu(waseru)*, to shake (v.t.) [2]	駐	CHŪ, to stop, to stay [2]
霊	REI, *tama*, soul, spirit, ghost [1]	魅	MI; *mi(suru)* (lit.), to fascinate, to enchant, to bewitch [1]
▲ 頬	*hō*, cheek	黙	MOKU; *dama(ru)*, to become silent, to close one's lips [1]

16 STROKES

儒	JU, Confucianism, Confucianist, scholar; cowardice, tenderness [1]	壇	DAN, platform, dais, raised floor
凝	GYŌ; *ko(ri)*, stiffness; *ko(ru)*, to be absorbed in, to elaborate, to grow stiff [1]	壊	KAI, to collapse, to be destroyed; to break, to destroy [1]
墾	KON, to cultivate, to farm, to reclaim [1]	壁	HEKI; *kabe*, wall [1]
壤	JŌ, earth, soil [1]	奮	976 page 196

嬢	JŌ, Miss (used as suffix), girl, unmarried lady, daughter [1]	曇	DON; *kumo(ri)*, cloudy weather, blur; *kumo(ru)*, to become cloudy, to become dim [2]
衡	KŌ, scale, beam; to measure, to weigh [1]	樹	897 page 180
衛	646 page 130	橋	277 page 56
憩	KEI, to take a rest; *iko(i)*, vacation; *iko(u)*, to take a rest [1]	機	476 page 96
憲	863 page 173	濁	DAKU; *nigo(ri)*, turbidity; voiced sound; *nigo(ru)*, to become muddy or cloudy [1]
憾	KAN, to regret, to be sorry for [1]	濃	NŌ; *ko(i)*, dark, deep, thick, heavy, strong [2]
憶	OKU, to remember, to keep in mind, to think [1]	激	859 page 172
懐	KAI, one's pocket; to think, to long for; *natsu(kashii)*, beloved, longed for [1]	燃	786 page 158
擁	YŌ; *yō(suru)*, to protect, to embrace, to hold [1]	獣	JŪ; *kemono*, beast, brute [1]
操	935 page 188	獲	KAKU; *e(ru)*, to get, to obtain, to gain [1]
整	345 page 70	磨	MA; *miga(ku)*, to polish, to improve [2]

穏	ON; *oda(yaka)*, calm, quiet, peaceful, mild [1]	▲ 膳	ZEN; small low table; tray
積	550 page 111	膨	BŌ; *fuku(ramu)*, to swell, to expand; *fuku(reru)*, to swell, to expand, to sulk [1]
篤	TOKU, genuine, sincere, hearty, cordial [1]	興	702 page 141
築	774 page 155	薦	SEN, to recommend; *susu(meru)*, to recommend [1]
糖	958 page 192	薪	SHIN, firewood; *takigi*, firewood [1]
緻	CHI; fine (not coarse)	薫	KUN, fragrance; to be fragrant; *kao(ru)*, to be fragrant [1]
縫	HŌ; *nu(u)*, to sew, to stitch [1]	薬	420 page 85
緯	I, parallels of latitude; cross-threads [1]	薄	HAKU; *usu(i)*, thin, light, pale, weak, small (profit, etc.) [2]
縛	BAKU; *shiba(ru)*, to bind, to tie, to arrest [1]	融	YŪ, to melt; to circulate, to ventilate [1]
繁	HAN, thick, many, much, thriving; troublesome, busy, mixed [1]	親	166 page 34
縦	903 page 181	諮	SHI, to consult, to ask counsel of; *haka(ru)*, to consult [1]

諦	TEI; *akira(meru)*, abandon; give up	錮	KO; to tie
謡	YŌ; *utai*, chanting of a *Noh* drama text [1]	錠	JŌ, lock, padlock; tablet (medical) (used as suffix for counting tablets) [1]
諭	YU; *sato(su)*, to admonish, to instruct [1]	録	640 page 129
諧	KAI; harmony, order	錯	SAKU, to be mixed together, to make a mistake [1]
謀	BŌ, MU; *haka(ru)*, to scheme, to conspire [1]	錬	REN, to temper or forge metal; to train, to cultivate, to polish, to drill morally [1]
賢	KEN; *kashiko(i)*, wise, intelligent, tactful, smart, shrewd [2]	錦	KIN; *nishiki*, brocade; fine dress, honors
賭	TO; *ka(keru)*, gamble; wager; bet	鋼	874 page 175
輸	819 page 164	隣	RIN; *tonari*, next door house; next to, neighboring [1]
避	HI; *sa(keru)*, to avoid, to keep away from, shirk [1]	隷	REI, servant, follower [1]
還	KAN, to return, to come back [1]	頼	RAI; *tano(mu)*, to request; *tano(mi)*, a request; *tano(moshii)*, trustworthy; *tayo(ru)*, to rely on [3]
醒	SE; *sa(meru)*, *sa(masu)*, awake, be disillusioned; sober up	頭	203 page 41

| 館 | 266
page 54 | ▲
麺 | MEN; noodles; wheat flour |
| ▲
骸 | GAI; bone, body, corpse | | |

17 STROKES

償	SHŌ; *tsuguna(i)*, indemnity, atonement; *tsuguna(u)*, to make up for, to atone for 1	▲ 曖	AI; *kurai*, dark, not clear 1
優	995 page 200	濯	TAKU wash, rinse 2
厳	865 page 174	燥	SŌ, to dry 2
嚇	KAKU, to threaten, to menace 1	爵	SHAKU, peerage, title and court rank 1
懇	KON kind, cordial, in love with, intimate 1	犠	GI, sacrifice, victim 1
▲ 戴	TAI; receive; be crowned with	環	KAN, ring, link; to surround 1
擦	SATSU, to rub, to scrub, to scratch; *su(reru)*, to rub, to become worn; *su(ru)* to rub, to chafe 1	療	RYŌ, to cure, to heal 2
擬	GI; *gi(suru)*, to point or aim (an object) at; to imitate; to compare 1	▲ 瞭	RYŌ; clear

瞳	DŌ; *hitomi*, pupil of the eye	謄	TŌ, to take a copy of, to transcribe [1]
矯	KYŌ; *ta(meru)*, to straighten, to correct [1]	謙	KEN, to humble oneself, to condescend [1]
礁	SHŌ, submerged rock, unknown reef [1]	謝	728 page 146
績	752 page 151	謹	KIN, to restrain oneself, to be respectful; *tsutsushi(mu)*, to be humble [1]
縮	904 page 181	講	703 page 141
繊	SEN, thin, slender, fine, small [1]	購	KŌ, to purchase, to buy [1]
翼	YOKU, to aid, to assist; *tsubasa*, wing [1]	轄	KATSU, control, management [1]
聴	CHŌ, to listen to, to comply with; *ki(ku)*, to listen to, to take notice of [1]	醜	SHŪ; *miniku(i)*, ugly, unseemly, ignoble [1]
臆	OKU; timidity, cowardly, fear	鍋	*nabe*, pot; pan; kettle
謎	*nazo*, riddle; puzzle; enigma; hint	鍵	KEN; *kagi*, key
覧	1,001 page 201	鍛	TAN; *kita(eru)*, to forge; to train, to cultivate (morally) [1]

闇	*yami*, darkness; gloom	鮮	SEN, fresh, new, clean, Korea, few; *aza(yaka)*, bright, clear, graceful [1]
霜	SŌ; *shimo*, frost [1]	齢	REI, age, years [2]
頻	HIN, frequent [1]		

18 STROKES

懲	CHŌ; *ko(rasu)*, to punish, to discipline, to chasten; *ko(riru)*, to learn from experience [1]	礎	SO; *ishizue*, foundation, cornerstone [1]
曜	236 page 48	穫	KAKU, to reap, to harvest [1]
濫	RAN, at random, wantonly; excessive; to overflow, to float [1]	簡	843 page 169
璧	HEKI; ball; sphere	糧	RYŌ, food, provisions [1]
癒	YU; *ier(ru)*, get well, recover; *i(yasu)*, to heal, cure, quench (one's thirst) [1]	繕	ZEN; *tsukuro(u)*, to patch up, to mend, to trim, to smooth over [1]
癖	HEKI; *kuse*, habit, peculiar way, frizz (of hair), weakness [1]	繭	KEN; *mayu*, silkworm cocoon [1]
瞬	SHUN, a short time; to wink, to twinkle, to flicker; *matata(ku)*, to wink, to twinkle, to blink [1]	織	742 page 149

翻	HON; *hirugae(ru)*, to flutter; *hirugae(su)*, to wave (v.t.); to change (one's mind) [1]	▲ 鎌	*kama*, sickle, scythe
職	743 page 149	鎮	CHIN, to calm, to quiet, to tranquilize; to suppress; *shizu(meru)*, to suppress, to pacify [1]
臨	1,004 page 201	闘	TŌ; *tataka(u)*, to fight [1]
▲ 藍	RAN, *ai*, indigo (blue); indigo plant	難	960 page 193
▲ 藤	TŌ; *fuji*, wisteria	離	RI; *hana(reru)* (v.i.), *hana(su)* (v.t.), to separate, to part, to divide, to keep apart
藩	HAN, Japanese feudal clan or domain [1]	韓	KAN; Korea
襟	KIN; *eri*, neckband, collar [1]	▲ 顎	GAKU; *ago*, jaw, chin
覆	FUKU; *ō(u)*, veil, conceal, wrap; *kutsugae(su)* (v.t.), *kutsugae(ru)* (v.i.), overturn [1]	額	665 page 134
観	468 page 94	題	360 page 73
贈	ZŌ; *oku(ru)*, to present as a gift [2]	顕	KEN, bright, clear, distinguished, manifest; to show, to manifest [1]
鎖	SA, hasp; to shut, to close; *kusari*, chain [1]	類	632 page 127

顔	103 page 21	騒	SŌ; *sawa(gi)*, noise, disturbance; *sawa(gu)*, to make a noise, to make a disturbance 1
験	500 page 101	騎	KI, suffix for counting horsemen; cavalry, saddle horse; to ride, to mount 1

19 STROKES

瀬	*se*, shallows, rapids 1	藻	SŌ; *mo*, seaweed 1
爆	BAKU, to burst, to explode 2	覇	HA, supremacy, domination 1
璽	JI, Imperial seal 1	譜	FU, music, musical score; family record, genealogy 1
簿	BO, notebook 1	識	725 page 146
繰	*ku(ru)*, to reel (thread, etc.), to gin (cotton), to turn over (pages, etc.) 1	警	857 page 172
羅	RA, silk gauze, thin silk 1	▲蹴	SHŪ; *ke(ru)*, kick
臓	937 page 188	鏡	486 page 98
▲艶	EN; *tsuya*, luster, gloss, polish, sheen	霧	MU; *kiri*, mist, fog, spray 1

韻	IN, rhyme, echo, taste, elegance [1]	鶏	KEI; *niwatori*, chicken [1]
願	469 page 94	▲ 麓	ROKU, *fumoto*, foot of a mountain
髄	ZUI, marrow, pith [1]	麗	REI; *uruwa(shii)*, fine, lovely, beautiful, elegant, graceful [1]
鯨	GEI; *kujira*, whale [1]		

20 STROKES

懸	KEN, KE to hang, to suspend; to offer a reward; to be anxious; to depend on [1]	議	477 page 96
欄	RAN, column (of, a newspaper, etc.); railing [1]	醸	JŌ to brew; *kamo(su)*, to brew, to distil, to bring about [1]
競	487 page 98	鐘	SHŌ; *kane*, bell [1]
籍	SEKI, census, register, membership [2]	響	KYŌ; *hibi(ki)*, sound, echo, vibration; *hibi(ku)*, to echo, to vibrate [1]
譲	JŌ; *yuzu(ru)*, to hand over, to concede to, to yield to, to reserve [1]	騰	TŌ, to rise, to ascend, to leap [1]
護	696 page 140		

21 STROKES

艦	KAN, warship [1]	顧	KO; *kaeri(miru)*, to look back, to reflect upon oneself, to think of, to heed [1]
躍	YAKU; *odo(ru)*, to leap, to jump; to rise, to go up [1]	魔	MA, devil, demon, evil spirit [1]
露	RO, to expose, to lay bare; to be exposed, to come to light; Russia; *tsuyu*, dew [1]	鶴	*tsuru*, crane; stork

22 STROKES

▲ 籠	RŌ, be crowded; *ko(moru)*, seclude oneself, be filled with; *kago*, cage; basket	驚	KYŌ; *odoro(ki)*, surprise; *odoro(ku)*, to be surprised or frightened, to marvel (at) [1]
襲	SHŪ, *oso(u)*, to attack; to succeed to; to make a surprise visit		

23 STROKES

鑑	KAN, model, pattern, example; *kanga(miru)*, in light of, in consideration of [1]		

29 STROKES

▲ 鬱	UTSU; depression, gloom, melancholy; *us(suru)*, *fusa(gu)*, to be depressed		

RADICAL INDEX

In this index, the **center column** provides this information:

- All Essential characters are referenced by their character number only.

- All General Use characters that are not Essential characters are referenced by their page number. Page numbers are followed by either "a" or "b" to indicate the left or right column on that page.

The **righthand column** provides the reference number that the *New Nelson Dictionary* assigns to the character.

1 一			**5 strokes**			**4 strokes**			任	785	136
1 stroke			丼	209a	37	互	205b	75	仰	213b	137
一	1	1	主	315	38	井	205b	76	伏	213b	139
2 strokes						五	5	77	仲	571	140
丁	367	2	**4 丿**			**7 strokes**			伝	580	141
七	7	3	**3 strokes**			亜	218a	81	休	80	142
3 strokes			久	676	47				会	93	143
丈	204a	5	**4 strokes**			**8 亠**			仮	656	144
与	204a	6	乏	205a	46	**3 strokes**			全	347	145
万	227	7	**9 strokes**			亡	985	86	**7 strokes**		
三	3	8	乗	336	54	**6 strokes**			似	724	138
下	24	9				交	128	90	但	219a	154
上	23	10	**5 乙**			**8 strokes**			佐	219a	155
4 strokes			**1 stroke**			享	226a	92	伺	219a	156
不	600	13	乙	203b	56	京	110	93	伴	219a	157
5 strokes			**2 strokes**			**9 strokes**			伯	219b	158
丙	208a	16	九	9	57	亭	235a	96	位	445	162
且	208b	17	**3 strokes**						伸	219b	163
丘	209a	19	乞	204a	59	**9 亻**			住	325	164
世	344	20	**7 strokes**			**2 strokes**			体	182	165
6 strokes			乱	999	60	人	39	99	低	575	166
両	434	23	**8 strokes**			**4 strokes**			作	141	167
8 strokes			乳	961	61	介	206a	108	余	820	168
並	977	24	**11 strokes**			仁	917	110	何	86	169
			亀	254a	62	仏	805	111	**8 strokes**		
2 丨			乾	254a	63	今	138	112	侮	226a	187
4 strokes						**5 strokes**			価	657	188
中	26	28	**6 亅**			以	443	109	舎	727	189
7 strokes			**2 strokes**			仙	209a	120	併	226a	190
串	218a	30	了	203a	67	令	633	121	依	226a	191
9 strokes			**4 strokes**			他	354	122	侍	226a	192
衷	235a	31	予	425	68	仕	301	123	例	635	193
			6 strokes			付	602	124	佳	226a	194
3 丶			争	558	69	代	358	125	供	850	195
3 strokes			**8 strokes**			**6 strokes**			使	303	196
丸	101	34	事	309	71	件	687	130	**9 strokes**		
4 strokes						伐	213a	132	侶	235a	205
丹	205a	36	**7 二**			伎	213b	133	侯	235a	211
			2 strokes			企	213b	135			
			二	2	72						

316

遣	280a	6100
遠	85	6101

14 strokes

遡	285b	6094
遜	285b	6098
遭	285b	6105
遮	285b	6106
適	778	6107

15 strokes

遵	291b	6112
遷	291b	6113
選	556	6114
遺	827	6115

16 strokes

避	295a	6120
還	295a	6121

163 阝 (right)

7 strokes

那	225b	6129
邦	225b	6130

8 strokes

邸	234b	6134
邪	234b	6135

9 strokes

郊	243b	6137
郎	243b	6138

10 strokes

郡	491	6143

11 strokes

郭	262b	6144
郷	852	6145
部	407	6146
郵	994	6147
都	376	6148

164 酉

10 strokes

酒	318	6160
酎	253a	6161
酌	253a	6162
配	388	6163

11 strokes

酔	263a	6166

12 strokes

酢	272b	6169

13 strokes

酬	280b	6171
酪	280b	6172

14 strokes

酵	285b	6175
酷	285b	6176
酸	715	6177

16 strokes

醒	295a	6185

17 strokes

醜	297b	6189

20 strokes

醸	301b	6197

165 釆

8 strokes

采	234b	6201

11 strokes

釈	263a	6203

166 里

7 strokes

里	238	6206

9 strokes

重	326	6207

11 strokes

野	233	6208

12 strokes

量	630	6209

167 金

8 strokes

金	18	6211

10 strokes

釜	253a	6215
針	916	6218

11 strokes

釣	263a	6224

12 strokes

鈍	272b	6235

13 strokes

鈴	280b	6247
鉢	280b	6249
鉛	280b	6251
鉱	700	6252
鉄	374	6253

14 strokes

銭	757	6264
銘	285b	6265
銅	781	6266
銃	286a	6267
銀	281	6268

15 strokes

鋭	292a	6279
鋳	292a	6280

16 strokes

鋼	295b	6286
錠	295b	6293
録	640	6298
錯	295b	6299
錬	295b	6300
錦	295b	6301
鋼	874	6302

17 strokes

鍋	297b	6315
鍵	297b	6317
鍛	297b	6318

18 strokes

鎖	299b	6325
鎌	299b	6326
鎮	299b	6328

19 strokes

鏡	486	6341

20 strokes

鐘	301b	6352

23 strokes

鑑	302a	6361

168 長

8 strokes

長	189	6379

169 門

8 strokes

門	231	6381

11 strokes

閉	979	6385

12 strokes

閑	272b	6390
間	100	6391
開	261	6393

14 strokes

閣	286a	6398
閥	837	6401
関	467	6402

15 strokes

閲	292a	6404

17 strokes

闇	298a	6414

18 strokes

闘	299b	6418

170 阝 (left)

7 strokes

阪	225b	6428
防	812	6429

8 strokes

阜	234b	6423
附	234b	6433
阻	234a	6434

9 strokes

限	691	6439

10 strokes

陛	978	6444
陥	253b	6446
院	249	6447
陣	253b	6448
除	910	6449
降	873	6450

11 strokes

陵	263a	6454
隆	263a	6455
険	689	6456
陳	263a	6457
陪	263a	6458
陶	263a	6459
陸	627	6461
陰	263b	6462

12 strokes

随	272b	6460
隅	272b	6467
隊	567	6468
階	262	6469
陽	429	6470

13 strokes

隙	280b	6471
隔	280b	6475

14 strokes

際	710	6478
障	913	6479
隠	286a	6480

16 strokes

隣	295b	6484

171 隶

16 strokes

隷	295b	6490

172 隹

10 strokes

隻	253b	6494

12 strokes

雇	273a	6497
雄	273a	6499
集	324	6500

13 strokes

雅	280b	6505

14 strokes

雌	286a	6506
雑	714	6507

18 strokes

難	960	6515
離	299b	6517

173 雨

8 strokes

雨	69	6518

11 strokes

雪	174	6520

12 strokes

雰	273a	6521
雲	83	6522

INDEX OF READINGS

This index contains an alphabetical listing of all Japanese readings given in the body of the book. Note that:

1. On readings are shown in capital letters and kun readings are shown in lower case letters.

2. All Essential characters are referenced by their character number only. For example:
   abiru 浴 625.

3. All General Use characters that are not Essential characters are referenced by their page number. These are preceded by the letter "p" and followed by either "a" or "b" to indicate the left or right column on that page. For example: A 亜 p 218b.

4. When readings include okurigana, these are not indicated by parentheses.

— A —

A 亜 p 218b
abaku, abareru 暴 814
abiru, abiseru 浴 625
abunai 危 844
abura 油 422
abura 脂 p 251b
agaru, ageru 上 23
agaru, ageru 挙 482
ageru 揚 p 266b
ago 顎 p 299b
AI, aisuru 愛 441
AI 哀 p 236b
AI 挨 p 247b
AI 曖 p 296b
ai 藍 p 299a
ai- 相 348
aida 間 100
aji, ajiwau 味 415
aka, akai 赤 51
akarameru, akaramu 赤 51
akarui, akasu 明 228
akatsuki 暁 p 267a
akeru 空 66
akeru 明 228
akeru 開 261
aki 秋 156

aki, akiru 飽 p 281b
akinau 商 333
akiraka 明 228
akirameru 諦 p 295a
akogareru 憧 p 288a
AKU 悪 241
AKU 握 p 266b
aku 空 66
aku 開 261
ama 尼 p 211b
amai 甘 p 212b
amari, amaru, amasu 余 820
ame 天 67
ame 雨 69
ami 網 p 284a
amu 編 806
AN 行 131
AN 安 242
AN 暗 243
AN, anjiru 案 442
ana 穴 860
anadoru 侮 p 226a
ane 姉 146
ani 兄 114
ao, aoi 青 52
aogu 仰 p 213b
arai, arasu 荒 p 242b
arai 粗 p 260a

arashi 嵐 p 265b
arasoi, arasou 争 558
aratamaru, arata메 aratameru 改 458
aratani 新 165
arau 洗 927
arawareru, arawasu 現 692
arawasu 表 402
arawasu 著 949
areru 荒 p 242b
aru 有 423
aru 在 711
aruku 歩 221
asa 朝 191
asa 麻 p 263b
asaeru 抑 p 222b
asai 浅 554
aseru 焦 p 268b
ashi 足 36
asobu 遊 424
ataeru 与 p 204a
atai 価 657
atai 値 946
atama 頭 203
atarashii 新 165
atari 辺 608
ataru, ateru 当 200
atatakai, atatamaru,

atatameru 温 257
atatakai, atatamaru, atatameru 暖 945
ateru 充 p 214a
ateru 宛 p 228b
ato 後 123
ato 痕 p 259b
ato 跡 p 280a
ATSU 圧 641
atsui 暑 329
atsui 熱 589
atsui 厚 698
atsukau 扱 p 216a
atsumaru, atsumeru 集 324
au 会 93
au 合 134
au 遭 p 285b
awa 泡 p 232a
awai 淡 p 258b
aware, awaremu 哀 p 236b
awaseru 合 134
awaseru 併 p 226a
awatadashii, awateru 慌 p 266a
ayamachi 過 659
ayamari, ayamaru 誤 868

319

itonami, itonamu
営 645
ITSU 一 1
ITSU 逸 p 262b
itsukushimu 慈
p 275b
itsutsu 五 5
itsuwaru 偽 p 254a
iu 言 118
iwa 岩 102
iwai, iwau 祝 533
iya 嫌 p 274b
iyashii, iyashimeru
卑 p 236a
iyasu 癒 p 298a
izumi 泉 926

— J —

JA 邪 p 234b
JA 蛇 p 261b
JAKU 弱 154
JAKU 若 896
JAKU 寂 p 255b
JI 耳 32
JI 字 78
JI 寺 149
JI 自 150
JI 時 151
JI 地 184
JI 仕 301
JI 次 308
JI 事 309
JI 持 310
JI 児 526
JI 治 527
JI, jisuru 辞 528
JI 示 723
JI 似 724
JI 磁 892
JI 除 910
JI, jisuru 侍 p 226b
JI 滋 p 268a
JI 慈 p 275b
JI 餌 p 286b
JI 璽 p 300a
~ji 路 439
JIKI 直 192
JIKU 軸 p 272a
JIN 人 39
JIN 神 340
JIN 臣 543

JIN 仁 917
JIN 刃 p 204b
JIN 尽 p 216a
JIN 迅 p 218b
JIN 甚 p 240b
JIN 陣 p 253b
JIN 尋 p 265b
JIN 腎 p 278a
JITSU 日 13
JITSU 実 312
JO 女 41
JO 助 330
JO 序 734
JO 除 910
JO 如 p 215b
JO, josuru 叙 p 236a
JO 徐 p 247a
JŌ 上 23
JŌ 場 161
JŌ 星 171
JŌ 乗 336
JŌ 定 371
JŌ 成 545
JŌ 静 548
JŌ 条 738
JŌ 状 739
JŌ 常 740
JŌ 情 741
JŌ 城 914
JŌ 蒸 915
JŌ 盛 921
JŌ 丈 p 204a
JŌ 冗 p 206a
JŌ 浄 p 240a
JŌ 剰 p 254b
JŌ 畳 p 269a
JŌ 縄 p 290a
JŌ 壌 p 292b
JŌ 嬢 p 293a
JŌ 錠 p 295b
JŌ 譲 p 301a
JŌ 醸 p 301b
JOKU 辱 p 252b
JU 受 319
JU 授 729
JU 樹 897
JU 就 900
JU 寿 p 221b
JU 呪 p 227a
JU 需 p 286b
JU 儒 p 292a

JŪ 十 10
JŪ 中 26
JŪ 拾 321
JŪ 住 325
JŪ 重 326
JŪ 従 902
JŪ 縦 903
JŪ 汁 p 212a
JŪ 充 p 214a
JŪ 柔 p 239b
JŪ 渋 p 258b
JŪ 銃 p 286b
JŪ 獣 p 293b
JUKU, jukusuru 熟
905
JUKU 塾 p 281a
JUN 順 534
JUN 準 733
JUN 純 906
JUN 巡 p 216a
JUN 旬 p 216b
JUN 盾 p 241a
JUN 准 p 245a
JUN, junjiru 殉
p 249a
JUN 循 p 266a
JUN 潤 p 289a
JUN 遵 p 291b
JUTSU 述 731
JUTSU 術 732

— K —

KA 火 15
KA 下 24
KA 花 70
KA 何 86
KA 科 87
KA 夏 88
KA 家 89
KA 歌 90
KA 化 258
KA 荷 259
KA 加 453
KA 果 454
KA 貨 455
KA 課 456
KA 可 655
KA 仮 656
KA 価 657
KA 河 658
KA 過 659

KA 佳 p 226a
KA 苛 p 234a
KA, kasuru 架
p 239b
KA 華 p 252a
KA 菓 p 261a
KA 鹿 p 263b
KA 渦 p 268a
KA 嫁 p 274b
KA 暇 p 276a
KA 禍 p 277b
KA 靴 p 281a
KA 寡 p 282a
KA 箇 p 284a
KA 稼 p 289b
-ka 日 13
ka 香 p 244b
ka 蚊 p 252a
kabe 壁 p 292b
kabu 株 839
kado 角 97
kado 門 231
kaerimiru 省 546
kaerimiru 顧 p 302b
kaeru 帰 106
kaeru 代 358
kaeru 変 609
kaeru 換 p 266b
kaeru 替 p 267a
kaesu 返 412
kagami 鏡 486
kagayaku 輝 p 291b
kage 陰 p 263b
kage 影 p 287b
kagi 鍵 p 297b
kagiri, kagiru 限 691
kago 籠 p 302a
kagu 嗅 p 274a
KAI 回 92
KAI 会 93
KAI 海 94
KAI 絵 95
KAI 界 260
KAI 開 261
KAI 階 262
KAI 改 458
KAI 械 459
KAI 街 461
KAI 快 661
KAI 解 662
KAI 灰 834

334

(Continued from front endpapers)

ナ *na*	一 ナ	な *na*	一 ナ な な
ニ *ni*	一 二	に *ni*	l lこ に
ヌ *nu*	フ ヌ	ぬ *nu*	l め ぬ
ネ *ne*	` ラ ネ ネ	ね *ne*	l れ ね
ノ *no*	ノ	の *no*	の
ハ *ha*	ノ ハ	は *ha*	l lこ は
ヒ *hi*	一 ヒ	ひ *hi*	ひ ひ
フ *fu*	フ	ふ *fu*	` ら ふ ふ
ヘ *he*	ヘ	へ *he*	へ
ホ *ho*	一 ナ オ ホ	ほ *ho*	l lこ にこ ほ
マ *ma*	フ マ	ま *ma*	一 二 ま

(Continued on next page)

SYLLABARY: KATAKANA AND HIRAGANA

(Continued from the previous page)

ミ *mi*	` ミ ミ		み *mi*	ス み	
ム *mu*	∠ ム		む *mu*	ー む む	
メ *me*	ノ メ		め *me*	∖ め め	
モ *mo*	ー ニ モ		も *mo*	し も も	
ヤ *ya*	ー ヤ		や *ya*	っ ゃ や	
ユ *yu*	フ ユ		ゆ *yu*	い ゆ	
ヨ *yo*	フ ヲ ヨ		よ *yo*	ー よ	
ラ *ra*	ー ラ		ら *ra*	` ら	
リ *ri*	｜ リ		り *ri*	い り	
ル *ru*	ﾉ ル		る *ru*	ろ る	
レ *re*	レ		れ *re*	｜ ｉ れ	